The Provincial Deputation in Mexico

Special Publication

Institute of Latin American Studies

University of Texas at Austin

The Provincial Deputation in Mexico

Harbinger of Provincial Autonomy, Independence, and Federalism

By Nettie Lee Benson

UNIVERSITY OF TEXAS PRESS
AUSTIN

First edition, 1992

Requests for permission to reproduce material from this work should be
sent to Permissions, University of Texas Press, Box 7819, Austin, TX
78713-7819.

All photographs courtesy of the Benson Latin American Collection,
University of Texas at Austin.

All maps provided by the Institute of Latin American Studies, University
of Texas at Austin. Cartography by Susan M. Long.

Library of Congress Cataloging-in-Publication Data
Benson, Nettie Lee.
    [Diputación provincial y el federalismo mexicano. English]
    The provincial deputation in Mexico : harbinger of provincial
autonomy, independence, and federalism / by Nettie Lee Benson. —
1st ed.
        p.   cm. — (Special publication / Institute of Latin American
Studies, University of Texas at Austin)
    Translation of: La diputación provincial y el federalismo mexicano.
    Includes bibliographical references and index.
    ISBN 0-292-76531-2
    1. Legislative bodies—Mexico—History—19th century.   2. Federal
government—Mexico—History—19th century.   3. State governments—Mexico—History—19th century.   4. New Spain. Diputación
Provincial—History.   I. Title.   II. Series: Special publication (University of Texas at Austin. Institute of Latin American Studies)
    JL1298.8.B46   1992
    328.72—dc20   91-43937
                                                                          CIP

ISBN 978-0-292-76363-0

First paperback edition, 2014

utpress.utexas.edu/index.php/rp-form

Contents

Maps

Illustrations

Introduction

When Napoleon invaded Spain in 1808 and placed his brother Joseph Bonaparte on the Spanish throne and held the former kings of Spain, Charles IV and his son Ferdinand VII, as hostages in Bayonne, France, the former Spanish kingdoms (now intendancies or provinces of Spain) rose up in protest. So did the Spanish territories in the New World. Many changes had occurred in the administration and institutions since the conquest of that territory in America later known as Mexico, which was earlier known as the kingdom of New Spain. As it grew and was brought under the control of Spain, New Spain's territory was divided into smaller kingdoms or provinces. When various conquerors won new territory, each one named the region he conquered, often after the region in Spain from which he came, and vied with the viceroy of New Spain, seated in Mexico City, to govern his newly conquered area. This happened with Nueva Galicia, with Guadalajara as its capital, to the west of New Spain. Some of these territories later conquered were Nueva Vizcaya with Arispe as its capital, Nueva Extremadura (which became Coahuila) with Monclova as its capital, Nuevo León with Monterrey as its capital, and Nuevo Santander (which became Tamaulipas after independence) with Aguayo as its capital. Some of these areas also were broken up into smaller provinces governed by a governor subject to the viceroy. Later, between 1767 to 1786, some of these kingdoms or provinces were changed into intendancies; however, the original term "province" and later term "intendancy" were frequently used interchangeably.

By 1808, this Mexican territory had been divided into the Viceroyalty of New Spain, the Commandancy-General of the Interior Provinces, and the Captaincy-General of Yucatán, all subject or semisubject to the viceroy of Mexico.

The Commandancy-General of the Interior Provinces went through various stages of division beginning on May 16, 1776, and running through 1821 related to the creation of the intendancy system.[1] The Interior Provinces of the Commandancy-General were composed of the provinces of

Texas, Coahuila, Nuevo León, Nuevo Santander, Durango, Chihuahua, and Sonora and Sinaloa as well as the territories of New Mexico and the Lower and Upper Californias. Sometimes there was more than one Commandancy-General—for instance, the Commandancy-General of the Eastern Interior Provinces composed of Coahuila, Nuevo León, Nuevo Santander, and Texas and the Western Interior Provinces composed of Sonora and Sinaloa, Durango and Chihuahua, and sometimes the territories of New Mexico and the Californias, with the Commandancy-General usually stationed at Chihuahua City, the capital of the province of Chihuahua.[2] Some of these provinces were also governed by intendants or by individual military governors subordinate to the Commandant-General, whose headquarters was at Chihuahua City.

When the intendancy system was introduced into Mexico between 1767 and the 1790s in New Spain, but mostly after 1786, it involved the provinces and Captaincy-General of Yucatán with its capital at Mérida, which also included the provinces of Tabasco and Campeche. Other intendancies were the province of Puebla, including Tlaxcala; the province of México, including the area surrounding Querétaro City; the province of Nueva Galicia, with its capital at Guadalajara; the province of Michoacán, with its capital Valladolid;[3] and each of the provinces of Guanajuato, Oaxaca, Veracruz, and Zacatecas with corresponding capitals of the same name. San Luis Potosí posed a special problem, because it was made an intendancy located at San Luis Potosí, but it was also supposed to be the headquarters for that system in several of the Interior Provinces; however, that process had not been carried out entirely by 1808. The first intendancy set up was that of Sonora and Sinaloa with its capital at Arispe, Sonora. In the Commandancy-General of the Interior Provinces the only other intendancy was at Durango, which had authority over the province of Chihuahua. The intendant also acted largely as governor over the province in which he lived. Although his primary responsibility was for the financial and economic resources of the territory under him, he also had some ecclesiastical, political, military, and judicial authority. Each intendant, including the one stationed in Mexico City, had a relationship with practically every individual in his intendancy. He was an appointee of the king of Spain and was directly responsible to him.[4] In fact, from the time of the creation of the intendancy system, especially in New Spain, the viceroy was further removed from the individual, who felt loyalty to the king of Spain more through the intendant than through the viceroy or Commandant-General over him, for the intendant had authority in everyday life.[5]

The intendants generally replaced the military governors of the provinces except in the military provinces, such as Coahuila, Nuevo León, Nuevo Santander, Texas, New Mexico, Tabasco, the Californias, Chihuahua, Sinaloa, and possibly other provinces that had not yet been made intendancies; the intendants were supposed to have learned or laid out the exact boundaries of their intendancies.

The news of Napoleon's having taken the kings of Spain hostages and placed his brother on the throne of Spain and the subsequent uprising of the provincial juntas in Spain reached Mexico City in mid-1808.[6] Thereafter, events immediately began to occur there. The well-known story of the overthrow of Viceroy José de Iturrigaray of New Spain and his replacement by the Audiencia of Mexico by Pedro de Garibay need not be told here. However, Garibay's recognition of the government that had been set up by the revolting juntas of Spain to govern Spain and the Indies through a Junta Suprema Central of Spain and the Indies seated at Seville does need to be taken into account here. It was composed of deputies or members from the various Spanish juntas rebelling against Napoleon's army and his brother Joseph Bonaparte on the throne of Spain.

That Junta Suprema Central of Spain and the Indies issued a decree in the name of Ferdinand VII, in whose name it was ruling, that the colonies of America were no longer to be thought of as colonies but rather as integral and equal parts of the empire. Now the Junta Suprema Central was so decreeing that the viceroyalties of New Spain, Peru, New Granada, and Buenos Aires and the independent Captaincy-Generals of Cuba, Puerto Rico, Guatemala, the Provinces of Venezuela, and the Philippines should put that resolution into effect by electing a deputy to represent their respective districts in this Junta Suprema Central now sitting in Seville. Then the decree proceeded to spell out how the elections were to be held for each specified territory and how New Spain, including its Interior Provinces, should elect one deputy to the Junta Suprema Central of Spain and the Indies.[7]

On April 4, 1809, Garibay issued the call for that election by the Municipal Council of Mexico City, the capital of New Spain, and by the Municipal Council of each *partido* (district) of New Spain and of each capital of an intendancy of New Spain and the Interior Provinces. The election was carried out on October 4, 1809, by twelve Municipal Councils of the existing intendancies and two additional provinces—Querétaro and Tlaxcala, which protested their omission. Miguel Larrázabal y Uribe of the province of Tlaxcala was the winner in the final draw to represent New Spain and the Interior Provinces in the Junta Suprema Central of the Superior Government of Spain and the Indies. He took his seat immediately, for he was already in Seville when elected.[8]

In late 1809, the Junta Suprema Central, which had been discussing the calling of a Spanish Cortes, fled before the French armies threatening Seville toward the Island of León and Cádiz. In February 1810, in great confusion and fear it named a five-member Regency, including the conservative Mexican Miguel Larrázabal, with instructions to call a Spanish Cortes to assemble in September 1810 at Cádiz on the Island of León.[9] A call for that election was issued, on February 1810, by the Regency. That decree, containing instructions for holding that election, reached Mexico City on May 16, 1810, and was printed in the official newspaper on May 18, 1810.[10]

The procedure in this election was relatively simple. It stated that each Municipal Council of each capital of each province or intendancy would meet and name three men, natives of the Mexican province or intendancy, who were endowed with integrity, talent, and education. Their names would be placed in a container from which one would be drawn. The man whose name was drawn would be deputy for that Mexican province to the Cortes of Spain. The Municipal Council would then certify the election and give the deputy instructions on matters that he should present to the Cortes.[11]

The Audiencia of Mexico acting with viceregal authority in May 1810 ordered the election to be held without the slightest delay by the Municipal Councils of the capitals of the provinces or intendancies of New Spain: México, Puebla, Veracruz, Yucatán, Oaxaca, Michoacán, Guanajuato, San Luis Potosí, Guadalajara, Zacatecas, Tabasco, Querétaro, Tlaxcala, Nuevo León, and Nuevo Santander. They were held in all of these provinces.[12]

The Commandant-General, Nemesio Salcedo, received the same decree and notified the provinces under his jurisdiction to hold the election immediately in the provinces of Coahuila, Sonora and Sinaloa, Chihuahua, Durango, Nuevo México, and Texas. They were so held enthusiastically.[13]

That Spanish Cortes met in September 1810 and continued to 1813 with twenty-two Mexican deputies, several of whom held the most prestigious positions, such as president and vice-president and chairmen of important committees, and helped produce the Spanish Constitution of 1812. According to Charles R. Berry in his study of "The Election of the Mexican Deputies to the Spanish Cortes, 1810–1822," five other Mexican deputies were elected but did not take part, for some of them died en route or failed to arrive in Cádiz. These deputies chose to serve their homeland during a time of fierce struggle not only for the independence of the Spanish empire from French domination but also during their own struggle for more local participation in the government of their own provinces, which they represented. They chose the legal path to achievement of their goal rather than the revolutionary road of Miguel Hidalgo and José María Morelos and the angry, bloody masses during the period late 1810 to 1814, at the same time that the Constitution was being debated and adopted. As we shall see, there were two roads to Mexican independence.

The Provincial Deputation of the Spanish world came from the debates of that Cortes and was constitutionalized through the Constitution of 1812. The following is the history of that short-lived institution. It is the story of its introduction into Mexico, its brief existence between 1812 and 1814, the forced reestablishment of the Constitution of 1812 by Ferdinand VII in early 1820, the Deputations' growth and development between 1820 and 1821 under the Spanish government and in Mexico under the brief rule of Emperor Agustín Iturbide, and the turbulent year (1823) of his overthrow and the still briefer government of the first Congress elected under his rule.

The history of this short-lived but extremely significant institution has been ignored by the contemporary historians, Lucas Alamán, Lorenzo de Zavala, and José María Luis Mora, all of whom were participants in its actions. Lucas Alamán did recognize its existence and was perhaps best prepared to tell its complete story in his five-volume *History of Mexico*. He, however, only mentioned it at the end of the fifth volume with the statement that its action brought a federal republic to Mexico rather than a strong central monarchy, which he thought would have been best for his native land. Lorenzo de Zavala in his *Historical Essay on the Revolutions in Mexico from 1808 until 1830* mentioned it in passing only once. Mora did not treat it in his work on the revolutions of Mexico.

Carlos María Bustamante cited some documents relative to its activities and its role in the 1820–1821 period in the fifth volume of his *Historical Picture of Mexico*. He, however, kept a manuscript diary of Mexico during the years 1821–1843. In it he recorded everything occurring in the part of Mexico in which he lived, mostly in Mexico City, or appearing in newspapers, broadsides, and pamphlets related to the events he recorded. This information too has lain largely unknown and unused in the Zacatecas Ar-

Agustín de Iturbide, General and
Emperor of Mexico, 1822–1823.
Lithograph, from Manuel Rivera
Cambas, *Los gobernantes de México*
(Mexico City: Imprenta de J. M.
Aguilar Ortiz, 1873).

chives for many, many years. It does contain much valuable material, for he
bound in each volume many extremely rare printed documents of those
years. It is cited here as his manuscript Historical Diary.

Later historians, Mexican as well as Anglo-American, have seldom mentioned the Provincial Deputation of Mexico; when they have, their assertions have been largely erroneous. Hubert Howe Bancroft, long the basic
Anglo-American historian, in the fourth volume of his six-volume *History
of Mexico* mentions the institution one time with the statement that Mexico
could have had many Provincial Deputations but chose to have only one.
This is a completely erroneous statement, as is thoroughly demonstrated
herein.

Practically all later historians continue either to be completely ignorant
of its existence or to ignore its significance. Yet the Provincial Deputation
in Mexico played an important role in bringing autonomy to the provinces
of Mexico, in contributing to the legitimization of the Iturbide independence movement with his ultimate success, in the creation of the Mexican
monarchical empire with Iturbide as emperor, then to his downfall, and
finally to the establishment of a federal republican system of government in
order to maintain Mexico as a single nation and not some eighteen different
nations, as occurred in Central America, largely as a result of the establishment of the Provincial Deputation in those provinces under Spanish rule.

The Provincial Deputation brought about in Mexico the creation of a
federal republican system under the Constitution of 1824 in order to maintain a united nation of all its provinces, which continues there to this day.
It was not a simple copy of the United States Constitution, as stated by
Michael Meyer and William L. Sherman in all three recent editions of *The
Course of Mexican History,* who simply repeat what most other histories
state when discussing the Mexican Constitution of 1824.

Here, therefore, is the documented history of the creation, implanta-
tion, and actions of the Provincial Deputation of Mexico. It begins with

1808 and moves on to its legitimization in Spain and carries the story to the passing of its duties to the Mexican State Legislatures in 1824. It is also the history of the actions and personalities of those involved in creating, implanting, and seeing it to its ultimate achievement, the largely independent State Legislatures. It is an exciting and interesting story of the Mexican nation that needs to be told and recognized.

ONE

Origin of the Provincial Deputations

From the standpoint of the role it played in Mexican political history and in the evolution of the Mexican federal state, the most interesting institution legalized by the Spanish Constitution of 1812 was the Provincial Deputation. This native Spanish institution had its genesis in the provincial juntas (governmental units) that sprang up throughout Spain in 1808 after Napoleon lured Charles IV and Ferdinand VII into captivity in France. From that time until the Spanish Cortes met in September 1810 to frame a Constitution for the Spanish monarchy, those provincial governing units, without legal or constitutional sanction, virtually governed a large portion of the individual provinces (formerly kingdoms or intendancies) of Spain.

Their legalization was one of the first matters brought up for consideration in the Cortes. A duly authorized committee presented a plan for the regulation and reorganization of the government of the provinces on November 13. It failed to win support, and another committee was appointed to study the subject in the light of the arguments advanced in the discussion of the report offered by the first committee and instructed to bring in a new plan.[1]

This second committee presented its report on March 4, 1811. Since conditions in the provinces demanded prompt action,[2] its provisions were rapidly pushed through in revised form. Approved by the Cortes on March 16, 1811, the complete bill, entitled "Regulation of the Provinces," appeared in the *Diario de las actas y discusiones de las Cortes,* on March 28, 1811.[3]

The "Regulation" provided for each provincial governing junta to be composed of a Captain-General and an intendant of the province, both of whom were to be appointees of the king, and nine other provincially elected members. In provinces having more than nine districts (*corregimientos* or *partidos*), there were to be as many members in the provincial junta as there were districts, with each district electing one member. To qualify for election each member had to have financial means or property and be a native or resident of the province for the previous ten years, in addition to meeting the qualifications required of a deputy to the Cortes. The term of office was three years, one-third of the membership being replaced each year. Members were to receive no salary, honors, or title; to wear no insignia or distinctive dress because of their position; to enjoy no special privileges in civil courts and in criminal courts to enjoy the privilege only of not being charged, except in the territorial courts or chancellories, while exercising their duties.

The Captain-General, where there was one, was to act as president, with each junta to elect, by plurality of vote, a vice-president from its membership, who was to serve for one year. Each of these bodies was also to name a secretary, who was to serve without salary or reward and would be ineligible for reelection until three years after his first term in office expired.

These provincial juntas were to be the medium through which the national government communicated to the people the orders and provisions necessary for the defense of Spain from the French and were to administer all business intrusted to them by the national Spanish government. They were (1) to aid the Captain-General and the military leaders in securing provisions and recruits—the assessment of the levies of provisions for the troops being the right of the junta; (2) to supervise the assessment and collection of public funds within their territory; and (3) to report to the Cortes the amount of money, provisions, and gifts that the Municipal Councils, other organizations, or private individuals had required of the people for the support of the troops and the use made of it. They were also (4) to see that the public funds were kept in one public treasury and (5) to publish and send to the national government monthly statements of income and expenditure and an annual report, including any protests against the monthly statements. They were, furthermore, (6) to make a census of the population and an annual statistical report on the agriculture, industry, and commerce in their province; (7) to encourage and establish primary schools for both sexes; and (8) to inform the Cortes of any positions or organizations that had outgrown their usefulness and to propose desirable new ones. The final article (9) stated that the "Regulation" was temporary and to be enforced only until the government of the provinces was provided for by the Constitution.

It was by no means the intent of either committee that the proposed plan of government for the provinces be applicable beyond the Spanish peninsula. An American deputy, José Mejía, representing New Granada, urged, during the discussion of the first plan, that it also apply to the Americas and suggested when the second committee was proposed that if the plan were to apply to all provinces some American[4] deputies should be included among the committee members.[5] At this time Agustín Argüelles and Evaristo Pérez de Castro, both members of the Constitutional Committee, said it was understood that the temporary plan was *not* to apply to

José Miguel Ramos Arizpe, Deputy to the Cortes of Cadiz, Mexican Congressman, Secretary of Justice and Ecclesiastical Affairs, 1825–1828. Lithograph, from Lucas Alamán, *Historia de Méjico* (Mexico City: Imprenta de J. M. Lara, 1850).

the Americas.[6] Argüelles did say, however, that the Constitution would make provision for the government of the American provinces. The American deputies apparently accepted the statements of these two men as final. No American deputies were appointed to the committee; and no further mention of the Americas was made in the later discussion of the plan adopted.

Just seven days before the approved version of the "Regulation of the Provinces" appeared in the *Diario de Cortes,* an American deputy from the Eastern Interior Provinces, probably Mexico's most ardent supporter of provincial autonomy, took his seat in the Cortes.

He was José Miguel Ramos y Arizpe (generally called Ramos Arizpe).[7] At that time he was thirty-six years of age. Born in the little town of San Nicolás de la Capellanía, on February 14, 1773, he had lived in the fertile agricultural valley of his birth, in the bustling commercial city of Saltillo, Coahuila, and in the small villages of Ciudad Victoria, Villagrán, Güemes, and Padilla, all in the Eastern Interior Provinces. He was well acquainted with both the urban and rural life of the region he represented. He had also spent several years in Guadalajara, a cultural center, while attending its university and practicing law. There he received the degree of bachelor of philosophy and of law and the doctorate in canon law. Nor was he a stranger to the capital of New Spain, Mexico City, for he had taken holy orders there in 1803 and was still a student in the law school of the Royal University of Mexico when elected as deputy to the Cortes in 1810. He was, therefore, well prepared by both experience and education to represent his beloved Interior Provinces.

Unquestionably he read the "Regulation of the Provinces" with great interest and at once began to make plans to secure more political freedom for his native region. By October 23, 1811, his plans had been given form in a proposal that asked that a superior junta be established at Saltillo in the Eastern Interior Provinces. This proposed body was to be composed of seven members, two each from the provinces of Coahuila, Nuevo León, and Nuevo Santander and one from Texas. At the same time, he asked that subordinate juntas composed of from three to five elected members be established in the capital of each of the four provinces.[8] This bill was referred to the Constitutional Committee for study.

In an effort to further his purpose, on November 1, 1811, Ramos Arizpe completed a long memorial addressed to the Cortes, in which he described in detail the geographical, historical, economic, political, and judicial conditions in the Eastern Interior Provinces and proposed methods whereby the evils from which those provinces suffered might be remedied. He asked again for the establishment of (1) a Superior Executive Junta for the four Eastern Interior Provinces of North America to be composed of seven citizens of the provinces with two elected by each of the provinces of Coahuila, Nuevo León, and Nuevo Santander and one by the province of Texas, because of its small population, and (2) a Provincial Deputation in each province to have charge of its administration.[9] This memorial, when presented to the Cortes, on November 7, 1811, was sent to the Constitutional Committee for study and action.

It is worth noting that the term "Provincial Deputation," which was to be applied henceforth to this institution, was apparently used for the first time in this document. The body had previously been referred to as a "provincial junta." Ramos Arizpe, however, used the term "Provincial Deputation" in the heading of section 25, and in the text he suggested that the governing junta be called a "Provincial Deputation."[10]

It has not been possible to determine whether this title was original with Ramos Arizpe. Probably he used the term "Deputation" deliberately. The Cortes was jealous of its legislative function. In the debate on the "Regulation of the Provinces" various deputies had emphasized that only the Cortes had the power to legislate. Some had questioned the advisability of establishing provincial governing units, alleging that such bodies would almost certainly assume some legislative powers. The term "junta," furthermore, connoted a Congress and was, therefore, not a politic term to be used in this situation. "Deputation," on the other hand, had no such connotation, being simply a group of deputies whose function could be specifically designated. By calling this institution a "Provincial Deputation," the Cortes could be sure that the name at least would not evoke precedents.

On December 26, 1811, the last part of the draft of the Constitution including Title VI, which dealt with the internal government of the provinces and municipalities, was read to the Cortes and printed copies were distributed to the members.[11] In this draft the term "Provincial Deputation" first appeared in the minutes of the Cortes. Thereafter it was used as the name of the institution whose influence in Mexico was to be so far reaching.

With the promise that some provision would be made for the Americas when the matter of provincial government was taken up in the Constitution, the American deputies began early to prepare themselves. Keenly aware of the potentialities of the proposed institution and seeing in it an opportunity to gain more political autonomy for the provinces, the American deputies, especially those from North America, centered their efforts upon this part of the Constitution and tried in every possible way during the debates to enlarge the membership and to increase the powers of the Deputations. On the other hand, they successfully restricted the power of the king's appointees, the Political Chief and the intendant, by denying them a voice and a vote in the deliberations of the Provincial Deputation. The only role these appointees of the king were given in the Provincial Deputation was that of presiding over the ninety annual regular sessions. Furthermore, if both the king's appointees were absent at the time of the sessions, the first elected member should preside.[12]

The debate on this section of the Constitution reveals that, while the American deputies saw in this institution a potential provincial Legislature, representative of the will of the provinces, the Spanish deputies regarded it as merely an administrative body of an advisory character, without legislative power.[13] While the Americans sought to make the Provincial Deputation representative of the province by having each district (*partido*) represented, the Spaniards objected, claiming that representation according to population or representation for all in the Provincial Deputation was the initial step toward federalism and untenable, on principle, in a monarchy. The Count of Toreno was so farseeing as to say, "the very expansion of the nation inclines it under a liberal system, toward a federalism, which, if not prevented, will come into existence above all in the overseas provinces—a federalism like that of the United States, which will unconsciously imitate that of the most independent of the ancient Swiss cantons and end by constituting separate states."[14]

Agustín Argüelles, one of the two Spaniards who had argued in 1810 that the "Regulation" should not apply to America, stated that "these Provincial Deputations would necessarily usurp more functions than the law gave them; and if the action of these small governing bodies were multiplied by an increase in membership, they would tend toward nothing short of federalism."[15]

The Spanish deputies, in their efforts to limit the establishment of these bodies in the Americas as much as possible, found a way to do so without being accused of discrimination by proposing that Provincial Deputations be set up only in the provinces named in Article 10.[16] That article of the Constitution, listing the component parts of the Spanish nation, named each province or intendancy of Spain individually, but in the New World it named provinces only under very broad groupings. Spanish North America—divided into six regions or divisions (New Spain, New Galicia, Yucatán, the Eastern Interior Provinces, the Western Interior Provinces, and Guatemala)—was, therefore, to be allowed six Provincial Deputations.

The American deputies disapproved the small number and at once began to try to increase it. By the time the enabling acts for the establishment of this institution had been drawn up and passed, the American deputies had succeeded in increasing the number on the continent of North America by two, one of which was San Luis Potosí in New Spain.[17]

Mexico was thus allowed the establishment of six Provincial Deputations: two in New Spain (one at Mexico City over the provinces or intendancies of México, Veracruz, Puebla, Oaxaca, Michoacán, Querétaro, and Tlaxcala, and another at San Luis Potosí over the provinces or intendancies of San Luis Potosí and Guanajuato); one at Guadalajara over New Galicia and Zacatecas; one at Mérida over the provinces of Yucatán, Tabasco, and Campeche; one at Monterrey over the Eastern Interior Provinces of Nuevo León, Coahuila, Nuevo Santander, and Texas; and one at Durango over the Western Interior Provinces of Durango, Chihuahua, Sonora, Sinaloa, and the Californias.[18] The Constitution of 1812 declared each Deputation politically independent of the others.[19] Each province (the Constitution did not differentiate between Spanish provinces or intendancies and the groupings in the colonies, a basic fact on which the American deputies would seize in their continued struggle to obtain deputations for each province in the colonies) was to be governed by a Political Chief, an intendant, and the provincially elected deputies of the Provincial Deputation, which was to deal directly with the national government in Spain through its Political Chief and the Minister of Overseas Affairs.

The functions of the Provincial Deputations as outlined in Article 335 of the Constitution were (1) to superintend and approve the assessment of taxes in the province; (2) to see to the proper expenditure of public funds by the municipalities; (3) to establish Municipal Councils wherever needed and in every community having a thousand inhabitants; (4) to propose to the government needed public works and the repair of old ones and to present methods for financing the same (in case of urgency of public works in overseas provinces, to proceed to finance and provide the same without awaiting approval of the Cortes); (5) to promote education and to encourage agriculture, industry, and trade, by protecting inventors in all fields of endeavor; (6) to inform the national government of any abuses in the administration of public funds; (7) to take the census and to draw up statistics of the province or intendancies; (8) to see that all charitable institutions fulfilled their functions and to propose rules or regulations to correct any abuses; (9) to inform the Cortes of any infractions of the Constitution; and (10) in overseas provinces to watch over the economy, order, and progress of the Indian missions. Article 323 gave the Provincial Deputation complete supervisory jurisdiction over the Municipal Councils.

Félix María Calleja, Viceroy of
Mexico. Lithograph, from Manuel
Rivera Cambas, *Los gobernantes de
México* (Mexico City: Imprenta de
J. M. Aguilar Ortiz, 1873).

These functions were defined in more detail in the enabling act issued by
the Cortes on June 23, 1813. Here the Provincial Deputation was declared
to be the final court of appeal in regard to assessment of taxes, supplies for
a municipality, and recruiting of soldiers or replacements for the army (the
military authority had the right to intervene only in regard to the aptitude
or physical fitness of the individuals). Also, the Provincial Deputation was
to set standards, examine, and license public school teachers in the province and to present to the government plans and projects for the improvement of agriculture, industry, the crafts, and commerce.[20]

The general powers of the Provincial Deputations just summarized were
increased by subsequent decrees of the Cortes. The Deputations were put
in charge of the distribution of public lands within their respective jurisdictions and authorized to intervene in certain judicial matters.[21] The
Audiencias were forbidden to concern themselves in any way with the governmental or economic affairs of the provinces or intendancies and instructed to turn such matters over to the Provincial Deputations, which
should determine whether the cases fell within their jurisdiction, that of
the Political Chiefs, or that of the Municipal Councils. The Audiencia, in
conjunction with the Provincial Deputation, was to determine the sched-
ule of fees to be collected by district or municipal judges, notary publics,
and other judicial officers. The Deputation, jointly with the Audiencia,
was to set up judicial districts within its jurisdiction and to propose to the
Cortes the number of officials other than the judge needed in each primary
court.[22]

This new system of government, established by the Constitution of 1812,
did *not* provide for a viceroy. The Political Chief became the exclusive
executive officer of the entire province or intendancy over which the Provincial Deputation exercised jurisdiction and was directly responsible to
the Minister of Overseas Affairs, who resided, not in Mexico City, but in
Spain. The Political Chief at Mexico City, who in effect replaced the viceroy, had no control over the Political Chiefs at Guadalajara, Mérida, San

Luis Potosí, Monterrey, or Durango. Each province was completely independent of the others.[23]

Félix María Calleja, when he assumed the office as Captain-General in Mexico in 1813, found that this was the opinion of the other Political Chiefs and Provincial Deputations. In an effort to retain the overall powers formerly pertaining to a viceroy, Calleja, on May 19, 1814, called upon his legal advisers to render an interpretation on the matter.[24]

His advisers informed Calleja that he had authority over the Provincial Deputation at Mexico City and at San Luis Potosí, but Calleja also wanted authorization to control those at Guadalajara, Monterrey, Durango, and Mérida and asked his advisers for an opinion.[25] Before the matter could be carried further, news of Ferdinand VII's abrogation of all acts of the Cortes reached Calleja. That the interpretation rendered by his legal advisers was unconstitutional is evident from the fact that in 1821, at the time of Juan O'Donojú's appointment, all twenty members of Ferdinand's advisory council concurred that under the Constitution there could be no viceroy, that the Political Chief of Mexico had jurisdiction only over the provinces composing the Provincial Deputation sitting in Mexico City, and that the other Provincial Deputations and Political Chiefs were completely independent of him. O'Donojú, therefore, was named Political Chief of only that area under the jurisdiction of the Provincial Deputation sitting in Mexico City.[26] Furthermore, when the Constitution of 1812 was reproclaimed in 1820, Viceroy Juan Ruiz de Apodaca ceased to use the title of viceroy, substituting the title of Political Chief and Captain-General.[27]

Thus it is that the genesis of federalism in Mexico, as will be shown, can be traced directly to the Constitution set up in 1812 for the government of Spain and its colonies. It provided for representative government and the political independence of each province. It created the Provincial Deputations, of which Mexico was granted six by 1814. This Constitution of 1812, when reproclaimed in 1820 by Ferdinand VII, played quite a significant role not only in bringing considerable autonomy to the Mexican provinces but in bringing national independence to Mexico.

It is quite doubtful that Ramos Arizpe, one of the oustanding liberal American deputies, who never lost an opportunity in the Cortes to uphold the interests of all the Americas, particularly those of the Eastern Interior Provinces, proposed and advocated these "Provincial Deputations" as a basis for the system that was to take form in the Mexican Constitution of 1824. But they played an extremely significant role in doing just that, as did Ramos Arizpe.

TWO

Establishment of the Provincial Deputations in Mexico, 1812–1814

The Constitution of 1812 was formally signed by the members of the Cortes and the members of the Regency on March 18 of that year. Immediately after its proclamation, the Cortes began work on the enabling acts needed to put it into effect. A decree was issued on May 23, 1812, calling for the election of deputies to the first regular Cortes, as provided by the Constitution. Articles 1 and 2 of the "Instructions to the Overseas Provinces for the Holding of Elections of Deputies to the Regular Session of 1813" ordered preliminary electoral councils formed in (1) Mexico City, the capital of New Spain; (2) Guadalajara, the capital of New Galicia; (3) Mérida, the capital of Yucatán; (4) Guatemala, the capital of the province of that name; (5) Monterrey, the capital of Nuevo León, one of the four Eastern Interior Provinces; and (6) Durango, the capital of New Vizcaya, one of the Western Interior Provinces. Each of these councils was to be constituted by the Political Chief; the archbishop, bishop, or whoever acted for him; the intendant, if there was one; the ranking alcalde; the ranking councilman or alderman (*regidor*); the procurator general; and two citizens of good repute, residents of the province, who were to be chosen by the aforementioned members. The Political Chief of Nuevo León was to preside over the preliminary electoral council of the Eastern Interior Provinces to be held at Monterrey and the Political Chief of New Vizcaya, over that of the Western Interior Provinces to be held at Durango. These councils were ordered established promptly on receipt of the decree; each Political Chief immediately on establishment was to inform the Regency, which, in turn, was to inform the Cortes.[1]

The meeting of the preliminary electoral council was to take place at once, and no member of this electoral body was to be excused from attending or granted permission to delay attendance. Using the latest census of its territory or the most accurate calculations available, on the basis of one deputy to every seventy thousand inhabitants, the body was to designate the number of regular deputies and alternates to which its jurisdiction was entitled. To facilitate the election, the body was, for this purpose only, to divide its territory into provinces and to designate the city in each to which the district electors were to repair to name the deputies of the province.

The preliminary electoral council was also to designate the number of deputies to which each of the provinces within its jurisdiction was entitled. If its provinces had not already been divided into districts, this body was to indicate them; but if such districts existed, the body was to recognize them and simply instruct them on the number of electors to which they were entitled according to the Constitution.[2] Furthermore, this body was to prepare beforehand to meet all problems that might arise in connection with the election. The decisions made were to be obeyed without question, but the body was in no way to interfere in the actual elections held in the parishes, districts, and provinces.[3]

On the day following the election of deputies to the Cortes of 1813, deputies were ordered elected to the Provincial Deputations. Overseas such bodies were ordered established in each of the provinces expressly named in Article 10 of the Constitution and an additional Deputation in New Spain, that of San Luis Potosí, to which Guanajuato was to be added. Until the new division of provinces was made overseas, Provincial Deputations were not to be established in all provinces electing deputies to the Cortes; hence the members of these Provincial Deputations were to be chosen in the capitals of the provinces making up the jurisdiction of each Deputation. If this jurisdiction extended over seven provinces, each provincial electoral body was to name one representative to the Provincial Deputation. If fewer than seven, each province was to elect one, then the province having the largest population should elect one, then the next most populous province, and so forth, until the required number was reached. But if the number of provinces should be greater than seven, the seven provinces with the largest population should each elect one deputy for the first biennium, provinces that had not elected in the past election should each elect in order of their population for the next biennium, and so on. Those provinces in which the population exceeded half again that of the smaller provinces were to have the privilege, however, of always electing a deputy. All districts of the province were to alternate in the election of members to the Provincial Deputation except in the case of the capital district, which should always have a deputy in that body.[4]

The two decrees of May 23 reached Mexico City in September 1812 and were turned over by the Political Chief, Francisco Xavier Venegas, to three attorneys (*fiscales*) for the crown for official interpretation. They informed Venegas on September 27 that he should send copies of the decree to the Political Chiefs of New Galicia, Yucatán, and the Eastern and Western Interior Provinces and should proceed to convoke the preparatory electoral council of New Spain. The title of "viceroy" was replaced by the title "Political Chief" under the Constitution of 1812 and Venegas' civil and political authority was now restricted to the six provinces of New Spain. Even though Venegas was reluctant to accept this fact, three days later, he ordered copies of the decrees sent to the Audiencias of Guadalajara and of Mexico; the three attorneys for the crown and other legal bodies in Mexico City; each of the intendants; the governors of Nuevo León, Acapulco, Tlaxcala, Perote, Yucatán, Tabasco, Nuevo Santander, Upper California, Lower California, and Colotlan; and the bishops of Puebla, Guadalajara, Michoacán, Oaxaca, Yucatán, and Nuevo León.[5]

The first Provincial Deputation to be installed within the bounds of present Mexico was that of Yucatán at Mérida, whose jurisdiction included the present-day provinces of Yucatán, Campeche, and Tabasco. Yucatán's preparatory electoral council was installed in Mérida on October 29, 1812.[6] Since the minutes of the meetings of that body have not been located, proof is lacking that the jurisdiction of the subdelegates was recognized as that of the electoral districts; but, as this policy was followed in New Spain and New Galicia, it was probably also true of Yucatán. That the steps in the electoral process were carried through expeditiously, however, is known. Before the end of 1812, the various municipalities had installed their constitutionally elected Municipal Councils; and on the second Sunday of March 1813, in accordance with Articles 61, 80, and 328 of the Constitution, the election of deputies to the Cortes took place.

On the following day, March 15, 1813, the deputies to the Provincial Deputation of Yucatán were chosen. They were Juan José Duarte of Mérida, Ignacio Rivas of Izamal, Diego de Hore of Valladolid, José María Ruz of Tekax, Manuel Pacheco of Tihosuco, José María Paula Villegas of Calkini, and Andrés de Ibarra of Campeche. José Joaquín Pinto, Francisco Ortiz, and José Francisco de Cicero were the alternates.[7] They called upon the Municipal Councils, as the principal supporters of the new institution and as its agents, to work for the well-being of the country and to give special attention to the advancement of public education.[8] Shortly afterward, this Provincial Deputation requested Venegas, now limited politically to controlling only the intendancies or provinces of New Spain, to forward to it, at the earliest possible date, all the files then in the Mexico City archives dealing with governmental, educational, and economic affairs pertaining to the provinces of Yucatán, Campeche, and Tabasco.[9]

The Provincial Deputation of New Galicia was also established in 1813. The decree of May 23, 1812, was published there on May 24, 1813, and the preliminary electoral council was soon in session.[10] On June 19, in regard to Article 10 of the decree relating to the election of the deputies to the Provincial Deputation, the Nueva Galicia electoral council ruled that since seven members were to be elected to this Deputation and there was only the other province or intendancy of Zacatecas, Zacatecas should elect three regular deputies and one alternate and the province of Nueva Galicia (frequently referred to as Guadalajara), four regular deputies and two alternates at an election to be held in the capitals in accordance with the Constitution.[11]

The electoral council set August 22 as the date for the district electors to report to the city of Guadalajara for the provincial elections. As its regular deputies, the province of New Galicia (referred to here as Guadalajara) elected José Simeón de Uría, Juan Manuel Caballero, Tomás Ignacio Villaseñor, and José Chafino, with Toribio González and Benito Antonio Vélez as alternates.[12] The province of Zacatecas, on September 12, 1813, elected the Conde de Santa Rosa, Jacinto Martínez, and Rafael Riestro as regular deputies and Felipe Chavarino as alternate.[13]

José de la Cruz, Political Chief of New Galicia, informed Venegas (now only the Political Chief of New Spain), on September 20, 1813, that the Provincial Deputation of New Galicia had that day been formally installed. On the same day, that Provincial Deputation named Pedro Vélez as its secretary and immediately began its work by requesting Venegas to forward to it all orders pending in regard to its jurisdiction.[14]

Since half of the membership of each Provincial Deputation was to be renewed every two years (Article 327), an election was called late in 1813 and held in the following spring. Guadalajara held its provincial election on March 12–24, 1814. On the last day, two regular deputies, Toribio González and Juan Coracura, were elected to replace Tomás Ignacio Villaseñor and José Chafino; and two alternates, Manuel Tuñón and José Crispín Velarde, to replace alternates Benito Antonio Vélez and Toribio González as deputies to complete the Provincial Deputation of New Galicia for the years 1814–1815.[15]

Zacatecas held similar elections on March 13–15 and on the last day elected Juan Francisco Calera and Juan Crisóstomo Dubal as regular deputies and Agustín de Iriarte as an alternate to the Provincial Deputation of New Galicia for the years 1814–1815.[16] These men probably never assumed office, because the decree issued by Ferdinand VII at Valencia on May 4, 1814, abolishing the Constitution of 1812 and annulling all acts of the Cortes from 1811 to 1814, reached Guadalajara on October 17 of that year.[17]

The third Provincial Deputation to be established within the bounds of Mexico was that of the Eastern Interior Provinces, with its capital at Monterrey.[18] During the period from 1810 to 1814, the Eastern Interior Provinces experienced repeated revolutionary upheaval. Especially in Nuevo León and Texas there was revolution and counterrevolution. That the Provincial Deputation was, nevertheless, established is not at all surprising in view of the fact that from April 1, 1811, until March 11, 1813, Nuevo León was governed by a provincial governing junta, a body similar to the Provincial Deputation and reminiscent of the juntas of Spain that gave birth to the Deputation.[19]

After the viceroy had named Ramón Díaz Bustamante provisional governor for Nuevo León, the junta surrendered its powers to him, on March 11, 1813; but in less than a month he was dead and Pedro Manuel de Llano, as ranking alcalde, became the acting governor. He was soon succeeded by Fernando de Uribe, newly elected ranking alcalde. He, as acting governor, called the meeting of the preparatory electoral council of 1813,[20] which on September 20 sent instructions to the governors of Nuevo Santander, Coahuila, Texas, and Nuevo León to forward to the council the census of their respective provinces at the earliest possible moment so that instructions for the holding of elections could be completed.[21]

Because the disturbed conditions in the provinces made it difficult for the governors to take a census,[22] the council, anxious to proceed with arrangements for the elections, formulated its instructions and designated electoral districts according to the latest ecclesiastical census reports of Bishop Marín de Porras of the diocese of Linares, whose jurisdiction coincided with that of the Eastern Interior Provinces. Texas, because of its limited population,[23] was assigned only one district with its capital at Béxar; Nuevo Santander, five; Nuevo León, four; and Coahuila, three. The council instructed the governors of each province to proceed with the parochial and district elections as soon as possible so that the district electors could be in Monterrey by February 15, 1814, at which time the election of deputies to the Cortes would be held.[24]

The parochial and district elections evidently did not proceed as rapidly as the council had hoped. Monterrey itself did not hold its district election until February 20, 1814, five days after the date set for the gathering of the district electors from all the provinces there. Prior to May 10, 1814, however, when most of the electors from Coahuila, Nuevo León, and Nuevo Santander had arrived, deputies to the Provincial Deputation were named. It was decided that Coahuila, Nuevo León, and Nuevo Santander should each be represented by two members and Texas by one; but, as that province was still fighting the invaders and had sent no district elector, it was decided that Nuevo León should have a third deputy to act for Texas. Coahuila, Nuevo León, and Nuevo Santander were each to have one alternate. Those elected as regular deputies were Dr. José Bernardino Cantú and Dr. José León Lobo Guerrero for Nuevo León; José Melchor Sánchez Navarro and Francisco Antonio Gutiérrez for Coahuila; Ylarión Gutiérrez and Pedro Paredes for Nuevo Santander; and Pedro Manuel de Llano to represent Texas. The alternates were Juan Isidro Campos, José Grande, and Bachiller José María Gutiérrez de Lara. After José Bernardino Cantú, José León Lobo Guerrero, Pedro Manuel de Llano, and Juan Isidro

Campos had taken the oath of office, the Provincial Deputation of the Eastern Interior Provinces was declared installed and immediately began functioning by naming Juan Bautista Arizpe as its secretary.

That area did not have an intendant living within its limits and the Commandant-General, Brig. Gen. Joaquín de Arredondo, who was off in Texas fighting the rebels during all of its existence, never attended any of its sessions as its Political Chief and executive officer. The Provincial Deputation of the Eastern Interior Provinces, with its capital in Monterrey, Nuevo León, met three days a week from June 10, 1814, until sometime after August 18, 1814, when it received a message from Arredondo ordering it to dissolve. This Provincial Deputation had strongly objected to some of Arredondo's measures, such as forced loans and calling up of troops. In its session of June 10, it had written a long letter to Arredondo, complaining of his nonattendance at its sessions. He had responded in a long letter of June 17, 1814, accusing the Deputation of not being a legitimate body, of interference, and of not respecting his authority. He even complained to Calleja about its activities. It was Calleja's sending him word on August 18, 1814, of the abrogation of the Constitution of 1812 by Ferdinand VII, on May 4, that gave Arredondo the power to dissolve the body.[25]

The Provincial Deputation of the Western Interior Provinces was to be composed of deputies from the provinces of Durango, Chihuahua, Sinaloa and Sonora, and New Mexico. The date of the establishment of this Provincial Deputation has not yet been found, but it can be assumed that it was established prior to April 13, for on that date the interim Political Chief, Don Juan Josef Zambrano of Nueva Vizcaya, reported to Spain on the election of deputies to that province (names not given) on March 15, 1814. Furthermore, the deputies to represent Chihuahua and New Mexico (Juan Ortiz of Santa Fé for New Mexico, Mateo Sánchez Alvarez for Chihuahua, and Francisco Xavier Chávez, alternate from Albuquerque) were elected at Paso del Norte, on March 14, 1814; and the deputies for the provinces of Sinaloa and Sonora were elected at Real de Alamos, on March 24, 1814 (names not found).[26] Though documentation has not yet been found, it was probably installed in April or May 1814.

The last of the Provincial Deputations known to have been established in Mexico in the period 1813–1814 was that at Mexico City. Francisco Xavier Venegas, as New Spain's Political Chief, on November 11, 1812, called the electoral council,[27] which drew up the necessary instructions for the holding of the elections in New Spain and signed them formally on November 14, 1812.[28]

The provinces of New Spain were stated to be México, Puebla, Valladolid (Michoacán), Guanajuato, Oaxaca, San Luis Potosí, Veracruz, Tlaxcala, and Querétaro.[29] The provincial electors were ordered to meet in the capital of each of these provinces. In regard to the division of each province into districts, the electoral council decided on "the existing divisions; that is, each subdelegation was to serve as the district division; except, in the province of Querétaro, there was to be a district made of San Juan del Río, Santa María Mealco, and Tequisquiapan; also, in the province of Guanajuato, because of the large population and the independent jurisdiction of the alcaldes, the city of Salamanca with Santiago and Irapuato and the city of Salvatierra with Yurirapundaro and Acambaro were each to form a district; and in Tlaxcala, Huamantla and San Agustín Tlaxco were to form one district."[30]

Article 10 of the official order of the electoral council dealt with the establishment of a Provincial Deputation. It authorized the intendancy of San Luis Potosí to name three members and one alternate and the intendancy of Guanajuato, because of its larger population, to name four deputies and two alternates to the Provincial Deputation of San Luis Potosí, which would have jurisdiction over those two provinces. In the remaining provinces of New Spain, forming the Provincial Deputation of New Spain, the council decided that since the intendancies of its jurisdiction, including the additional provinces of Tlaxcala and Querétaro, were seven in number, each should elect one deputy and México, Puebla, and Oaxaca should each elect an alternate.[31]

The Constitution of 1812 provided in detail for the method of holding these elections. They were to be indirect. The citizens of the parish were to choose parish electors, who, meeting with other parish electors, were to name district electors. Those, in turn, were to meet at the capital of each province to choose its deputies to the Cortes and to the Provincial Deputation.[32] The parish elections for Mexico City were held on November 29, 1812. The electoral council, in its official order of November 27, 1812, had set February 1, 1813, as the date for the district electors of the province of México to meet at Mexico City to name deputies to the Cortes.[33]

According to Article 328 of the Constitution, the provincial deputy for the province of México should have been elected on February 2, 1813; but he was not, because the parish elections held on the preceding November 29 were immediately contested.[34] As a result, no steps toward convening the parish electors in these provinces of New Spain were taken as long as Venegas remained in command there. He continued to publish the decrees and orders of the Cortes but made no move to obey them and thus, in fact, suspended them.[35] It was another case of "I obey but do not comply" (*obedezco pero no cumplo*).

Venegas was replaced by Félix Calleja on March 4, 1813, when the insurgents were still strong enough to control virtually all of Oaxaca, harass parts of most of the central provinces, and frequently infiltrate into the outskirts of Mexico City itself. Calleja, therefore, in an effort to placate the malcontents and wavering factions among the loyalists, decided to reestablish the suspended Constitution of 1812 and to enforce the decrees of the Cortes.[36] To do so, he had to proceed with the election of deputies, which Venegas had refused to do, even after repeated requests from the parish electors.[37]

Following the instructions of the attorneys for the crown, Calleja called a meeting of the parochial electors for Sunday, April 4, 1813.[38] At that time members of the Municipal Council, but not district electors, were elected, although the announced purpose of the election at its inception in September 1812 was to elect deputies to the Cortes and to the Provincial Deputation. Apparently the parish electors were dismissed after the election of the municipal councilmen.

At the next meeting of the electoral council, called by Calleja for April 20, 1813, it was decided that the respective intendants of the provinces of Puebla, Veracruz, Oaxaca, Michoacán, Guanajuato, México, and San Luis Potosí, together with the governors of Tlaxcala and of Querétaro, should be instructed to proceed at once with completing the elections of deputies to the Cortes and to the Provincial Deputations. Deputies to the Cortes were to go immediately to Veracruz to sail for Spain, and deputies to the Provincial Deputation of New Spain were to present themselves in Mexico City within two months.[39]

Receiving no reply concerning elections from the province of Oaxaca, which was completely dominated by the insurgents, Calleja, on April 23, 1813, called another meeting of the electoral council at which it was decided that, in the absence of a deputy from Oaxaca to the Provincial Deputation of New Spain, the province of México, because of its larger population, should elect two deputies to the Deputation and Michoacán should elect an alternate, in addition to its regular deputy.[40] Thus the body would be assured of a full membership—seven deputies and three alternates.

In accord with the directive of April 20, parochial elections were ordered for July 4.[41] Parish electors for Mexico City chosen on that date met on July 11 and named district electors; these met with the other district electors of the province of México on July 18 and chose deputies to the Cortes and, on the following day, deputies to the Provincial Deputation. The province of México chose Dr. José Miguel Guridi y Alcocer and José María Fagoaga as deputies and José Antonio Cristo y Conde as alternate.[42]

In the province of Puebla, parish elections were held in the city of Puebla on April 25 and district elections on May 1; these first two steps of the electoral process were also carried out in the other districts of the provinces not in the hands of the insurgents, and the provincial elections were set for May 9.[43] In reply to a query from José Mariano Marín,[44] who was elected deputy for Puebla to the Provincial Deputation of New Spain, Calleja stated that he had set July 19 as the date for the installation of that body.[45] The province of Querétaro, on June 4, 1813, elected Col. Pedro

Acevedo y Calderón as its deputy,[46] and Tlaxcala elected Lic. Bernardo González Pérez de Angulo.[47]

By August 1, the provinces of Puebla, Querétaro, México, and Tlaxcala had elected deputies to the Provincial Deputation of New Spain, and the impossibility of Oaxaca's doing so had been recognized. Oaxaca and Michoacán, then almost entirely in insurgent control,[48] had been unable to do so, and no records that Veracruz held such an election in 1813 have been found.

Even the provinces or intendancies that had elected deputies had trouble in seating their representatives. When Bernardo González Pérez de Angulo arrived in Mexico City to represent Tlaxcala, he was promptly arrested on the charge of having been involved in sedition earlier. In spite of his appeal to Calleja for immunity, his arrest was confirmed and his election declared null; Tlaxcala was instructed to reconvene the provincial electors to elect a new deputy.[49] Juan Madrid Quiñónes protested the election of Guridi y Alcocer as deputy for the province of México; and, on July 23, Calleja called for a complete report from the intendant on the election of members of the Provincial Deputation of New Spain and for a legal opinion on the charge against Guridi y Alcocer.[50] No explanation of the charge is given, but since he was not a native of the province of México,[51] it is possible that the election was challenged on the basis of residence: a member of the Provincial Deputation was either to have been a native of the province or to have resided in it for seven years.[52]

Probably the underlying cause of the challenge was political affiliation, for all three men elected by the province of México were supported by the insurgent force through the organization in Mexico City known as Los Guadalupes. Its members reported to José María Morelos, the insurgent leader, that, despite the concerted efforts of Calleja and the bishops, their candidates as deputies in the Cortes had been victorious and that the severest defeat received by the royalists was the election to the Provincial Deputation of New Spain of Guridi y Alcocer, ex-deputy to the Cortes, and of José María Fagoaga, European by birth, but reared and educated in Mexico and "addicted to liberal ideas and a good man, in the eyes of our enemies, worse than the most insurgent American." They continued that, as for the alternate deputy elected, "José Antonio del Cristo y Conde, a native of Havana," was "a proper person for the place to which elected."[53]

The year 1813 passed without the installation of the Provincial Deputation of New Spain, but efforts toward the consummation continued. The province of Tlaxcala reported on May 18, 1814, that it had elected Lic. José Daza y Artazo, an attorney of the Audiencia of Mexico and a former member of the Tlaxcala Municipal Council, as its deputy.[54] The intendancy of Veracruz, on March 15, 1814, elected Dr. Antonio Manuel Couto.[55] The intendancy of México, on March 16, 1814, in accord with the Constitution,[56] elected as new deputies to the Provincial Deputation of New Spain José Angel Gazano and Juan Bautista Lobo, along with Ignacio García Illueca as alternate.[57] Thus, by the end of May 1814, six of the seven deputies and two alternates had been named: Guridi y Alcocer and Fagoaga for México, Marín for Puebla, Acevedo y Calderón for Querétaro, Daza y Artazo for Tlaxcala, and Couto for Veracruz, with Cristo y Conde alternate for México and Tomás Rodríguez Pontón alternate for Puebla.

The question then arose as to whether the Provincial Deputation of New Spain should be formed with some of the deputies elected to that body in the years 1813–1814 and others for 1814–1815. It was finally decided by the preparatory electoral council of April 18 that, if the Deputation was installed prior to June 7, 1814, it should be composed of those already elected; but, in any case, on that date, its membership should be renewed by newly elected deputies.[58]

The Provincial Deputation of New Spain was not installed before June 1814; nor had it been installed on June 7, when Calleja called another meeting of the preparatory electoral council to decide whether the installation should take place without representation from the intendancy of Michoacán. It was decided that with the five deputies already present in Mexico City—two deputies and one alternate from the intendancy of México and one deputy each from Querétaro and Tlaxcala—the Provincial Deputation of New Spain should be installed at once and the orders should be sent instructing those absent deputies and alternates to come to Mexico City immediately. When the regular deputies arrived, the alternates and the second deputy from México should retire.[59]

In an official order, dated July 11, 1814, Calleja called upon the five deputies already in Mexico City and the intendant, Ramón Gutiérrez del Mazo, to appear at the government palace on July 13 to take the oath of office as members of the Provincial Deputation of New Spain. Instructions were also sent to the governors and intendants of Puebla, Oaxaca, and Michoacán, stating that the Deputation would be installed immediately and that the deputies for those intendancies should set out at once for Mexico City to take their place in that body.[60]

Thus, over a year after the date originally set for the event, the Provincial Deputation of New Spain was officially installed, on July 13, 1814.[61] On the following day, announcements of its installment were sent to the Municipal Councils of its jurisdiction.[62] The newspaper *Diario de México,* on July 18, 1814, after announcing that the Provincial Deputation of New Spain would hold its first session on that day and listing the names of its members, added: "The establishment of this Provincial Deputation is one of the greatest benefits that the Spanish Constitution has contributed in favor of the people who through their representatives have sanctioned it in conformity with the express law of nations. . . . Its powers and duties are well explained in the article of the *Catecismo de la constitución,* which we copy." This was followed by two pages dealing with the composition, sessions, powers, and duties of the Provincial Deputation.

At the first session on July 18, 1814, the Provincial Deputation of New Spain elected José María Martínez del Campo as its secretary.[63] Whether it ever exercised any other function is unknown, since no record of any sessions for this period has been found either in Mexico City or in the Archives of Toluca, México. Probably it never did hold other sessions, for less than a month later, on August 11, the royal decree nullifying the Constitution of 1812 and all of the acts of the Spanish Cortes of 1810 to 1814 reached Mexico City.[64]

Possibly the body was not immediately dissolved, for, on August 18, Calleja issued an official order that, in order not to disrupt the political and judicial administration of the dominion, no governmental changes were to be made until further instructions were received from the king.[65] If the newly installed Deputation continued, it must have enjoyed a passive existence until October 5, 1814, when the *Diario de México* carried a royal order to the effect that the Provincial Deputations of America should cease and the governors of the respective jurisdictions should take custody of their archives.

While the provinces of San Luis Potosí and Guanajuato had been authorized to establish a single Provincial Deputation with its capital in San Luis Potosí, little information concerning either its installment, if it occurred, or its activities has been found. It is clear, however, that deputies were elected in both 1813 and 1814. The exact date of the first election has not been established; but they were held before October 1, 1813, because on that date one of the deputies selected for Guanajuato was notified of his election and instructed to proceed at once to San Luis Potosí.[66] And, on March 15, 1814, two of the three deputies formerly elected for San Luis Potosí were replaced by the election of Lt. Col. Miguel Flores, ranking mayor of San Luis Potosí, and Francisco Gordoa.[67] Guanajuato, on March 15, 1814, renewed half its membership by electing Lt. Col. Manuel Marcelino de los Fuentes as regular deputy and Juan José García Castillo as alternate.[68] Nevertheless, Calleja was informed a week later that no deputies from Guanajuato had arrived in San Luis Potosí and that the body had not been installed.[69]

Chiapas, which later became a state of Mexico under the Constitution of 1812, at this time formed part of the Captaincy-General of Guatemala. It was made an intendancy in 1790, with jurisdiction specified to include the districts of Chiapa, Tuxtla, and Soconusco, with the capital located at Ciudad Real.[70] Under the decree of May 23, 1812, Chiapas was one of the intendancies to be represented in the Provincial Deputation of Guatemala, which was installed on September 2, 1813.[71] Details concerning the election of its members and its activities have not been found. It is known, however, that Chiapas was dissatisfied, for it wanted a Provincial Deputation of its own. Mariano Robles Domínguez, deputy for Chiapas in the Spanish Cortes, on May 18, 1813, presented a proposal to the Cortes that a Provincial Deputation for that intendancy, separate from that of Guatemala, be established at Ciudad Real.[72]

This proposal was referred to the Constitutional Committee,[73] and later to the Committee on Overseas Affairs. The latter's report, submitted November 18, 1813, recommended: (1) that the Municipal Councils of Ciudad Real should get the opinion of the principal Municipal Councils of the intendancy of Chiapas—Santa María Comitan, Tapachula, Tonala, Tuxtla, and Palenque—concerning the need for and the benefit to be derived from the establishment of such a body and the amount of territory to be included in its jurisdiction; and (2) that the Municipal Council of Ciudad Real should present all of this information to the Provincial Deputation of Guatemala for study and recommendation. That body, through its Political Chief, should then present the report with all these opinions to the Cortes for its final decision.[74] This was very obviously a delaying tactic to limit the number of Provincial Deputations in the Americas.

By August 1814, five of the six Provincial Deputations authorized for Mexico had been installed in Mérida, Yucatán; in Guadalajara, Nueva Galicia, and in Monterrey, Nuevo León, of the Eastern Interior Provinces; in Durango, Nueva Viscaya, of the Western Interior Provinces; and in Mexico City of New Spain. The members of the Deputation for San Luis Potosí had been elected, but available evidence casts some doubt on whether it was really installed and functioned for any length of time.

Chiapas, then a part of Guatemala, was represented in the Provincial Deputation of Guatemala, but was even then demanding a body of its own. Extremely significant, furthermore, in the light of future developments is the fact that, in the election of members to these bodies and to the Cortes and in the debates of the latter, it had been made clear that in the New World, especially in Spanish North America, there were many other recognized provinces and intendancies.

In the realm of New Galicia, there were Guadalajara and Zacatecas. In the Western Interior Provinces, there were Sonora, Sinaloa, Durango, Chihuahua, New Mexico, and the Californias. In the Eastern Interior Provinces, there were Coahuila, Nuevo León, Nuevo Santander, and Texas. And in New Spain there were the intendancies of México, Oaxaca, Puebla, Michoacán, and Veracruz and, since 1809, Querétaro and Tlaxcala. Each of these intendancies and provinces was recognized as an integral part of the Spanish nation. Most had had a long history as a province, and the limits of each were known.

It is true that during the brief period of the Constitution of 1812 the in-

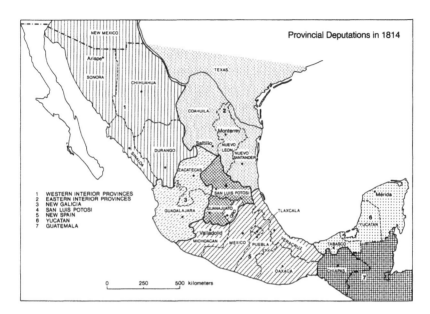

stitution of the Provincial Deputation led a brief and erratic existence (1812 to 1814). But it is also true that many Mexicans even at that date recognized it as a means to obtain more local and provincial autonomy. They had had an opportunity through the many local and provincial elections held from 1809 to 1814 to exercise their right to political expression and did so enthusiastically when permitted.

When Ferdinand VII returned to rule Spain again in May 1814, he abrogated the Constitution of 1812 and all the acts of the Cortes from 1810 to 1814 along with all the institutions created by them.

The government reverted back to what it had been prior to Napoleon's invasion of Spain in 1808. Calleja reassumed his position of viceroy of Mexico and was replaced by Juan Ruiz de Apodaca on September 16, 1816. The provinces and intendancies reverted back to government by the intendants and the military governors who had been in control of the intendancies and provinces during most of the time of the revolutionary wars of Mexico. A check of those individual intendants and governors listed in a broken but rather extensive file of Felipe de Zúñiga y Ontiveros, *Calendario, manual y guía de forasteros para el año del señor* . . . for the years 1788 to 1821 shows that many of the intendants and military governors assigned to a certain place served in that intendancy or province for years. That was true of Fernando Pérez de Marañón of Guanajuato, 1811–1820; Manuel Jacinto Acevedo of San Luis Potosí, 1810–1821; José Gallagos of Zacatecas, 1816–1821; Brigadier Diego García Conde of Durango, Nueva Vizcaya, 1816–1821; Francisco Rendón of Oaxaca, 1815–1821; Miguel de Castro y

Araoz of Mérida, Yucatán, 1816–1821; Antonio Cordero of Sonora and Sinaloa, 1816–1821; Ciriaco de Llano of Puebla, 1816–1821; and Ramón Gutiérrez del Mazo of México, 1811–1821. There was more of a turnover of intendants in the provinces or intendancies of Valladolid of Michoacán, Veracruz, and Nueva Galicia with its capital at Guadalajara.[75]

Ricardo Rees Jones, in *El despotismo ilustrado y los intendentes de la Nueva España,* cites the names of the intendants by dates and intendancies and in the text comments on the work of each and on the unenthusiastic reception by many of the viceroys and their subjects.[76]

What this means in relation to the Provincial Deputation is hard to say, for the intendant had only a single role in that institution. He was the presiding officer in its meetings if the Political Chief was absent. If both he and the Political Chief were absent, the senior member of the elected Deputation presided at the meeting. Neither the intendant nor the Political Chief could vote on any matter being resolved in the meeting. In other words, they could not have any input in the matters handled by the Provincial Deputation; but they were to carry out its decisions on matters pertaining to their authority.

In this chapter we have seen the foundation of at least five of the six Provincial Deputations of Mexico. We have also introduced the activities of Chiapas, a future territory of Mexico, and the attitude of the intendancies and provinces toward the desire for more Provincial Deputations. In the next chapter we shall see the attitude of the Mexican intendancies and provinces toward increasing the numbers of this institution in Mexico, when the Constitution of 1812 was restored in the Spanish dominion in 1820.

THREE

Growth of the Provincial Deputations in Mexico, 1820–1821

Absolutism reigned in Spain and its colonies from mid-1814 to the end of 1819. During those years Ferdinand VII successfully quelled the annual revolts against his autocratic rule and apparently did not consider them to be demands for governmental reform. By 1820 dissatisfaction had become so general throughout Spain that municipality after municipality joined in the demand for a restoration of constitutional government as set forth in the Constitution of 1812. The revolt of troops led in Spain by Rafael de Riego and Antonio Quiroga initiated a movement so powerful that Ferdinand VII, on March 7, 1820, felt it expedient to yield. Two days later, before a provisional council, which he set up to advise him until the Cortes could meet, he took an oath to support the Constitution of 1812.[1]

News of these events began to reach Mexico in late April, but those in authority were reluctant to make such facts known. Campeche, one of the first Municipal Councils in Mexico to take the oath of allegiance to the reestablished Constitution, did so on May 8, 1820, and on the following day installed its constitutional Municipal Council. Just five days later, on May 13, Yucatán, the pioneer in installing the first Provincial Deputation, was the first to reinstall it.[2] The Municipal Council and Consulate of Veracruz forced José Dávila, the governor there, to proclaim the Constitution on May 25.[3]

In Mexico City, Viceroy Juan Ruiz de Apodaca, Conde de Venadito, had held a meeting (*acuerdo*) as early as May 4, 1820, at which it was decided to wait for official orders from Spain before taking any action. But after the news arrived on May 30 of the proclamation of the Constitution by Veracruz, Apodaca felt himself forced to action. On May 31, without orders, he took the oath.[4]

Apodaca, no longer viceroy but rather Captain-General and Political Chief of New Spain, moved so slowly, however, in putting the provisions of the Constitution into effect that the Provincial Deputation of New Spain, the only constitutional body not yet established, was not reinstalled until July 20. It elected José Manuel de la Sierra as its secretary in its sec-

Juan Ruiz de Apodaca, Viceroy of
Mexico. Lithograph, from Manuel
Rivera Cambas, *Los gobernantes
de México* (Mexico City: Imprenta
de J. M. Aguilar Ortiz, 1873).

ond session. Its membership was composed of Political Chief Apodaca and
intendant Ramón Gutiérrez del Mazo, as well as voting deputies Juan
Bautista Lobo (and his alternate, retired sergeant-major José Ignacio García
Illueca), both for the intendancy of México; Dr. Francisco Pablo Vásquez,
for the intendancy of Puebla; Col. Pedro Acevedo y Calderón, for the province of Querétaro; Lic. José Julián Daza y Artaza for the province of Tlaxcala; and Dr. Manuel Antonio Couto, for the intendancy of Veracruz, all
of whom had been in office in 1814. Deputies to be elected at elections already called for September would replace these provisional members on
September 30.

This Provincial Deputation of New Spain held twenty-one sessions in
the government palace between July 20 and September 26, 1820. Apodaca,
now as Political Chief, presided at all of these meetings except that of August 29, 1820, at which the intendant, Ramón Gutiérrez del Mazo, presided. Sometimes Apodaca suggested subjects that the Provincial Deputation should handle. The Provincial Deputation frequently referred matters
to the Political Chief when its voting members did not believe the matter
fell within its jurisdiction. It did, however, handle very assiduously all
matters referred to it by any body that it believed was within its jurisdiction. According to the minutes of its meetings, it was quite active and ex-
peditious. It was complimented by Apodaca for its good work at the end
of its term in office.[5]

No evidence has been found that the Provincial Deputations of the Eastern Interior Provinces, the Western Interior Provinces, San Luis Potosí, or
New Galicia were reestablished immediately or that the deputies in office
in 1814 were reinstalled. Since the new order for reinstallation of the 1814
members was approved by King Ferdinand VII, it is possible that they
were. On the other hand, it is also possible that their Political Chiefs and
Commandants-General, such as Joaquín de Arredondo of the Eastern Interior Provinces and José de la Cruz of Nueva Galicia, received the word so

late that they considered the period between possible installation and new elections too short to warrant taking such action.

Elections in these political divisions, as well as in Yucatán, New Spain, and Guatemala, were held and deputies elected in 1820 to all seven Provincial Deputations. Instructions for holding these elections, issued by Ferdinand VII, on March 24, 1820, authorized the initiation of the process upon receipt of the instructions by the Political Chiefs at México, Guadalajara, Mérida, Guatemala, Monterrey, and Durango.[6]

The preparatory electoral council of New Spain, when convoked by Apodaca, on July 11 issued an election proclamation setting forth the governing regulations. The territory under the jurisdiction of the council was described as that of the Audiencia of New Spain, except that of the intendancy of Yucatán and that of the Eastern Interior Provinces, which were each authorized by the royal instructions of March 24 to hold their own preparatory electoral councils.[7] The electoral divisions of New Spain were declared identical with those of 1812–1813, and all the electoral districts, with a few exceptions, were to have the same boundaries as those of the subdelegations or *corregimientos*. In Oaxaca the district of Jalapa was disallowed, and its parochial elector was ordered to meet with the electors of its nearest neighboring district.

Article 8 of the same proclamation dealt with the naming of deputies to the Provincial Deputation. It pointed out that two such bodies were to be established again in New Spain, one at Mexico City and the other at the intendancy of San Luis Potosí. It ordered that on Monday, September 18, following the elections of deputies to the Cortes, the district electors, meeting in the capitals of the intendancies of México, Puebla, Oaxaca, Michoacán, and Veracruz and the provinces of Querétaro and Tlaxcala, should proceed to name a deputy (México, Puebla, and Oaxaca each also to name an alternate) to the Provincial Deputation of New Spain. District electors meeting at the capital of the intendancy of San Luis Potosí should name three deputies and an alternate; and district electors meeting at the capital of the intendancy of Guanajuato, four deputies and two alternates to the Provincial Deputation of San Luis Potosí.[8]

The official instructions of the preparatory electoral councils of the intendancy of New Galicia, the intendancy of Yucatán, the provinces of Campeche and Tabasco, and the military Eastern Interior Provinces, the Western Interior Provinces, and Guatemala have not been located, but such councils were convened and deputies elected to the respective Provincial Deputations. All deputies elected in 1820 were to serve during the remainder of the year 1820 and all of 1821. By November 26, a completely new membership had been installed in all six of the Provincial Deputations allotted to Mexico (see appendices for names of deputies).

Dates of Election and Installation of Deputations in 1820

Deputation	*Date of Election*	*Date of Installation*
New Galicia	Aug. 28, 1820	Sept. 12, 1820[9]
Yucatán	probably Sept. 1820	(not ascertained)[10]
New Spain	Sept. 18, 1820	Sept. 30, 1820[11]
San Luis Potosí	Sept. 18, 1820	Nov. 17, 1820[12]
Eastern Interior Provinces	Oct. 3, 1820	Nov. 20, 1820[13]
Western Interior Provinces	Oct. 7, 1820	Nov. 26, 1820[14]

Not only were those six Provincial Deputations in Mexico and that of Guatemala established in that year, but further steps were taken to increase the number allotted in both Mexico and Guatemala. The American deputies in the Cortes had consistently held that the provinces of the New World should be granted Provincial Deputations on the same basis as the provinces of Spain, where each had such a body, and they continued to work toward that end. On October 4, 1820, Ramos Arizpe and José Mariano Michelena[15] introduced into the Cortes a bill proposing (1) that a Provincial Deputation be established in the city of Arispe, capital of the intendancy of Arispe, embracing the provinces of Sonora and Sinaloa; (2) that the Provincial Deputation have jurisdiction over Sonora and Sinaloa and the territory of Upper and Lower California; (3) that Upper and Lower California be added to the intendancy and military and political command of Arispe; (4) that a Provincial Deputation be established in Valladolid of Michoacán with jurisdiction over that intendancy and the intendancy of Guanajuato; and (5) that the Provincial Deputation of San Luis Potosí be given jurisdiction over the province and intendancy of Zacatecas.[16]

Ramos Arizpe said that the purpose of these changes was to give better direction to the affairs of the intendancies of Zacatecas, San Luis Potosí, and Michoacán and, by promoting the prosperity and settlement of the Californias, to raise an impenetrable barrier against other countries. He declared that the Florida Treaty had thrown the doors to Spanish territory open to foreigners and urged that care be taken to prevent foreign nations from getting possession of the mouth of the Colorado River.[17]

When this bill was read for the third time, on November 2, 1820, the Joint Committee on Provincial Deputations and on Overseas Affairs, which had studied the matter, reported that they had offered no opinion on the first three paragraphs, because they lacked the necessary topographical knowledge of the city of Arispe, but suggested that the views of the Secretary of Overseas Affairs be considered. They gave full approval, however, to the establishment of a Provincial Deputation in Valladolid (later known as Morelia) of Michoacán with jurisdiction over the territory of the intendancies of Michoacán and of Guanajuato and to the transfer of the intendancy of Zacatecas to the jurisdiction of the Provincial Deputation of San Luis Potosí.[18]

Ramos Arizpe, who had been prevented by illness from attending the committee hearings and thus from furnishing the information the committees lacked, then took the floor. After giving a brief description of Sonora and Sinaloa, he warned again of the danger threatening the northern border of New Spain as a result of the Florida Treaty and argued for a chain of settlements to the south of the Colorado River. Reminding the Cortes that the Russians had made a naval settlement only twenty-five leagues from San Francisco, he concluded that the best way to meet the threat was to establish a Provincial Deputation at Arispe with jurisdiction over Sonora, Sinaloa, and Lower and Upper California. This body would be able to promote the settlement of the entire region and make it the needed bulwark against foreign intruders.[19]

The Secretary of Overseas Affairs favored the Provincial Deputation for Valladolid of Michoacán, because, as the seat of an intendancy and with a Political Chief, a Deputation could immediately function constitutionally in it. In the case of Arispe, he argued that establishment of such a body was impossible at the moment, because an intendancy would have to be established or transferred and a Political Chief placed there. In the choice of Chihuahua, Arispe, or some other place as the capital of Sonora and Sinaloa, he himself regarded Arispe as the most suitable. He agreed that the establishment of a Provincial Deputation in that section would be in the best interests of the region and of the nation as a whole and promised that, if the necessary preliminary steps were taken, he would give the Provincial Deputation his full support.[20]

Ramos Arizpe then showed that Arispe had been designated the capital and the seat of the intendancy embracing the provinces of Sonora and Sinaloa, during the administration of José de Gálvez and that a Political Chief, a military commandant, and an intendant had continued to function there, only the seat of the Commandant-General of the Western Interior Provinces having been transferred to Chihuahua. As proof he offered Felipe de la Zúñiga y Ontiveros' *Guía de forasteros de Nueva España* of 1820, which listed Arispe as headquarters of Antonio Cordero, intendant and political and military governor of the intendancy of the provinces of Sonora and Sinaloa. Since the position of the intendant had been separated only recently from that of the governor and military commander, Ramos Arizpe argued that Arispe met all the requirements for the seat of a Provincial Deputation.[21]

In spite of his efforts, the establishment of a Provincial Deputation for Sonora and Sinaloa at Arispe was not authorized at that time; instead, the report of the Joint Committees was approved in its entirety.[22] Four days later, on November 6, 1820, México was granted its seventh Provincial Deputation—seated at Valladolid for the capital of the intendancies of Michoacán and Guanajuato—and the intendancy of Zacatecas was transferred to the jurisdiction of the Provincial Deputation of San Luis Potosí.[23]

During the period the Cortes was not in session, from November 10, 1820, to March 1, 1821, the position of the American deputies was strengthened by newly arrived deputies from New Spain and by petitions addressed to the Cortes by various political bodies in the New World. Even prior to the July 11 proclamation of the preparatory council of New Spain, the Municipal Council of Puebla de los Angeles had written Ramos Arizpe asking him to work for the establishment of a Provincial Deputation in that intendancy[24] and had demanded, in a seven-page printed protest, the repeal of the decree of May 23, which granted New Spain only one Provincial Deputation, at Mexico City.[25]

In that document the Puebla council showed that the decree was unconstitutional, on the ground that Article 325 of the Constitution provided that each intendancy should have a Provincial Deputation and that Veracruz, Michoacán, Querétaro, Puebla, Oaxaca, México, and Tlaxcala had each elected its own deputies to the Cortes, who had been seated as representatives of the province electing them—ample evidence that each one was recognized as a separate province—and yet had been permitted no individual Provincial Deputation. Articles 326 and 328 were also violated when each province was allowed to elect only one deputy to the Provincial Deputation, for those articles stated expressly that the district electors of each province should elect seven individuals to compose its Provincial Deputation. It was pointed out, furthermore, that the jurisdiction of one Deputation over seven recognized provinces not only violated the Constitution but made it an instrument of injustice rather than of public benefit. The document noted that the province of Puebla was twice as large as the province of Madrid and had more than double its population.

The *Representación* next attacked the reasons given for the combination of the seven provinces into a single Deputation—the lessened control of the Captain-General and the fear that the intendancies of Puebla, Veracruz, and so forth, under separate Provincial Deputations, would tend to become independent from Mexico. Puebla replied that there was no more cause to fear that the Mexican provinces would become independent than that the provinces of Spain, which were self-governing in provincial matters, would become independent of the king, to whom they were directly subject. The relation between the provinces under individual Provincial Deputations would be the same as under the intendant system—reciprocal independence. In conclusion, the Pueblan Municipal Council stated that the existing situation was an impossible one, for no single body composed of seven members could possibly cope, in ninety sessions annually, with the problems of 3,485 municipalities. The constitutional answer to the problem was the revocation of the decree of May 23. A copy of the *Representación* was sent the following week to the Municipal Councils of the capital of each of the other six provinces concerned. With it went a letter asking that these bodies study the document and offer suggestions for improvement and recommending that each send a similar protest to the Cortes.[26]

The response was prompt and definite. The Municipal Council of Mexico City was advised by its legal counsel that, while Puebla had gone too far in terming the May 23 decree unconstitutional, because it was based on the understanding that in America a kingdom (*reyno*) was a province,[27] more Provincial Deputations in New Spain were necessary. This increase neither could nor should be obtained through the revocation of the cited decree as unconstitutional, but new and proportionate divisions of the provinces, provided by the Constitution, should be urged. The attorneys saw no cause for fear of federalism in the increase in Provincial Deputations, because all, while independent in themselves, remained subject to the supreme government. They urged the Municipal Council of Mexico City to support the movement for more Provincial Deputations.[28] This opinion was approved by the Mexico City Council, on August 18, 1820, and a copy was sent to Puebla.[29]

The Municipal Council of Valladolid approved the Puebla *Representación* and instructed the deputies to make this issue their first responsibility in the Cortes.[30] The Municipal Council of Veracruz asked Ramos Arizpe for support in obtaining additional Provincial Deputations and addressed to the Cortes an appeal similar to that of Puebla; and Oaxaca instructed its deputies to press for additional Provincial Deputations in New Spain.[31]

The concern of the province of Puebla in this matter was also demonstrated in the action of its provincial electoral council, which, at its meeting on September 18 to elect its deputy to the Provincial Deputation at Mexico City, drew up a memorial to the Cortes, which bluntly stated: "the twenty-one electors of this province and their constituents address the Cortes to demand the prompt installation of the Provincial Deputation which belongs to it according to Article 113."

Subsequently, arguments similar to those offered earlier were advanced. This memorial was freely distributed in printed form both in Mexico and in Spain.[32] Some members of the group did not think it had gone far enough. José Nepomuceno Troncoso, one of the provincial electors, published a broadside addressed to the public in which he criticized that body for not having proceeded to elect deputies to the Provincial Deputation at the city of Puebla, for he said that the Constitution authorized it to do so.[33]

By March 1, 1821, when the second session of the general Cortes of 1820–1821 reconvened, the American deputies had gained considerable support for their demand for more Provincial Deputations in Mexico. Deputies Joaquín Maniau and Pablo de la Llave of Veracruz, Lorenzo de Zavala and Juan López Constante of Yucatán, and Julián Urruela of Guatemala all brought instructions to demand more Provincial Deputations in the New World. Michelena, an alternate in 1820 but now a representative of his native province of Michoacán, was likewise instructed to secure more Provincial Deputations. Ignacio de Mora, similarly instructed by Puebla, added still another voice to the demand.[34]

During the first session of 1820 the Mexican deputies had gained valuable experience and had won important concessions. The admission by the Secretary of Overseas Affairs that the prerequisites for a Provincial Deputation were a Political Chief and an intendant functioning at the capital of the province formed the basis of the next bill, which proposed that, since each intendancy overseas had the character and was in fact a real province, according to Article 325 of the Constitution, a Provincial Deputation should immediately be established in each province not having one and that provincial electors in each intendancy should meet to elect the individuals needed, in accord with Article 326, to form those bodies.[35]

After the bill was read a second time, on March 21, 1821, Ramos Arizpe emphasized the fact that the intendancies of the New World met all the requirements of provinces; while there had been many more provinces in America before the intendant system was instituted, he was willing to accept the intendant system as the most legal existing division, especially in New Spain and in Spanish North America. Each of these had a large population and covered an extensive region, and those that did not have a Provincial Deputation wanted one, as evidenced by the demands of Michoacán, Veracruz, and Puebla. His request that the bill be sent to the Joint Committee on Provincial Deputations and Overseas Affairs was granted.[36]

Oaxaca, through its deputy Patricio López, was the next to enter the struggle. He pointed out that the intendancy of Oaxaca was 108 leagues from Mexico City, the capital of New Spain, that the province had 931 municipalities, 117 parishes, and 510,000 inhabitants, and that since it should have its own Provincial Deputation according to Article 325 of the Constitution, he had been instructed to ask for authorization for installation of a Deputation. He asked for a quick report from the Committee on Overseas Affairs, to which his request on the application of Article 325 on the establishment of Provincial Deputations in America was referred.[37]

The report of the Joint Committee was given in detail on April 30, at a special session, to which the Secretary of Overseas Affairs had been formally summoned. When informed that he would not be present, Ramos Arizpe opposed postponement, declaring the cabinet member's presence unnecessary for only after having heard his views had the eighteen members of the Joint Committee voted unanimously. Ramos Arizpe offered to

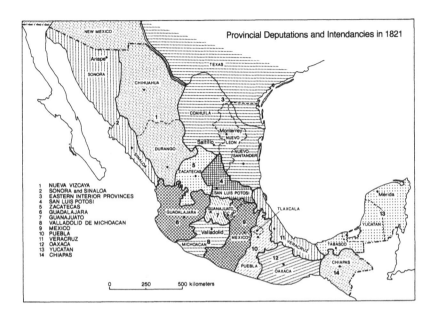

Provincial Deputations and Intendancies in 1821

1 NUEVA VIZCAYA
2 SONORA and SINALOA
3 EASTERN INTERIOR PROVINCES
4 SAN LUIS POTOSI
5 ZACATECAS
6 GUADALAJARA
7 GUANAJUATO
8 VALLADOLID DE MICHOACAN
9 MEXICO
10 PUEBLA
11 VERACRUZ
12 OAXACA
13 YUCATAN
14 CHIAPAS

assume the responsibility of answering any questions that might arise in the course of the discussion. He continued:

> New Spain, the most important part of America, . . . has believed firmly that, in the Constitution and according to Article 325, she has the right to profit from the benefits to be derived from the establishment of Provincial Deputations. Veracruz, Oaxaca, Guanajuato, and above all Puebla have claimed the right with great energy, and both the good judgment of some and the military display on the part of others have been necessary to prevent the naming of the members of the Provincial Deputations at the time of the election of deputies to the Cortes with the hope of obtaining this justice from that body. . . .
>
> The warship *Asia,* which will at last carry the most important officeholder of New Spain, is ready to leave any day, and it would be very opportune for Juan O'Donojú, worthy successor to Señor Apodaca, to carry with him the order establishing Provincial Deputations in all the intendancies. . . .[38]

At his request the opinion of the Joint Committee was then considered. Acknowledging that each intendancy in America was in every sense a large and true province, it recommended (1) that a Provincial Deputation be established at the capital of each intendancy with jurisdiction over all the territory within it; (2) that the deputy or deputies elected to the Provincial Deputation by the last provincial electoral body held within the territory of each intendancy continue to serve as members of these Deputations; (3) that, in order to complete the membership of those bodies, the district

electors in each of the intendancies meet in the capital on the day designated by the Political Chief and elect the deputies and alternates needed;
and (4) that in the future biennium the election and renewal of members
of the Provincial Deputation be in accord with the Constitution and the
existing laws.[39]

After lengthy speeches in favor of the committee's recommendations by
La Llave, Montoya, José Moreno Guerra of Córdoba, and Luis Hermosilla
and Juan Esteban Mills of Guatemala, all four of the recommendations
were approved. Printed copies of the decree, issued on May 9, 1821, ordered
the establishment of Provincial Deputations in all the overseas intendancies
in which such bodies had not already been established.[40] Copies were sent to
the Political Chiefs of the overseas provinces and 200 copies were distributed on May 17 among the members of the Cortes.[41]

Michoacán was the first province in Mexico to attempt to establish its
own Provincial Deputation under these new provisions. The decree of
May 6 was known in Mexico before O'Donojú arrived there. The mayor of
the Municipal Council of Valladolid, Michoacán, on February 21, 1821, informed that body that, since official news had been received through the
Gaceta del gobierno of Madrid that the Cortes had approved the request of
their province for the establishment of a Provincial Deputation, Apodaca
should be asked to put the decree into effect immediately at the elections
to be held in March 1821.[42]

The council voted to take such action. On February 25, it sent the request to Juan José Pastor Morales, deputy for Michoacán to the Provincial
Deputation of New Spain, with instructions to deliver it.[43]

Apodaca referred this matter to the Provincial Deputation of New
Spain, on March 10, 1821. That body concurred with Apodaca that no action could be taken because the official decree and instructions had not
been announced.[44] The Municipal Council of Valladolid, nevertheless, on
March 7, 1821, requested the intendant and Political Chief of Michoacán, in
view of the need for the Provincial Deputation and the fact that the establishment had been decreed, to set the election of members for March 12,
1821.[45] They were held at least in Michoacán on that date. Dr. Manuel de la
Bárcena, Don José María Cabrera, Bachiller Don Lorenzo Orilla, and
Don José Ignacio del Río were elected as regular deputies for Michoacán
and Lic. Juan José Zimbela and Don Antonio de la Haya as alternates. But
they were not installed, because the official decree did not arrive before the
province joined the Iturbide independence movement in May 1821.[46]

Apparently Michoacán's deputy in the Spanish Cortes, José Mariano
Michelena, was aware of this election but not of the failure to install the
members, for he made two references to the Provincial Deputation of
Valladolid in his speech to the Spanish Cortes on June 4, 1821, after news
of the Iturbide revolt had reached it. Michelena stated that he had ad-

Mariano Michelena, Deputy to the Cortes, 1820–1822. Lithograph, from Manuel Rivera Cambas, *Los gobernantes de México* (Mexico City: Imprenta de J. M. Aguilar Ortiz, 1873).

dressed a letter to that Deputation on April 25, 1821, and another letter on May 23, 1821.[47] Furthermore, Michoacán's deputy to the Provincial Deputation of New Spain, Juan José Pastor Morales, asked the New Spain Deputation to be permitted to return for a month to his home in Michoacán on April 10, 1821. He never returned to reassume his seat in the New Spain Provincial Deputation. He was known to have been a very independent thinker and had earlier been tried by the inquisition for ideas on Mexican independence.[48] It is quite possible that he was already supporting the Iturbide revolt.

In the province of Puebla, which had been so active in demanding a Provincial Deputation, Iturbide's revolt accelerated the establishment of the Provincial Deputation. Puebla had resorted to appeals to the deputies and to the Cortes, to letters to the other provinces, and to the distribution of pamphlets and broadsides in making its position known and now was quick to grasp the opportunity to establish this body.

Iturbide entered Puebla triumphantly, on August 2, 1821. When the Municipal Council appealed to him four days later for permission to establish a Provincial Deputation to have jurisdiction over the province of Puebla, Iturbide granted the request.[49] It is not known whether the council made the recognition of Iturbide contingent upon the request for permission for the establishment of the Provincial Deputation. It is known, however, that this request and the granting of permission both came prior to Iturbide's being officially accepted by the Puebla Municipal Council. Carlos García, Political Chief and intendant of Puebla, a week later ordered Iturbide's reply printed and circulated throughout the province.[50]

The electoral machinery was set in motion and, on September 1, seven deputies were elected to the Pueblan Provincial Deputation: Joaquín de Haro, José María Ollér, Juan Nepomuceno Troncoso, Juan Wenceslao Gazca, José María Lobato, Juan José Mariano Santa Cruz, and José Vicente Robles, and alternates Matías García, José María Ovando, and Juan González.[51] The Provincial Deputation of Puebla was duly installed shortly thereafter and began functioning with the approval of the entire province.[52]

At the same time that all this action to increase the number of Provincial Deputations was going on in the Spanish Cortes, the Provincial Deputation of New Spain was exercising its authority in sessions in Mexico City. That body, newly installed on September 30, 1820, was composed of José María Fagoaga, representing México; Lic. Juan Pastor Morales, representing Michoacán; Lic. Francisco Ignacio Mimiaga, representing Oaxaca; Don Patricio Furlong, representing Puebla (with Dr. José Mariano Amable as its alternate deputy), Lic. Juan Wenceslao de la Barquera, representing Querétaro; Dr. José Miguel Guridi y Alcocer, former deputy to the Spanish Cortes and a signer of the Constitution of 1812, representing Tlaxcala; and Don Juan Bautista Lobo, representing Veracruz.

Everything went smoothly with this body through session 65, on February 27, 1821, with the Political Chief, Apodaca, and the intendant, Ramón Gutiérrez del Mazo, attending all sessions of the previous Provincial Deputation of New Spain. It was kept extremely busy attending to the internal functioning of its seven provinces, especially relating to the growing problems occurring in the increasing numbers of municipalities.[53] Indeed, things went smoothly between the Provincial Deputation and Apodaca as long as he observed the articles of the Constitution of 1812.

Apodaca, on March 1, 1821, directed a report to the Provincial Deputation, telling it of his actions taken with the Mexico City Municipal Council on his learning from the archbishop and the Regent of the Audiencia of Iturbide's project of independence from the Spanish monarchy. Apodaca presided at the March 2 session of the Deputation when this report was read along with these reports of the Municipal Council and the archbishop and ecclesiastical chapter of the bishopric and the territorial Audiencia. He then left the meeting for the Provincial Deputation to respond as it thought best. That body immediately protested to him that, since it had first become aware of the Iturbide plan, it had been disposed to fulfill its duties and offered again to collaborate with him in all measures to insure the prosperity and security of the provinces; however, the body regretted that it had not been the first in manifesting these sentiments. There can be little doubt that the Provincial Deputation felt that it should have been consulted before the others.

Apodaca, on March 5, directed and signed a report to that body, in which he stated that Iturbide was approaching the capital city; he was taking every precaution to prevent Iturbide's entry and was calling on that body to fulfill its duties. After its reading on the same day at the 67th session, Apodaca left the meeting. The Provincial Deputation responded that it would collaborate in every way constitutionally possible to preserve public tranquillity and praised Apodaca for the prompt and proper mea-sures that he had taken.[54]

Nearly two months passed before the Provincial Deputation of New Spain and the Political Chief again found themselves in disagreement. On May 31, 1821, after notifying the Deputation that on April 29 and 30 Iturbide had printed his insidious propaganda on the press of Alejandro Valdés in Mexico City, that the commandant of Valladolid had joined Iturbide as well as the province of Guanajuato, and that the measures he had ordered were not being heeded, Apodaca called for a special meeting of the Deputation to give its opinion that freedom of the press could be suspended for one month under Article 170 of the Constitution.

The Provincial Deputation on the same day responded that it knew free-dom of the press had been abused, but that neither Article 170 nor any other article gave even the king the right to suppress freedom of the press; it was basic to the Constitution and could not be suspended. It continued: "Those who abuse freedom of the press should be tried and punished, but suspending a basic constitutional right would simply give the dissidents a new argument for opposing the constitutional government."

That body then reminded Apodaca that it was its duty to report infrac-tions of the Constitution immediately to the government in Spain. Never-theless, on June 5, Apodaca ordered the suspension of freedom of the press. That action was taken up by the Provincial Deputation on June 16, when it drew up its protest that was to be transmitted to the Spanish Cortes. It sent a copy of the protest to Apodaca for him to respond to the Cortes as he saw fit.[55]

From that date forward, hardly a session took place in which the Provin-cial Deputation did not find Apodaca issuing unconstitutional orders. It protested Apodaca's order, on June 7, for general mobilization for all men from sixteen to fifty years of age and his annulment of all licenses for travel to Spain, and again when he requisitioned arms, horses, and saddles on June 16—all of these acts attacked individual liberty and property and were unconstitutional. The Deputation's protests occurred almost daily. Apodaca, however, did not consult the Provincial Deputation of New Spain, whose authority he was ignoring, on any of these orders. Nor did he respond to any of its protests, as that body frequently reminded him.[56] He made no protest in the *Gaceta del gobierno de México* and very rarely mentioned the Provincial Deputation of New Spain in that official news-paper. The Mexico City Council was notified by the Provincial Deputation of these protests; the councils within its jurisdiction were probably also notified even though the documentation of general notification is not so far known to this author.

By July 5, 1821, Apodaca, who had taken over the viceroyalty of New

Spain from Félix María Calleja in 1816, now with Iturbide confronting him, the political institutions under him challenging him, and the military under him pressing him to take even stronger measures, decided he had had enough. He addressed a letter to the Provincial Deputation of New Spain, on July, 1821, notifying it that on that day he had agreed with Field Marshal Francisco Novella that "for the good of the nation" Apodaca had turned over the military and political commands of those kingdoms to Novella.[57]

The Deputation, in the early morning of July 6, 1821, the same day the message was received, in a special session, immediately responded to Apodaca that he had no authority to do what he had done and that his action naming Novella militarily and politically in command was null. It pointed out that under Article 10 on the royal and constitutional instructions for the economic and political government of the provinces, in case of resignation of the Political Chief, the intendant should succeed to that office unless the royal government had already named another person. The Deputation stated that, if this had occurred, it wished to see the document and said that the matter of military command was out of its jurisdiction. After taking this action, the Deputation notified the Territorial Audiencia, the Mexico City Municipal Council, and the mayors (*alcaldes*) under its jurisdiction of Apodaca's action and its response to him.[58]

In an extraordinary session on the following day, the Provincial Deputation received a communication from Novella notifying it that Apodaca had transferred to him the military and political commands of the Kingdoms of New Spain. The Deputation immediately responded to Novella that, following the constitutional provisions of governance, it was sending him the documents already forwarded to Apodaca and to the Territorial Audiencia relative to the Deputation's interpretation of Apodaca's power to transfer his political power.

In the evening of the same day, the Provincial Deputation received another communication from Novella informing it that he would take the oath of office of political and military commander of the kingdoms before the Provincial Deputation of New Spain and the Mexico City Municipal Council and military officials at 9:30 the next morning and expected its members to be present. In a special session the following day, the Deputation again renewed the statement of the nullity of Novella's accession to power. In order, however, to avoid confusion and to maintain order and tranquillity in the capital, the members were present when the oath was taken.[59]

By this date, communication with the other provinces of New Spain was virtually nonexistent; for that reason the Provincial Deputation of New Spain decided, following Article 334 of the Constitution of 1812, not to continue its weekly meetings and so informed Novella.[60]

Juan O'Donojú, Captain-General
and Political Chief of Mexico.
Lithograph, from Manuel Rivera
Cambas, *Los gobernantes de México*
(Mexico City: Imprenta de J. M.
Aguilar Ortiz, 1873).

When Novella invited that body, on July 17, to be present at the cathedral to ask for divine help in his new office, the Provincial Deputation, meeting in special session on that day, responded that it would not assist as a body at such a mass. However, the members presently available would assist individually in order not to create confusion.[61] By this date, only five of the seven members were attending the special meetings.

While all this was happening in New Spain, in Spain Ferdinand VII and the deputies in the Cortes, especially the Mexicans, were also taking action. On January 16, 1821, Juan O'Donojú was named to the position first of Captain-General of New Spain to replace Juan Ruiz de Apodaca and then, on January 24, 1821, as Political Chief of New Spain. However, his instructions for his duties in this second position were not presented to him until March 2, 1821, and he did not set sail on the frigate *Asia* until May 30, 1821.

According to Jaime Delgado in *España y México,* O'Donojú's nomination to the position had been influenced by Ramos Arizpe, Michelena, José María Couto, Manuel Cortazar, and other Mexican deputies known as insurgents. O'Donojú did not deny it, but said that he had accepted the position because of their insinuations.[62]

Another action that began probably in late 1820 and at least by early 1821 among some of the Mexican deputies was proposing a plan for not only provincial autonomy but also a form of dominion autonomy of the New World. Exactly how early this planning began is not presently known; however, it originated among the alternate American deputies, at meetings held in the home of deputy Francisco Fagoaga. Michelena referred to it in his speech to the Cortes on June 4, 1821, when Apodaca's report on Iturbide's revolt was read.

Michelena at that time said that his ideas had been written down by Ramos Arizpe and given to the Conde de Toreno as a result of some proposals by Deputy Felipe Fermín de Paúl. Michelena stated that he had sent them to the Provincial Deputation of Valladolid, on April 11, 1821, and that

Lucas Alamán, Secretary of Internal Affairs and Foreign Affairs of Mexico and Historian. Lithograph, from Manuel Rivera Cambas, *Los gobernantes de México* (Mexico City: Imprenta de J. M. Aguilar Ortiz, 1873).

they had been approved by the newly arrived deputies by May 23, 1821, and he hoped the Cortes would approve them soon.[63]

Michelena's idea or plan, revised by Lucas Alamán and dated June 21, 1821, was presented to the Cortes on June 25, 1821. It called for the establishment of three Cortes in America, one in Mexico City, the capital of New Spain, for all of Spanish North America; one in Santa Fé, the capital of New Granada, for all of New Granada and Tierra Firme; and one in Lima, the capital of Peru, for all of Peru, Buenos Aires, and Chile. These Cortes would meet at the same time as the Cortes of Spain set forth under the Constitution of 1812 and would have the power to pass laws for the internal government of the provinces under the jurisdiction of each except for certain laws relating to the entire empire. There would be four ministries of government—government, finance, grace and justice, and war and navy—in each of them. Each would have its own supreme court, composed of a president, eight judges, and an attorney. An executive who might be from the royal family or a Regency of three would be appointed by Ferdinand VII to rule over each of them under the Constitution. Each would have its own council of state of seven members to assist the executive.

Trade between the peninsula and the American sections would be treated like that between provinces in the monarchy; consequently, the Spaniards of both hemispheres would enjoy the same advantages. In the same manner all civil employment would be open to all natives of the empire wherever born. New Spain and other American sections would help finance the empire, sending the peninsula the sum of a hundred million reales in six years beginning in January 1823 (the total to be reached by 1828) and other financial aid for the military and the protection of the sovereignty of the realm. Finally, the deputies of these three Cortes, when taking the oath of office, would swear to uphold the Constitution of 1812 and to uphold the law establishing this system. Some fifty American deputies, most of them from Mexico, signed this proposal, among them Ramos Arizpe, who did it on condition that he present a slightly different plan on the following day.[64]

Ramos Arizpe presented his plan, dated June 24, 1821, and signed only by him and José María Couto, on the following day. It differed from the earlier plan in that it proposed a Cortes only for Mexico and did not refer to the Spanish possessions in the southern hemisphere. It also stated that at least five of the deputies elected to the Mexican Cortes should attend the general Cortes held in Madrid; the Mexican Cortes was to decide on the exact number of these deputies and the mode of designating them at its first meeting. Also, in the choice of an executive to rule in Mexico, Ferdinand VII was not to name a "member of the royal family in order to assure the integrity of the monarchy and the constitutional rights of Ferdinand VII."[65] In this matter Ramos Arizpe and Couto must have known that Ferdinand VII had rejected for this reason a plan proposed to him in mid-May by the Minister of Overseas Affairs for three kingdoms in America ruled by three princes under him.[66] No further action was taken in the Cortes in regard to either the plan read on June 25 or Ramos Arizpe's plan.

The idea of kingdoms in the New World under Spanish princes had been around for a long, long time whether included in the purported Conde de Aranda plan or not. During the time of Manuel de Godoy and Charles IV, a number of plans had been prepared. For instance, Godoy proposed the kingdom of Louisiana in 1797, with a Spanish prince on the throne. In 1804, Godoy proposed Spanish princes as Regents, similar in many respects to the American proposal. On October 7, 1806, Charles IV proposed hereditary viceroyalties or kingdoms ruled by Spanish princes for New Spain, New Granada, Peru, La Plata, and so forth. There was also the plan of a treaty of Fontainebleau of October 1807 with Charles IV as emperor of Spain, Portugal, and Spanish America. Then there was the plan offered by the Mexican deputy, Ignacio Beye de Cisneros, in 1811 to the Spanish Cortes for the formation of independent governing juntas in the Americas, to which the king of Spain could flee to take charge as emperor in case the French captured all of Spain.[67]

Furthermore, in mid-May 1821, at a meeting presided over by the Minister of Overseas Affairs, former viceroys, Captains-General, and ex-inspectors then resident in Madrid considered a project for overseas government, which recommended to Ferdinand VII the division of America into three kingdoms: one in North America and two in South America, governed by princes under the constitutional system and, in case of lack of princes, by Regents. When it was approved, Mexico was to take charge of some of the Spanish debt. Ferdinand VII rejected the proposal for the reason stated above. Finally, there is the letter of Ferdinand VII of December 24, 1820, addressed to the Conde de Venadito, Don Juan Ruiz de Apodaca, telling him of Ferdinand's thoughts of fleeing Spain to take refuge in Mexico, where he believed he would be well received and could govern the empire as he thought best under his divine right.[68]

It has not yet been verified when the news reached Mexico of O'Donojú's appointment to the office of Political Chief and Captain-General of New Spain. The first mention of it in the *Actas de la diputación provincial de Nueva España* occurred on June 2, 1821, when the Municipal Council of Puebla, on May 22, 1821, requested information from the Provincial Deputation of New Spain as to whether he should be received as Political Chief or as Captain-General and what the cost of the reception should be. The Provincial Deputation responded that he should be received according to the laws and to past practices.[69]

O'Donojú arrived at Veracruz harbor, on July 30, at 1:15 P.M. and almost immediately transferred to the Castillo de San Juan de Ulúa. Veracruz was still in the hands of the Spanish government; however, it had been under siege since July 7, and all communication from the interior was cut off. When he was appointed to the position, he had been told that there existed only a few spots where insurrection continued in the provinces assigned to him.[70] With no military forces except those he found still loyal in San Juan de Ulúa and Veracruz and a small force in Mexico City, he found the contrary to be true.[71]

In this situation, he issued a proclamation addressed to the inhabitants of New Spain on August 3, at Veracruz, in which he told them that he had come to New Spain to bring to it tranquillity and peace, to put an end to the disastrous wars. He appealed to them to allow him to reach his destination, Mexico City, peacefully to take charge of the position to which he had been named, and repeated that he was alone and without any forces to cause hostility. He promised that if the Mexicans did not find him a just leader who merited their general approval he would himself allow the people to make their own choice of a leader.[72]

On the following day, O'Donojú issued a second proclamation addressed to the "worthy military and the heroic inhabitants" of Veracruz, in which he praised the city and the military forces for the great defense that they had offered to the enemy, but at the same time spoke of the need for peace and tranquillity for all the land. According to Carlos María Bustamante, who reproduced both of these proclamations in full, the loyal Veracruzanos said at that time that O'Donojú had sold out to the Americans.[73]

O'Donojú must have known of the 23-article Plan of Iguala, issued by Iturbide and Vicente Guerrero, on February 24, 1821, before he left Madrid for Mexico, for Iturbide had sent his plan to Ferdinand VII and to the Spanish Cortes as early as March 16, 1821. In this plan, Iturbide and Guerrero invited Ferdinand VII to come to Mexico to rule as emperor. On the following day, they sent to Juan Gómez Navarrete, a Mexican deputy in the Spanish Cortes of 1821, a copy of it plus his proposal for the members of the Governing Junta of Mexico; all of this had reached Madrid before O'Donojú's departure.[74] However, O'Donojú indicated in his message from Veracruz on August 6 to Iturbide that he had learned about Iturbide's ideas communicated to Apodaca through the newspaper *México independiente* (no. 4) and military newssheet no. 6 of June 1821. O'Donojú said he had been in correspondence and had friendships with the most distinguished Americans in the empire and it had been because of their insinuations and encouragement that he had accepted the position in the first place. In his heart, he was glad that Iturbide had not delayed his proclamation that was sent to Apodaca on March 18, for it concurred with O'Donojú's ideas to bring peace and tranquillity to Mexico. He finished by telling Iturbide that his safe arrival in Mexico City to take over his office and carry forward conciliation was in Iturbide's hands.[75]

Iturbide, then at Puebla, was quick to grasp this opportunity to legalize his movement and responded about August 11, arranging to meet O'Donojú at Córdoba, where the two of them signed the Treaty of Córdoba, on August 24, 1821. Its seventeen articles recognized Mexico as a sovereign independent nation to be governed by a moderate constitutional monarchical system, preferably headed by Ferdinand VII, or on his renouncement by one of the Spanish princes. It contained most of the provisions of the Plan of Iguala and provided for the immediate establishment of the Provisional Governing Junta, of which O'Donojú would be a member, or a Regency to exert executive power until the arrival of Ferdinand VII or one of the princes. O'Donojú offered to employ his position and authority to see that the Spanish troops controlling Mexico City left without unnecessary shedding of blood and then to allow the establishment of the new provisional government.[76]

By signing this, O'Donojú, at least for the moment, had gained safe passage through that part of Mexico under the control of the independence forces. He next had to win safe passage through the forces under the control of Novella. He would be able to achieve this through the help of the constitutional institutions within Mexico City, especially the Provincial Deputation of New Spain and the Municipal Council of Mexico City. Both bodies had never recognized the authority of Novella to govern politically and were anxious to collaborate with the royally appointed O'Donojú.

Also, in February 1821, Iturbide had suggested the names of three members of the Provincial Deputation of New Spain—José Miguel Guridi y Alcocer, José María Fagoaga, and Juan Bautista Lobo—as deputies among the nine-member proposed Provisional Governing Junta of Mexico and Juan José Pastor Morales as one of the four alternate deputies to the same junta. He also had suggested Juan Francisco Azcárate of the Municipal

Council as a deputy to the junta and alderman Francisco Sánchez de Tagle as an alternate deputy.[77]

When the junta later met on September 22, Guridi y Alcocer, Lobo, and Fagoaga were all present, as well as José Ignacio García Illueca of the Provincial Deputation and Azcárate and Sánchez de Tagle.[78] All of these played a significant role in opening the way for both O'Donojú and Iturbide to enter Mexico City.

Apparently Novella first learned of O'Donojú's arrival in Veracruz on August 12, when two different messengers sent by Iturbide arrived in Mexico City. The first brought the original proclamation issued by O'Donojú. The second brought the same proclamation published in Puebla with the addition of a notice that Iturbide had sent messengers to O'Donojú suggesting that he come to Córdoba, a more healthy and comfortable place, where they would be able to lay the basis for Mexican independence. Two days later, the priest Pedro Fernández, sent by Iturbide, arrived in Mexico City from Puebla, bearing a parcel of letters from O'Donojú to Novella, telling of his arrival in Veracruz and his actions there, including his letters sent to Iturbide. On that same day, Lt. Domingo Noriega, sent by Iturbide with a parcel of letters to Novella, was badly treated by Novella's forces.[79]

Novella did not want to believe what he was being told about O'Donojú. But these messengers were pouring into the city; by late evening of August 14, Novella addressed a letter to Iturbide asking for permission to send messengers to Veracruz to consult with O'Donojú and verify that he had really arrived in Veracruz. The permission was granted and ultimately three commissioners were sent, but Iturbide did not allow them to pass through his lines, alleging that the reason they were called back was because Novella had not called a cease-fire.[80] Iturbide's forces were moving closer and closer to Mexico City daily. As stated above, Iturbide and O'Donojú had, in the meantime, signed the Treaty of Córdoba.

On August 21, 1821, a lengthy article entitled "A Mexican Patriot to Those Who Want Independence" appeared in the Mexico City newspaper *Noticioso general* (no. 103), asking why O'Donojú, appointed by the liberal Spanish government, who had accepted what Iturbide had proposed to Apodaca, was not allowed to enter Mexico City. It praised O'Donojú's actions and called for his admission to Mexico City and his recognition as Captain-General and Political Chief.

Novella purportedly received a copy of the Treaty of Córdoba early in the morning of August 30 and immediately called upon each governmental, ecclesiastical, and military body to send two of its members to a meeting that afternoon to advise him on what to do under the circumstances. The Provincial Deputation met and voted unanimously to send Guridi y

Alcocer and Lobo to the meeting with the understanding that they had no power to vote on any action.[81]

At the meeting of the representatives of those corporations, the representatives of the Provincial Deputation, the Municipal Council, the Audiencia, and the Ecclesiastical Council all abstained from voting. Isidro Yañez, of the Audiencia, said that, as an individual, he felt that O'Donojú was authorized to treat with the head of the independent forces, adding that O'Donojú was "authorized by the king to be Captain-General and Political Chief of these dominions." "The archbishop said that," as a citizen, "he felt that the presence of O'Donojú in the capital was necessary in order to remove any doubt of his position and actions," and Gen. Pascual Liñán held that, until O'Donojú was present in Mexico City, nothing could be resolved. Guridi y Alcocer, representative of the Provincial Deputation, said, speaking as an individual, that "he approved of whatever O'Donojú had done, because he had acted under instructions he had received from the Spanish government." At that moment, the sound of cannon shots terminated the meeting.[82]

On the following day, the Provincial Deputation of New Spain addressed two letters to O'Donojú, one welcoming him to the country and another including the account of its meeting and that called by Novella. O'Donojú responded from Puebla on September 5 with two letters of thanks for the actions of the Provincial Deputation and for the copy of the meeting with Novella.[83]

Novella, on the other hand, replied to O'Donojú to advise him that he had the idea that O'Donojú, being in enemy territory, was forced to sign the Treaty of Córdoba and would not have done the same in territory under the control of the Spanish government. O'Donojú, addressing Novella simply as field marshal, sub-inspector of artillery, and commandant of Mexican troops, responded from Puebla, on September 4, that he had informed the messengers what he expected of Novella and they would so inform him.[84]

On September 9, Novella called another meeting of the representatives of the various Mexico City corporations to ask them how he should reply to the suggestion of an interview with O'Donojú and Iturbide and under what title he should attend such an interview. He had been using the title of viceroy and Political Chief and wanted that group to confirm those titles. Again the Provincial Deputation, the Municipal Council, and the ecclesiastical representatives were of the opinion that the interview should be held. Guridi y Alcocer and Col. Blas del Castillo Luna were chosen to take a copy of an account of the meeting to O'Donojú[85] and to report to him on it.[86]

The Provincial Deputation of New Spain wrote to O'Donojú on September 9 that it was far from believing that O'Donojú approved of the events that had transpired on July 5 (the replacement of Apodaca by Novella) and that it was solidly behind O'Donojú and his Treaty of Córdoba and had explained its ideas to Guridi y Alcocer, who had been chosen by the Novella junta to negotiate the problem with O'Donojú.[87]

O'Donojú, on September 12, reported that Guridi y Alcocer had explained to him the "scandalous" events occurring in Mexico City, that he told Guridi y Alcocer that he would never recognize Novella as legitimate Captain-General and Political Chief, but that he would propose to Novella that they meet solely as military generals.[88] O'Donojú wrote to Novella on the same day that Apodaca was the only one in Mexico City eligible to restore his office; that the office of viceroy no longer existed under the Constitution; and that Novella had broken many constitutional laws as well as military ones from July onward. O'Donojú cited the constitutional and military articles broken and said that, unless he received a satisfactory response within twenty-four hours, all of those criminal acts by Novella and his supporters would be reported to the Spanish government and they would suffer the consequences. O'Donojú did say that if Novella cooperated with him all such acts could be forgotten.[89]

The interview between O'Donojú and Novella was held on September 13. Novella agreed to do all that O'Donojú recommended and on the following day, at a joint meeting of the Provincial Deputation and the Municipal Council, Novella told them that he had agreed henceforth to carry out the orders of O'Donojú, Captain-General and Political Chief of New Spain.[90]

On the following day, September 15, 1821, a supplement to number 111 of the newspaper *Noticioso general* of Mexico City carried an order addressed to the army and to the public, signed by Novella on that date, to the effect that he had officially recognized O'Donojú as Captain-General and Political Chief of New Spain as a result of their interview and, in the interim prior to his arrival in Mexico City, Field Marshal Pascual de Liñán would take command of the army and intendant Ramón Gutiérrez del Mazo would serve as Political Chief. On the same page of the supplement appeared Liñán's order to the army to maintain peace and to recognize Juan O'Donojú as Captain-General and Political Chief.

In the same supplement on the last page appeared three notices to the public, all signed in Mexico City by Ramón Gutiérrez del Mazo on September 15, 1821. The first announced that on the previous day he had received appointment as interim Political Chief in Mexico City from Captain-General and Superior Political Chief Don Juan O'Donojú until he arrived in Mexico City. Gutiérrez del Mazo promised that he would obey the Constitution of 1812 and the laws of the Cortes in the conservation of public tranquillity. The other two notices lifted the requirement of having a passport to enter or leave Mexico City and having a license to mount or ride a horse within the city.[91]

Next O'Donojú, on September 17, 1821, at Tacubaya, addressed the "Inhabitants of the Kingdom of New Spain," to the effect that Mexicans of all the provinces of the vast empire owed the civil liberty that they now enjoyed to one of their own worthy sons and he wished to be the first to let them know that the war was over. O'Donojú continued that he was now in full possession of the military and political commands of the kingdom as its Captain-General and Superior Political Chief named by His Majesty and recognized by the authorities and corporations of the city, and the army that defended it was now obeying his orders. "Once installed, the government agreed to in the Treaty of Córdoba, which is now known to all, will be the legitimate authority. I shall be the first to offer my respect to the public representation. My function remains reduced to representing the Spanish Government, by occupying a place in yours in conformity with the said Treaty of Córdoba, to be useful in every way I possibly can to the Americans, and to gladly sacrifice myself in every way possible for the Mexicans and the Spaniards."[92]

On September 25, O'Donojú wrote a letter to the Provincial Deputation of New Spain from Tacubaya, to the effect that he had complied with Article 17 of the Treaty of Córdoba, which called for the evacuation of the Spanish troops from the capital city. He stated that on the following day he would leave Tacubaya at 4:00 P.M. to make his entrance into the city as Captain-General of the kingdom named by His Majesty.[93] He entered the city at five in the afternoon and was welcomed by the firing of artillery and the ringing of church bells, similar to the welcoming of viceroys, according to Bustamante. He was wined and dined by the Mexico City Municipal Council and was complimented by the Provincial Deputation and other corporations for his cooperation in Mexican independence and lodged in the home of the Conde de Berrio.[94]

On the following day, O'Donojú and the members of the Provincial Deputation of New Spain welcomed Agustín Iturbide to the former vice-regal palace in Mexico City, where he was received with great enthusiasm. After a *Te Deum* in the cathedral nearby, Iturbide and his welcomers returned to the palace, where they were entertained by the Mexico City Municipal Council. At the dinner Don Francisco Sánchez de Tagle in a lengthy ode to the occasion said that "the superhuman O'Donojú assures us peace."[95]

Independence came to Mexico at this time not only because of Iturbide, the Plan of Iguala, and the union of the early independence forces represented by Vicente Guerrero, Nicolás Bravo, and others, but also through the efforts of the Mexican deputies who represented Mexico in framing the

Constitution of 1812 (the institutions created by it—the Provincial Deputations and the popularly elected municipal govermments), the enabling acts of the Cortes in 1820–1821, and the naming of O'Donojú as Captain-General and Superior Political Chief of New Spain. Henceforth, the Constitution of 1812 and the enabling laws of the Spanish Cortes thus far created along with its institutions and all those individuals who had striven so many years, legislatively or militarily, for autonomy both provincial and national or for Mexican independence would play a significant role in establishing the system of the Mexican independent government.

FOUR

Continued Development of the Provincial Deputations in Mexico, 1821–1823

The sovereign Provisional Governing Junta that Agustín de Iturbide had earlier promised was assembled on the day following his entrance into Mexico City to begin its sessions to organize the interim government. On the following day, September 29, 1821, since four members of the Provincial Deputation of New Spain were now members of that junta, it was recognized that it would be necessary to fill their former positions on that Provincial Deputation in some way. Hence, on that day the junta named those four former members (José Miguel Guridi y Alcocer, José María Fagoaga, Juan Bautista Lobo, and José Ignacio García Illueca) as a committee to recommend how their replacement in the Provincial Deputation should be handled until new popular elections could be held.[1] This committee reported to the October 4 session, recommending various persons to fill the places; the following were elected by the junta: Col. Pedro Acevedo y Calderón, Lic. José Mariano Fernández Arteaga, Lic. José Ignacio Espinosa, Lic. Mariano Primo de Rivera, and Capt. Pedro Pablo Vélez.[2]

Thus, by October, 1821, there were at least eight Provincial Deputations functioning in Mexico: those of Guadalajara, the Eastern Interior Provinces, the Western Interior Provinces, México, San Luis Potosí, Yucatán, Puebla, and Chiapas. Six other intendancies—Arispe for the provinces of Sinaloa and Sonora, Guanajuato, Michoacán, Oaxaca, Veracruz, and Zacatecas—by the Spanish decree of May 8, 1821, had the right to establish their own Provincial Deputations, which would bring the total to fourteen. They did not delay long in doing so. Iturbide, as noted, had recognized the right of the institution to exist when he authorized creation of a Provincial Deputation in the province of Puebla in August 1821.

The province and intendancy of Chiapas, in August 1821, formed a part of the Audiencia and Captaincy-General of Guatemala. However, since it was an intendancy, its right to establish a Provincial Deputation was authorized in the Spanish decree of May 8, 1821, published on August 7, 1821, in *El amigo de la patria* of Guatemala City. However, before steps could be taken to put that decree into effect, the Municipal Council of Comitan declared independence from Spain on August 28 and the province of Chiapas, on September 3, declared its independence not only from Spain but also from Guatemala.[3]

Events then moved rapidly. Chiapas elected Juan Nepomuceno Batres, José Anselmo de Lara, Pedro José de Solórzano, José Liño García, Manuel Ignacio Escarra, José Vivis, and Francisco Antonio Guillén deputies to its Provincial Deputation, which was installed on October 19, 1821.[4] That body, "representing the sentiments of the province," immediately began not only to take steps to insure the province's complete independence from Guatemala but also to bring about its union with Mexico.[5] Ten days after installation, the Provincial Deputation of Chiapas appointed Pedro José de Solórzano to confer with Iturbide on this important matter.[6]

The Treaty of Córdoba had provided that existing Spanish laws and decrees should be preserved until a Cortes could be convoked to form a national Constitution. Iturbide, on September 24, 1821, made public the names of thirty-eight persons who were to compose the Sovereign Provisional Governing Junta,[7] which was invested with all the powers formerly held by the Spanish Cortes not in conflict with the Treaty of Córdoba.[8] The main duty of this junta was to draw up instructions for the holding of elections for deputies to a Constituent Cortes or Congress for independent Mexico.

Ten days after it began its regular session on September 28, 1821, a committee to draw up the electoral procedure for the first Mexican Congress was named. Discussion on its report began on November 10, 1821; on the following day, José Mariano Almanza of Veracruz proposed that the matter of the election of provincial deputies to their individual Provincial Deputations (which, according to the Spanish Constitution of 1812, should take place on the day following the election of deputies to the national Congress) should be settled. José María Fagoaga protested that the division of the provinces was pressing, implying that this was necessary before taking up the subject of Provincial Deputations. However, José Mariano Sardanete, the Marqués de Rayas, of Guanajuato, said that the provinces that did not yet have Provincial Deputations were clamoring for them. After lengthy discussion, provisions for the election of deputies to the Provincial Deputations were adopted.[9]

The complete instructions for elections to the new Congress were issued by the Regency on November 18, 1821. Article 14 ordered the Provincial Deputations already established to be continued, new ones to be established at once in the intendancies that had not already done so, and the future Congress to designate others that might be necessary for the well-being of the country. Article 15 ordered the membership of the established Provincial Deputations to be completely renewed at the time of the elections; however, half of the old members could be reelected, as long as they were from the province reelecting them.[10] Article 16 provided that the deputies in the newly created Provincial Deputations must be from the respective provinces. And Article 17 stated that the election of deputies to these provincial bodies should take place in the capital of the province on the day following the election of deputies to Congress.[11]

According to that decree, therefore, on January 29, 1822, deputies to the Provincial Deputations of Chiapas, the Eastern Interior Provinces, Guadalajara, Guanajuato, México, Michoacán, New Vizcaya, Oaxaca, Puebla, San Luis Potosí, Sonora and Sinaloa, Veracruz, Yucatán, and Zacatecas were to be elected. There seems to be no question that Tlaxcala was expected to install a Provincial Deputation, although it was not mentioned in the decree and evidence of the source of its right to do so has not been found. Tlaxcala was not an intendancy. The so-called province of Tlaxcala was brought into existence in 1809. The preliminary electoral council of New Spain in its formal instructions of November 27, 1809, for the holding of the elections under the Constitution of 1812, had designated for New Spain the nine provinces of México, Puebla, Oaxaca, Michoacán, Guanajuato, Veracruz, San Luis Potosí, Tlaxcala, and Querétaro.[12] All of these except Tlaxcala and Querétaro were intendancies, which at that time were also called provinces. However, the province of Tlaxcala, encompassing the Gobierno de la Ciudad de Tlaxcala, plus the *alcaldía* or *distrito* of Huexotzingo, was removed from the intendancy of Puebla and designated a province for the sole purpose of electing a deputy to the Cortes and to the Provincial Deputation of New Spain.[13] In all subsequent elections Tlaxcala continued to be designated as one of the seven provinces subject to the Provincial Deputation of New Spain and elected its deputy to that body.

When the Spanish Cortes, on April 30, 1821, voted to allow each intendancy in the New World to establish a Provincial Deputation, Tlaxcala, basing its right largely on the fact that it had been considered a province for the purpose of electing deputies to the Cortes and to the Provincial Deputation of New Spain, at once asked permission to have its own Deputation.[14] The Cortes, as far as has been learned, never granted that request. It is possible that Iturbide awarded Tlaxcala a Provincial Deputation, as he did Puebla. Whatever the reason, Tlaxcala's right to a Provincial Deputation was not questioned and it came into existence at the same time as those of the intendancies of Mexico. This brought the total number of Provincial Deputations to fifteen.

Another province believed so strongly that it should have a Provincial Deputation that it elected its deputies without even asking for permission to do so. Nuevo Santander (later known as Tamaulipas), one of the Eastern Interior Provinces, elected seven deputies to the Provincial Deputation of Nuevo Santander, in March 1822, on the day following the election of its deputy to the national Congress, and officially reported that action to the national government at the same time that it reported the election of its deputy to the Congress.[15] Furthermore, it installed the members of its Provincial Deputation and then appealed to Congress to legalize its action.[16] Response to this appeal, which arrived on March 22, 1822, was slow; but on June 21 this bill passed, and on August 26 Nuevo Santander's congressman, José María Gutiérrez de Lara, reported that the sixteenth Deputation in Mexico had been legally established.[17]

Even prior to the elections in January 1822, still another request for a Provincial Deputation had been received by the Mexican government. Querétaro, like Tlaxcala, had come into existence as a province of New Spain by the act of the preliminary electoral council of November 27, 1809. Encompassing the *corregimiento* of Querétaro and the *alcadías* of Cadereyta and Zacanela and carved from the intendancy of México, this province was so designated that it might have the right to elect deputies to the Spanish Cortes and to the Provincial Deputation of New Spain.[18] In all succeeding elections before 1822, Querétaro continued to be designated as a province, but the failure of the Sovereign Provisional Governing Junta to include Querétaro in drawing up its decree for the holding of elections in November 1821 deprived it of this rank.[19] Querétaro's protest and demand for provincial rights went unheeded by the junta,[20] which left the matter to the incoming Cortes or Congress. Until then Querétaro's status was established by the decree issued by the Regency on November 18, 1821.[21]

Shortly after Congress began its sessions in 1822, Querétaro renewed the demand for a Provincial Deputation through a petition sent to the constitutional committee, which was announced on March 12, 1822.[22] There it remained until June 7, when the matter was brought to the attention of Congress, by Iturbide's ordering Field Marshal Luis Quintanar to duty in Guadalajara. Quintanar had been elected as Querétaro's deputy in the Provincial Deputation of México, and his departure from Mexico City left Querétaro unrepresented in that body. After another unsuccessful attempt to secure its own Provincial Deputation,[23] Querétaro finally demanded it on the ground of lack of representation in the Mexico City body. This demand was read on August 1, 1822.[24] Twenty-one days later, the Congressional Committee on Government recommended that Querétaro should have its own Provincial Deputation and that its deputies should be elected immediately by the same electors who had named its deputies to the Congress then in session, and the bill was so approved.[25] The exact date of its installation and its total membership are unknown. No doubt, however, it was installed very soon thereafter.

Therefore, by November 1822, seventeen Provincial Deputations had been authorized in Mexico, and eighteen had been established. The un-

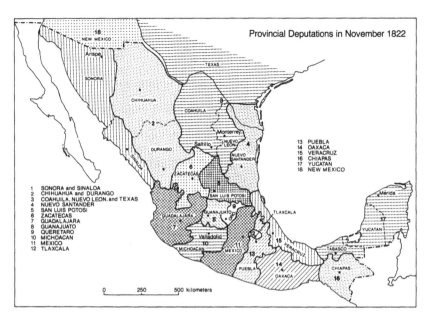

Provincial Deputations in November 1822

1 SONORA and SINALOA
2 CHIHUAHUA and DURANGO
3 COAHUILA, NUEVO LEON, and TEXAS
4 NUEVO SANTANDER
5 SAN LUIS POTOSI
6 ZACATECAS
7 GUADALAJARA
8 GUANAJUATO
9 QUERETARO
10 MICHOACAN
11 MEXICO
12 TLAXCALA

13 PUEBLA
14 OAXACA
15 VERACRUZ
16 CHIAPAS
17 YUCATAN
18 NEW MEXICO

authorized one was that of New Mexico; its members were elected in the early part of 1822 and it held its first session in Santa Fé, on April 25, 1822. Its deputies were Francisco X. Chávez, Pedro Ignacio Gallegos, Juan Bautista Virgil, Juan Estevan Pino, Agapito Alba, and Manuel Rubí; and its alternates, Juan Rafael Ortiz and Captain Bartolomé Baca.[26]

Available evidence indicates that New Mexico, like Nuevo Santander, proceeded in 1822 to establish its Provincial Deputation based on its belief that it had the right to do so as a province. A petition from the Municipal Council of Santa Fé asking for authorization to establish such a body was read on March 21, 1822, in the national Congress and sent to a committee;[27] however, there is no evidence that it was granted. Furthermore, in the 1822 *Actas del congreso constituyente mexicano,* New Mexico is consistently referred to as one of the component parts, with Durango and Chihuahua, of the Provincial Deputation of Nueva Vizcaya. The New Mexico Provincial Deputation was, nonetheless, established and functioned throughout 1822,[28] apparently officially unrecognized but also unmolested by the national government. The felicitations that the New Mexico Provincial Deputation offered to Congress in honor of its establishment were received and read on June 4, 1822; on July 2, Congress heard the petition of that same Provincial Deputation for permission to enjoy freedom of trade between New Mexico and the United States and sent it to the Committee on Commerce and Finance for consideration.[29]

Before the end of 1822, requests for the establishment of a Provincial

Deputation in each of the provinces of Tabasco, Sinaloa, Sonora, Chihua-hua, New Mexico, Nuevo León, Coahuila, and Texas had been presented in Congress.

Tabasco for many years had been under the jurisdiction of Yucatán and had no other representation in Congress. A proposal on August 22, 1822, by Manuel Crescencio Rejón, a Yucatecan deputy, that the province of Ta-basco be created, a Political Chief named, and a Provincial Deputation es-tablished in San José Bautista de Villahermosa,[30] was read for the second time on September 9 and referred to the Committee on Government. However, there is no further mention of the matter in the subsequent *Actas del congreso constituyente mexicano* before it was dissolved by Iturbide in late 1822, although Rejón, speaking in the restored Mexican Constituent Congress a year later, said that the Junta Nacional Instituyente had issued the decree creating the province of Tabasco.[31] The Provincial Deputation of Tabasco was functioning by the end of April 1823, and its members were José Antonio Rincón (Political Chief), Antonio Sierra, Lorenzo Ortega, José Puich, Nicanor Hernández Bayona, Pedro López, José María Cabral, and Ignacio Prado (deputies), and Juan Esteban Campos (secretary).[32] No facts concerning the date of the decree or the election of its members have yet been found.

Sinaloa, Sonora, Durango, Chihuahua, and New Mexico were the five provinces that had been under the jurisdiction of the Provincial Deputa-tion of the Western Interior Provinces, with its capital in Durango until 1821, when Sinaloa and Sonora were awarded a Provincial Deputation, with its capital at Arispe, and Durango, Chihuahua, and New Mexico the Provincial Deputation of Nueva Vizcaya, with its capital at Durango. Agi-tation for the establishment of a Provincial Deputation in each of them began in 1822, after New Mexico had established one without authoriza-tion. Juan Miguel Riesgo, Salvador Porras, Francisco Velasco, and Manuel José de Zuloaga, deputies in the Mexican Constituent Congress, drew up a 62-page memorial in which existing conditions in the Western Interior Provinces were described and desirable changes were outlined. Especially urged was the need for the division of the government of each province of the region and the establishment of Provincial Deputations and intendan-cies in each. This lengthy printed document, signed by the aforemen-tioned deputies on July 22, 1822,[33] and circulated in 1822, appears to have been written as a memorial to the Congress in session at that time; how-ever, the congressional records contain no mention of its formal presenta-tion. The first evidence of an effort to establish more Provincial Deputa-tions in the Western Interior Provinces appears in the statements of Carlos Espinosa de los Monteros (deputy for the province of Sinaloa and Sonora) made on February 22, 1823, in the course of debates in the Junta Nacional Instituyente, that not all the provinces had Provincial Deputations and of

Salvador Porras, who said that the separation of Chihuahua and Durango was pending.[34]

A week later, Espinosa de los Monteros published and circulated a 44-page document, in which he gave a detailed description of conditions in Sonora and Sinaloa and, among proposals for their improvement, urged the division of the two provinces and the immediate establishment of a Provincial Deputation in each.[35] In still another representation to the restored Mexican Constituent Congress on May 5, 1823,[36] Manuel Terán de Escalante, Simón Elías González, Juan Miguel Riesgo, Manuel Ximénez de Bailo, and Antonio de Iriarte took issue with some of the proposals of the exposition of July 1, 1822, and argued instead for a single Provincial Deputation with more extensive powers.[37] This was referred to a special Committee on Affairs of the Interior Provinces,[38] which reported promptly, for when discussion finally began six weeks later, Lorenzo de Zavala said that the report on the projected electoral law had been written long before that.[39] The urgency of other matters had evidently delayed submission of the report for discussion.

Among the more pressing matters was that of the electoral law to convoke a new Constituent Congress. The Plan of Casa Mata had called for a new Congress;[40] but, after Iturbide had recalled the members of the first Mexican Constituent Congress, its members had been reluctant to take the step and only after pressure from the provinces (presented in the following chapter) voted on May 21, 1823, to issue a call for such elections.[41] A committee immediately began the task of drafting an electoral law.

Discussion on the proposed electoral law was barely underway before the question of more Provincial Deputations was injected. Francisco Velasco urged the separation of Chihuahua from Durango, seconded by Florentino Martínez.[42] Juan José Espinosa de los Monteros joined in pressing for an addition to Article 10,[43] by which Durango should be divided into two parts for election purposes, one consisting of the territory from Paso del Norte to the Río Florido, with its capital at Chihuahua City, and the other, the remainder of the territory with its capital at Durango City.[44]

Throughout the discussion of the electoral law, Espinosa de los Monteros and the other deputies from the Western Interior Provinces insisted on the separation of those provinces. On June 15, when Congress reached Chapter VII, Articles 84 and 85, which dealt with the election of members to the Provincial Deputations, Espinosa immediately asked what course the provinces listed in Article 10 that did not have those bodies should take and pressed for a definitive statement concerning their position. These articles were referred back to the committee for further study, and discussion on the electoral law continued. When Article 88, which said that the Provincial Deputations should assume the functions of the preparatory electoral councils, was reached, Espinosa insisted that the article confirmed the necessity for the establishment of Provincial Deputations in all of the provinces still without them; with the reading of each succeeding article, he offered it as further proof for his argument. Finally his proposal, as an amendment to Article 92, that, in the provinces listed there separately,[45] Provincial Deputations be established to function according to the provisions of the Spanish Constitution of 1812 until the future Congress should otherwise provide was sent to the Electoral Committee.[46]

The recommendation of the committee that the proposed division of the provinces of New Vizcaya into two parts take place and each elect deputies according to Article 8 of the electoral law was approved by Congress;[47] it became Article 86 of the electoral law of June 17, 1823.[48] Congress first approved the committee's recommendations that the question of separating Chihuahua from Durango and Sinaloa from Sonora and granting each a Provincial Deputation be deferred and that the amendment of Article 92 calling for a Provincial Deputation in all provinces listed in Article 10 be referred to the Committee on Government.[49] However, after lengthy discussion of this matter from June 18 through July 12, Congress finally granted each a separate Provincial Deputation.[50] The location of the capital of Sinaloa at Culiacán and that of Sonora at Ures, with the provision that each might be moved, was approved on June 18, as was Article 10, which provided that New Mexico should have a Provincial Deputation with the same powers as that of Sonora.[51] Then, on July 14, 1823, Congress approved the establishment of a Provincial Deputation in each of the capitals of the provinces of Durango and Chihuahua.[52]

Durango elected Gaspar Periera, Diego García Celis, Esteban del Campo, Juan Mansonera, Vicente Elizalde, José Ignacio Iturrivarría, and Juan José Escovar as deputies; and Miguel Molina, Miguel Alcalde, and Santiago Sada y Ortiz as alternate deputies. New Mexico elected Antonio Ortiz, Pedro García, Jesús Francisco Baca, Mariano de la Peña, Jesús Francisco Ortiz, Pedro Jesús Perea, and Jesús García de la Mora as deputies; and Jesús Antonio Chávez, Pedro Bautista Pino, Matías Ortiz, Juan Tomás Terrazas, Juan Bautista Pino, and Juan Rafael Ortiz as alternate deputies. The names of the deputies for Sonora have not been found, but they were elected and installed, as witnessed by the correspondence of that body with Congress. Chihuahua elected José Ignacio Urquidi, José Ignacio Ochoa, Mariano Horcasitas, Mariano del Prado, Estevan Aguirre, Francisco Loya, and José María Echevarría as deputies and José María Irigoyen, Joaquín José Escarcega, and José Miguel Salas Valdéz as alternate deputies; the Deputation was installed on October 4, 1823. The names of the Sinaloa deputies have not been found, but they were elected and installed at Culiacán on October 8, 1823.[53]

The Eastern Interior Provinces had greater opposition to overcome. They were jointly granted a Provincial Deputation with its capital at Monterrey in the province of Nuevo León when Provincial Deputations were first instituted under the Constitution of 1812. The first of these provinces to break away was Nuevo Santander, which established its own Provincial Deputation in early 1822. This separation became the source of much trouble for the three remaining provinces—Nuevo León, Coahuila, and Texas. There had long been great competition between Monterrey, the capital of Nuevo León, and Saltillo, the principal municipality of Coahuila, to become the center of activity of the whole group. After Monterrey became the seat of the See of Linares, Saltillo was unceasing in its efforts to have it moved there. Ramos Arizpe not only requested that the Spanish Cortes move the seat of the See of Linares to Saltillo but proposed and had a law passed providing for the establishment of an intendancy of the Eastern Interior Provinces with its capital in Saltillo. This law, however, was never put into effect. From the time of the legalization of Provincial Deputations, he urged the Cortes that the Deputation be located at Saltillo. It should have been located there because that city had been named the capital of the intendancy. At the time of the establishment of the Provincial Deputation of the Eastern Interior Provinces, Monterrey had been named the capital; and, even after Ramos Arizpe induced the Cortes to change it to Saltillo, that body continued to sit at Monterrey.

Then, too, that Provincial Deputation of the Eastern Interior Provinces had Joaquín de Arredondo, the Commandant-General in charge of the four provinces, to contend with. He resented having to deal with this new institution; while it existed during 1814, he did not preside at any of its meetings, nor encourage any of its activities. He did allow it to be reestablished in 1820, however, after the Constitution of 1812 was reproclaimed. The members elected to it in November 1820 were to serve during the year 1820–1821. After serving their appointed time, they informed Political Chief Gaspar López, who had been named provisional Commandant-General in August 1821 to succeed Arredondo and, much to the disgust of the Monterrey officials, had established his headquarters at Saltillo,[54] that, since their term of office had expired, they were turning that body's archives over to him.[55]

Seven members of the Provincial Deputation—one from Texas and two each from the other three provinces—for the biennium 1822–1823 were to be elected on January 22, 1822. Prior to that date, however, petitions began to reach the Sovereign Provisional Governing Junta asking for changes. In its session of January 10, 1822, it referred to the Minister of Domestic and Foreign Affairs a petition from the Provincial Deputation of the Eastern Interior Provinces that its residence be changed to Saltillo.[56] Gaspar López, the Political Chief and Commandant-General, recommended, in a communication read on January 29, 1822, that a Provincial Deputation neither be established in Saltillo nor be permitted to be established at all.[57] The request of the Municipal Council of Saltillo that the body be established in that city, read on February 6, 1822, was sent to the Joint Committees on the Calling of Congress and on Internal Affairs.[58] To the same committee of the newly installed Mexican Constituent Congress on March 20, 1822, went Nuevo Santander's appeal for recognition of its seven deputies and three alternates, elected without authorization on January 29, 1822, to its Provincial Deputation. In the meantime, Gaspar López neither attended the sessions of the Provincial Deputation of the Eastern Interior Provinces, sitting at Monterrey, nor took any steps to install its members elected in January 1822. Since neither the junta nor Congress took any action on the various proposals made in regard to it, López doubtless felt that he was justified in not installing it.

Since José Antonio Gutiérrez de Lara of Nuevo Santander continued to press for the recognition of its elected Provincial Deputation, José Bautista Arizpe, deputy to Congress from Nuevo León, made a formal proposal that each of the other three Eastern Interior Provinces be authorized to establish such bodies.[59] He apparently suffered a change of heart soon afterward, for he later favored the recommendation of the Committee on Government that only the one at Monterrey be authorized and that the two deputies elected by Nuevo Santander proceed to Monterrey to assume their duties.[60] This recommendation was approved by Congress on June 20, 1822.[61]

Gutiérrez de Lara, who was absent from Congress on that day, heard the committee opinion that a Provincial Deputation should be established in Nuevo Santander approved on the following day by Congress. Ramos Arizpe then explained that the Eastern Interior Provinces were suffering from the delay in the establishment of a Provincial Deputation at Monterrey. He added that he had never been opposed to such a body for Nuevo Santander but had only objected to the crippling of the Monterrey body by such action. He believed it highly desirable that one Deputation for the four provinces be established at once in order to prevent further delay and that separate Deputations be established gradually in each province. When the vice-president of Congress observed that the difficulties Ramos Arizpe mentioned could be satisfactorily overcome, the matter of Provincial Deputations for the three remaining provinces was referred to the Committee on Government.[62]

The question of the continued delay in the establishment of the Provincial Deputation at Monterrey, when raised again on July 22, was simply referred to the Committee on Government, as all others had been.[63] On August 21, José San Martín proposed that the government provide an intendant and a Political Chief for Monterrey, that the Provincial Deputation be established, that López be removed as Commandant-General, and that the charges against his secretary, Padilla, be investigated. When the

José Servando Teresa de Mier Noriega, Historian and Member of Congress, 1823–1824. Undated postcard, miscellaneous postcard collection.

proposal was read the second time on September 12, it was sent to the Committee on Government.[64]

Finally, on October 7, 1822, the Joint Committees on the Constitution and Government ruled that the decrees of June 20 and June 21 concerning the Provincial Deputations of the Eastern Interior Provinces should be held valid and that a body composed of the members elected by the province of Nuevo Santander should be established at San Carlos,[65] and another be established at Monterrey, made up of the deputies elected in Nuevo León, Coahuila, and Texas, the vacancies caused by the withdrawal of Nuevo Santander being filled by two of the alternate deputies of the three provinces.[66] The enabling decree was formally issued on October 14, 1822,[67] and was published in the *Gaceta del gobierno imperial de México*, on February 5, 1823, just four days after the proclamation of the Plan of Casa Mata.

From August 1821 to February 1823, Nuevo León, Coahuila, and Texas knew no form of government other than the orders of Commandant-General Gaspar López until news of the Plan of Casa Mata reached Monterrey. Under the leadership of Ramos Arizpe, some members of the Municipal Council of Monterrey, ecclesiastical and military officials, and various citizens of Monterrey voted on March 6, 1823, to adhere to the Plan and, in the absence of a Provincial Deputation, to appoint a provisional governing council (junta) to assume the political and economic administration of the province. That council was named at once, with Ramos Arizpe (president), José León Lobo Guerrero (vice-president), José Rafael de Llano (secretary), and José Vivero, Rafael González, Julián de Arrete, José Antonio Rodríguez, and Francisco Eusebio de Arizpe; it assumed its duties on the same day. It was to serve until the national Congress stipulated in the Plan of Casa Mata had been installed and made provision for the government of those provinces.[68]

Some of the citizens of Monterrey did not entirely approve of the establishment of this provisional governing council. The Monterrey Municipal

Council, which had frequently been in conflict with the earlier Provincial Deputation of the Eastern Interior Provinces, refused to take orders sent to it from the newly installed governing council.[69] The Monterrey Municipal Council wrote to José Servando Teresa de Mier, its deputy in the reassembled national Constituent Congress, asking that this new governing council be dissolved. Mier proposed (April 2, 1823) that Congress order the immediate installation of the Provincial Deputation at Monterrey, composed of the members elected to it in January 1822, as provided by the decree of October 14, 1822.[70] While this matter rested in the hands of the Committee on Government,[71] the provisional governing council in Monterrey, after having taken the necessary steps during the last days of March, on April 1 installed the Provincial Deputation of the Eastern Interior Provinces with the membership as specified in the decree of October 14, 1822, and turned over to it the administration of the Eastern Interior Provinces in conformity with the Plan of Casa Mata.[72]

Paradoxically, the further dismemberment of these provinces resulted from the efforts of Mier. He had censured Juan Bautista Arizpe for having asked in Congress for a Provincial Deputation for each of these provinces, in June 1822.[73] Yet on July 5, 1823, Mier himself had proposed that a Provincial Deputation be established in every province except Texas, which, because of its limited population, should be joined to that of Nuevo León with the capital at Monterrey.[74]

The events that had taken place in that region during May and June 1823 prompted Mier's proposal. Ramos Arizpe, after having installed the Provincial Deputation of the Eastern Interior Provinces at Monterrey on April 1, 1823, had, much to Mier's displeasure, continued to direct political affairs in that area. During the latter part of May and the first days of June, the Provincial Deputation in Monterrey and the Municipal Councils of those provinces not only had proclaimed a federal republic for Mexico but had begun to take steps to constitute a "centralized federal state of the Eastern Interior Provinces." This filled the national government and Mier with alarm. He proposed (July 5) the separation of these provinces in order to forestall that movement toward a centralized state.[75] As usual, his proposal was sent to the Committee on Government.

Nine days later, during the discussion on the government of the Western Interior Provinces, Mier's proposal, as an addition to Article 18 of the electoral law then under discussion, was also admitted and sent to committee.[76] The committee's recommendation that deputations be established in the provinces of Nuevo León, Coahuila, and Texas was approved by Congress, and the decree was issued. Both the recommendation and the decree granted Texas a Provincial Deputation.

Juan A. Mateos, in *Historia parlamentaria de los congresos mexicanos de 1821 a 1857*, says that the committee's report was rejected. This is obviously

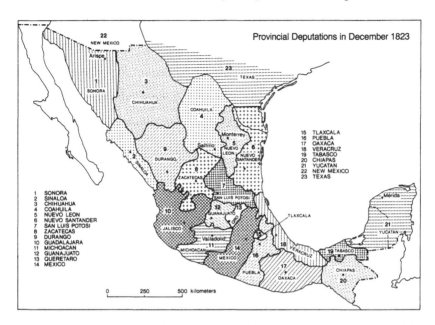

an error, for the congressional session of August 18, 1823, was printed in both the newspapers *El sol* and *Aguila mexicana*. They each reported the approval two days after it occurred. Furthermore, the decree to this effect was issued on the same day and the Deputations were established.[77]

Each of the provinces elected deputies at an election held on September 8, 1823. Nuevo León elected Eusebio Gutiérrez, Andrés Sobrevilla, Juan José de la Garza, Bernardino Güimbarda, Joaquín García, Pedro de la Garza, and Pedro González and alternate deputies Francisco Mier, José María Cárdenas, and Pablo Cabazos.[78] Coahuila elected Rafael Eça y Múzquiz, Francisco Fuentes, Juan Vicente Campos, Félix Malo, Melchor Sánchez Navarro, Agustín de la Garza, and José María Viezca and alternate deputies Victor Blanco, Joaquín de Arce, and Mariano Varela.[79] Texas elected José Antonio Saucedo, José María Zambrano, Ramón Múzquiz, Juan José Hernández, Miguel Arciega, Baron de Bastrop, and Mariano Rodríguez and alternate deputies José Salinas, Juan Veramendi, and Gaspar Flores.[80]

The first named deputy of each became the Political Chief of the province. Texas installed the Deputation in Béxar on October 31, 1823, with José Antonio Saucedo as Political Chief.[81] The Coahuila installation took place on December 3, 1823, with Rafael Eça y Múzquiz as Political Chief.[82] The exact date of the installation of the members of Nuevo León has not been found, but it took place prior to the middle of October 1823.[83]

Thus, by December 1823, Provincial Deputations had been authorized and established in twenty-three provinces of Mexico: Chiapas, Chihuahua,

Coahuila, Durango, Guadalajara (which by this date had changed its name to Jalisco), Guanajuato, México, Michoacán, New Mexico, Nuevo León, Nuevo Santander (later Tamaulipas), Oaxaca, Puebla, Querétaro, San Luis Potosí, Sinaloa, Sonora, Tabasco, Texas, Tlaxcala, Veracruz, Yucatán, and Zacatecas. (For the deputies elected to each of these provincial deputations by this date, see appendix B.) The powers of the Provincial Deputations had been broadened since their creation in the Constitution of 1812. And some of them by that date had gone further and assumed full powers over the government within their individual provinces.

FIVE

Assumption of Power by the Provincial Deputations

Before the action of the Provincial Deputations in existence by the close of 1823 can be more closely scrutinized, the general state of Mexican political thought needs to be reviewed.[1] At the time of independence, at least three distinct political groups existed: (1) those who favored a monarchy headed by a European prince, (2) those who wanted a monarchy headed by an American native, and (3) those whose efforts were specifically directed toward the establishment of a republic; the last group included most of the old insurgents. Each of these groups attempted to mold public opinion through the issuance of books, pamphlets, and other literature on the science of government. Such was the announced purpose of the weekly *Semanario político y literario* and of *El conductor eléctrico* of José Joaquín Fernández de Lizardi.

Among publications that especially praised the republican form of government of the United States were the *Abispa de Chilpancingo*, edited by Carlos María Bustamante, a great admirer of George Washington, and *El hombre libre*, a newspaper that supported republicanism.[2] The *Semanario político y literario* published translations of various political documents of the United States, including the Declaration of Independence, the Articles of Confederation, the Constitution of the United States, and the Bill of Rights.[3]

José Servando Teresa de Mier was an active contributor to this type of literature with his *Memoria instructiva*, published in Philadelphia in 1821 and sent to Mexico for distribution.[4] Its second printing in Mexico was on sale by June 1822.[5]

The ideas advanced in this work by Mier aroused much discussion. The magazine *Sabatina universal* attempted in its issue of June 15 to defend Iturbide and to answer the arguments advanced by Mier against any form of monarchy for Mexico,[6] but in so doing gave publicity to Mier's views. The newspaper *Noticioso general* further helped in this direction by commenting on the rejoinder of the *Sabatina universal* to Mier's denunciation of monarchy and his impassioned appeal to Mexican leaders to study the

Carlos María Bustamante, Congressman, Editor, and Historian. Lithograph, from Manuel Rivera Cambas, *Los gobernantes de México* (Mexico City: Imprenta de J. M. Aguilar Ortiz, 1873).

political ideas and practices of the United States.[7] Vicente Rocafuerte's *Ideas necesarias a todo pueblo americano independiente, que quiere ser libre,* first printed in 1822 in Philadelphia, set forth the political organization of the United States as a model for the nascent Latin American countries and included translations of many important documents. Its popularity in Mexico necessitated a reprinting in Puebla in 1823. Another book by Rocafuerte, his *Bosquejo ligerísimo de la revolución de México,* recounted the events leading to Iturbide's coronation as emperor in 1822 and denounced his double dealing since 1810.[8] Undoubtedly this literature exalting republicanism helped to arouse opposition to Iturbide's autocratic rule, an opposition that was greatly increased by his suppression of the newspaper *El sol,* which advocated a monarchy with a European prince on the throne, and *El hombre libre,* which supported republicanism.[9]

By this time, the idea of revolt against the newly crowned emperor was brewing. A republican conspiracy in Michoacán had been nipped in time; but the discovery of another, fomented by the same faction and nearer the capital, led to the arrest of fifteen deputies of the Imperial Constituent Congress on August 26 and 27, 1822, including Mier and Carlos María Bustamante.[10] When a congressional demand for their liberation went unheeded by Iturbide, public resentment increased.

As a result, an open revolt broke out in the province of Nuevo Santander. It was led by Felipe de la Garza, its Political Chief, who had the support of the Provincial Deputation of Nuevo Santander, the Municipal Council of Soto la Marina, and the provincial electors. From that place, on September 26, 1822, a representation was addressed to Iturbide, signed by Felipe de la Garza, the members of the Provincial Deputation, the provincial electors, the parish priests, the officers of the militia, and prominent citizens.[11]

This representation reached Mexico City on October 6, 1822.[12] Direct and forceful, it called upon Iturbide (1) to set the imprisoned deputies at liberty immediately, (2) to install Congress at whatever place it might

José Antonio Echávarri, Spanish
General. Lithograph, from Manuel
Rivera Cambas, *Los gobernantes
de México* (Mexico City: Imprenta de
J. M. Aguilar Ortiz, 1873).

choose, where it might deliberate with absolute freedom, (3) to depose the
acting ministry, making its members subject to trial by law, (4) to suppress
all military courts of public security wherever established, (5) to release all
other prisoners arrested on suspicion in Mexico City or in the provinces
under the provisions of the circular issued by the Secretary of State on August 27, (6) to bring to legal trial those known to have committed crimes,
and finally (7) to observe the fundamental laws that had been adopted
provisionally.[13]

The ministry charged with exercising powers detrimental to both Iturbide and the nation was held completely responsible for the criminal viola-
tion of the political liberty of the country.[14] Held blameless for previous
events, Iturbide was warned of future responsibility. Nuevo Santander informed the emperor that it would not allow Col. Pedro José Lanuza, his
nominee, or anyone else to take command of the province or permit
troops to enter it. Any such attempt would be repelled by force.[15]

Iturbide, ignoring the warning, immediately dispatched troops to suppress the revolt, and de la Garza, receiving no support from other provinces, soon had to give up the fight. By October 19, all appeared calm in
the provinces. The Nuevo Santander revolt, however, was a portent of the
future.

The next revolt broke out, not because of political indignation, but because of a personal feud between two of Iturbide's officers. José Antonio
Echávarri and Antonio López de Santa Anna, imperial commander of
troops in Veracruz, became suspicious of each other. General Echávarri,
suspecting that Santa Anna had tried to deliver him into enemy hands,
wrote to Iturbide accusing Santa Anna of double dealing. Iturbide, in an
effort to remove Santa Anna, asked him to come to Mexico City for a personal interview.

Santa Anna, however, hurried from Jalapa to Veracruz and, on December 2, 1822, issued a proclamation denouncing the arbitrary dissolution
of Congress by Iturbide. The shrewd rebel declared that, since all the prov-

Guadalupe Victoria, General and President of Mexico, 1824–1829. Lithograph, from Manuel Rivera Cambas, *Los gobernantes de México* (Mexico City: Imprenta de J. M. Aguilar Ortiz, 1873).

inces had proclaimed in favor of a republic with the government vested in the people and not in a single authority, he favored that form of government and had, with the approval of the Provincial Deputation of Veracruz, provisionally adopted all the measures necessary for the security of the city.[16] According to Santa Anna, an uprising was already being planned for 1823, but the orders that he appear in Mexico City decided him to declare at once for liberty or death.[17] He was joined almost immediately by Guadalupe Victoria, who had been in hiding near Veracruz, and by many of the republicans who had fled from Mexico City.

On December 6, in order to formalize the movement, Santa Anna issued the Plan of Veracruz, setting forth the platform of the rebels. This poorly organized, verbose document of seventeen main and twenty-two additional explanatory articles, drawn up by Miguel Santa María, outlined a political program framed to attract adherents. It was a hodge-podge of the Plan of Iguala, the representation of de la Garza, and the Santa Anna proclamation of December 2.[18] The first two main articles were copied almost verbatim from the Plan of Iguala. The twenty-first explanatory article quoted and ordered observed the provisions adopted by Santa Anna with the consent of the Veracruz Provincial Deputation. The third through the seventeenth main articles dealt with Iturbide and Congress. All its acts to that date, including the coronation of Iturbide and his decrees, were declared null and void, because they had been adopted under duress. Similar to the de la Garza representation, the Plan of Veracruz called for the reinstallation of the full membership of the old Congress in a place of its own choosing to insure untrammeled deliberations and the free designation of a council or Regency to exercise executive power until a Constitution could be drawn up.[19]

Although it seemed that this revolt, too, would be short-lived, it apparently gained more support. Vicente Guerrero and Nicolás Bravo fled from Mexico City to the south, where they collected some followers, seconded the Plan of Veracruz, and on January 13, 1823, from Chilapa, distributed printed copies of their adhesion.[20] The armies Iturbide sent quickly defeated the rebels. Santa Anna, then at Jalapa, retreated precipitously to Veracruz. Guerrero was believed killed, and Bravo went into hiding. By the end of January, the revolt had been restricted to the Veracruz area, where Guadalupe Victoria and Santa Anna were being so closely besieged by Echávarri that Santa Anna was preparing to flee to the United States.[21]

Iturbide was momentarily expecting word of the complete quelling of the revolt when an event occurred that completely changed the picture. A Plan was signed at Casa Mata in the state of Veracruz, on February 1, 1823, not by Santa Anna and Victoria, as has frequently been stated, but by Echávarri and his officers,[22] under circumstances which have long been debated. It was written by Col. Gregorio Arana,[23] Echávarri's secretary and honor guard. The groundwork for the Plan is said to have been laid, however, in the masonic lodges of the country by such men as Ramos Arizpe and Michelena, for whom Echávarri and his officers served merely as the mouthpiece.[24] Although there is no documentary proof of this, it may be accepted as fairly accurate, because Carlos María Bustamante and Lorenzo de Zavala, the first to make the assertion, were on the scene at the time and the latter was a very active member of a masonic lodge. The further fact that Ramos Arizpe and Michelena directed the trend of events after proclamation of the Plan tends to confirm their earlier participation in it.

It can be shown, however, that Santa Anna and Guadalupe Victoria had no hand in its origin, although it was the hope of all concerned that the Plan of Casa Mata would meet with their approval. Article 8 provided that a delegation should carry a copy to Veracruz with the hope of securing the adherence of the governor and official bodies there.[25] Echávarri at once sent Luis Cortazar to Santa Anna with a copy, prefaced by a letter inviting him to join the Plan of Casa Mata in order to prevent the disasters that threatened the country.[26] At the same time, Echávarri sent Lt. Col. Manuel María Hernández to deliver to the Municipal Council of Veracruz the Plan and a letter similar to that sent to Santa Anna, both of which were printed the next day as an extra by the *Diario de Veracruz*.[27] Santa Anna and his officers on the same day (February 2) signed a statement addressed to Echávarri in which they promised adherence,[28] as did the Municipal Council of Veracruz and other official bodies but with some modifications, in the form of additions.[29] One of these provided that, until Congress should meet, the Spanish Constitution of 1812 and the decrees of the Cortes should be strictly followed.[30] On the following day, February 3, the official bodies of Veracruz sent a delegation to Casa Mata to escort Echávarri to the city to preside over a joint meeting of the Provincial Deputation of Veracruz and the Veracruz Municipal Council, and the enthusiastic welcome he received there was "out of this world."[31]

Three days later, on February 6, Echávarri and Guadalupe Victoria had a meeting at El Puente and came to an agreement.[32] Victoria asked that if any changes were to be made in the Plan, as issued at Casa Mata, a council of war composed of all the commanders and officers of the united forces, including generals Vicente Guerrero and Nicolás Bravo and their officers, should be held to consider the matter.[33] Echávarri, on his return from this meeting, wrote Gen. José María Lobato that he could announce, with the greatest pleasure, that they had the support of the forces at Veracruz.[34]

On the same day that Echávarri sent copies of the Plan of Casa Mata to Veracruz, he sent copies to all of the Provincial Deputations of Mexico, to the Municipal Council of the capital of each province, and to the military leaders throughout the country. The rapidity with which these were delivered and the immediate adhesion to the Plan of Casa Mata tend to substantiate the claim that the groundwork had been well laid.[35]

Bravo accepted the plan on February 7, 1823, and entered Oaxaca without firing a shot.[36] Both the Oaxacan Provincial Deputation and the Municipal Council adopted it and at once began to make provisions for the government of that province.

Disturbing rumors of the Plan of Casa Mata quickly reached Puebla and began to arouse such conflicting attitudes among the people that the Commandant-General, José María Morán, Marqués de Vivanco, on February 8, 1823, issued a proclamation announcing that Echávarri and all his army had agreed that Congress should be installed as soon as possible, the convocation to be on the basis of the elections of deputies to the Spanish Cortes and the provinces to have the right to re-elect the worthy members of the dissolved Congress and to replace the others.[37] The emperor, who was thought to favor national representation, was to be spared all personal harm. Morán insisted that these were simple facts, distorted by some in an attempt to bring misfortune to the country. He urged all to await the reply of Iturbide in tranquillity.

Morán himself, on the contrary, three days later issued a broadside, addressed to the inhabitants of the province of Puebla, stating that he, with the Provincial Deputation of Puebla and the Municipal Council of Puebla, was espousing the Plan of Casa Mata. He interpreted Article 10,[38] which provided that the Provincial Deputation of Veracruz should handle administrative affairs, to mean that, as each successive province adopted the Plan of Casa Mata, its Provincial Deputation should have jurisdiction over its provincial administrative affairs. In Puebla all actions taken by its Political Chief were first sanctioned by its Provincial Deputation.[39]

The acceptance of the Plan of Casa Mata was gaining momentum. The province of New Galicia, after three days of consultation between the forces of Captain-General and Political Chief Luis Quintanar and the Provincial Deputation, accepted it on February 26, and a proclamation to that effect was issued the following day.[40]

The act of adherence of the province of Guanajuato has not been located; neither has its exact date been established. It took place between February 23 and 26,[41] for on the earlier date the secretary of the Provincial Deputation of Guadalajara informed Quintanar that Guanajuato was ready to join and three days later the Political Chief said Guanajuato had already taken such action.[42]

Querétaro knew at an early date of the action taken by Echávarri and of the rapidity with which the country had followed his lead, but waited quietly for the emperor to save the country a second time by the prompt installation of Congress. When its Provincial Deputation received word, on February 25, 1823, of the action of the Provincial Deputation of Puebla, it immediately took up the matter and, although it proposed that other bodies and individuals be called in for consultation, voted not to make the news public. The facts became public, nevertheless, and the next day the proposed joint meeting was held. It was unanimously agreed to announce that the province had adopted the Plan of Casa Mata and that consequently the administration of the province would devolve upon its Provincial Deputation until Congress should meet. The official act was signed on February 26 by the Political Chief, Juan José García, all members of the Provincial Deputation, and representatives of the city, the church, and the army.[43]

Four days later, at three o'clock in the morning, a group of army officers from Zacatecas and Querétaro proclaimed their solemn adherence to the Plan of Casa Mata and called upon the Commandant-General and Political Chief of Zacatecas, Mariano González Laris, to place himself at the head of the movement. On his refusal, the adherents to the Plan asked Col. Pedro de Iriarte to take the lead; but instead, he urged, as had González Laris, that Zacatecas await the action of México or Guadalajara before committing itself. José Antonio de Saldana, then named to leadership, in conjunction with a committee appointed to aid in establishing unity throughout the city and province, called upon the Provincial Deputation and all official bodies of the city to adhere to the Plan. After the Provincial Deputation, on March 1, decided to wait, Saldana and his supporters continued to campaign for the Plan of Casa Mata. They sent a report of their action to Aguascalientes, to Guanajuato, and to various towns in Zacatecas, urging all to join them. When word arrived, on March 2, that the Provincial Deputation of Guadalajara and the other bodies of New Galicia favored the Plan, the Deputation was called into session at once. The communications from Guadalajara were read to the members of all the official bodies of the city; all adhered to the Plan.[44]

On the same day, the Provincial Deputation, the Municipal Council, and the military garrison of San Luis Potosí voted adherence and removed from office its Political Chief, Gen. Juan José Zenón Fernández, when he opposed it. The Provincial Deputation, in conformity with Article 10 of the Plan of Casa Mata, took over the administration of the province and, on March 4, named Ildefonso Díaz de León as its Political Chief.[45]

The Provincial Deputation of Michoacán and the army stationed at Valladolid accepted the Plan on March 1. Two days later, the Provincial Deputation advised the ecclesiastical chapter of the cathedral of its action and that it, as supreme authority, had assumed control of the province.[46] Carlos María Bustamante reported on March 3 that a copy of the adhesion of Valladolid, Michoacán, signed by the members of its Provincial Deputation, had arrived in Mexico City.[47] And, on March 4, Francisco Argandar, deputy from Valladolid, read to the Junta Nacional Instituyente a printed manifesto of the Provincial Deputation of Valladolid proclaiming its adhesion.[48]

The Provincial Deputation of Yucatán voted unanimously on March 4 to adopt the Plan of Casa Mata with the amendment made to Article 5 by the Mérida Municipal Council and the civil, ecclesiastical, and military authorities of the province to celebrate the action taken.[49] Three days later, the Political Chief of that province declared all legislative decrees issued by the Junta Nacional Instituyente null and void.[50]

Durango adhered to the Plan on March 5. The Commandant-General, Antonio Cordero, was too ill to take any part in public affairs at the time, and the Political Chief, Brigadier Ignacio del Corral, tried to prevent such action. But the Provincial Deputation of Durango and its Municipal Council, the clergy, and other public officials all voted in favor of the Plan. In the face of this action Corral resigned and the Provincial Deputation named the intendant, Juan Navarro, as Political Chief of New Vizcaya, and Col. Gaspar de Ochoa, military commander. When news reached Durango on the following day that Guadalajara, Guanajuato, and Zacatecas had adopted the Plan, Corral promised adherence and asked to be reinstated, but the Provincial Deputation refused to restore him.[51]

In the Eastern Interior Provinces, where the Provincial Deputation had as yet not been installed by López, its Commandant-General and Political Chief, Ramos Arizpe headed the movement in favor of the Plan of Casa Mata and took matters into his own hands. He had been in the region since August 1822, but little is known of his activities during the intervening months other than those connected with the de la Garza revolt.[52] It has been generally agreed, however, that he was busy preparing for a revolt of those provinces; and the events of March 1823 tend to substantiate that fact.[53]

Ramos Arizpe was in Monterrey directing a meeting of the members of the Municipal Council of that city, the ecclesiastical chapter, the provisional governor of the province, public employees, and prominent citizens on March 6, who voted to adopt the Plan of Casa Mata with two additional articles.[54] In the absence of a Provincial Deputation, those participating in that meeting decided to establish a provincial governing junta composed of seven members to govern until the installation of the Congress demanded by the Plan of Casa Mata. Members of this junta were named at once, took the oath of office immediately, and began to take steps to unite the four provinces in support of the Plan.[55] The junta dispatched copies of the action taken at Monterrey to all towns of the region, calling on them to proclaim acceptance of the Plan of Casa Mata. This most of them did immediately.[56]

Trouble arose in Saltillo, where López, a staunch supporter of Iturbide, had his headquarters. Rumors of the Monterrey proceedings of March 6 reached Saltillo on the following day. López convoked the usual council of military, ecclesiastical, and municipal officials and prominent citizens, stated that rumors that Monterrey had adopted the Plan of Casa Mata were abroad but they did not have full particulars, and asked for the complete facts, if known. None being given, the council voted to send Dr. Rafael Ramos y Valdés, Ramos Arizpe's cousin, to San Nicolás de la Capellanía for more detailed information. On the following day, the junta of Saltillo heard his report and received official communications from the newly installed provincial junta of Nuevo León calling upon Saltillo to proclaim adhesion to the action taken both at Casa Mata and at Monterrey. A special committee of nine members named to study the matter recommended that Saltillo adhere to the Plan of Casa Mata and endorse the action of Monterrey, and this report was approved.[57] It was further agreed to invite the committee offered by the provincial governing junta of Nuevo León to confer concerning steps to unify and consolidate public opinion within the two provinces.

From these proceedings it seemed that Saltillo was going to join the movement peacefully and quietly; López, however, did not intend to desert his friend Iturbide without a fight. In spite of having signed the acts of March 6 and 7 and having offered his resignation and stated his intention to leave the province at once, he remained in command of the troops and with them swore allegiance to Iturbide and ordered reinforcements from Monclova to proceed to Saltillo. The appointees of the Nuevo León junta (en route to Saltillo) learned at Rinconada of his attitude.[58]

The Nuevo León junta had realized from the first that López would probably offer resistance, and with foresight had dispatched Lt. Col. Pedro Lemus with troops to offer the Saltillians aid, if needed, but had recalled him on receiving word that López had acquiesced in the movement.[59] At Rinconada, Lemus learned of his resistance and, reinforced by thirty-five men from Santa Catarina and Pesquería, continued his march toward Saltillo, arriving in San Nicolás de la Capellanía, on March 11, 1823.[60]

On that same day, Ramos Arizpe and Llano were welcomed on the outskirts of Saltillo by representatives of the Municipal Council and escorted, amidst applause, to the lodgings of López, where they met with him and a group of citizens named to confer on difficulties that had arisen since the meeting on March 7. Ramos Arizpe spoke at length on the necessity of adopting the Plan of Casa Mata and of taking the oath of allegiance to the Plan immediately. He also requested the prompt departure of López and his forces from the Eastern Interior Provinces. López asked if the province of Nuevo León would recognize him as Commandant-General, to which Ramos Arizpe replied that the Nuevo León junta had assumed full political, economic, and military control and did not recognize him in any capacity. López then said he had decided to leave, but certain matters relative to his surrendering command would have to be dealt with in other conferences.[61]

His subsequent actions belied his words, for, on the following day, one of the city aldermen was shot by one of his officers and three residents were arrested without legal procedure. Ramos Arizpe ordered Lemus and his forces to take up their position on the outskirts of Saltillo and to be ready to come to its immediate assistance,[62] informed the Municipal Council of this order, and notified López that he and Llano were retiring until order had been restored and those guilty of unwarranted attacks on citizens of Saltillo had been apprehended and punished.[63]

From the Arizpe mills where Lemus and his forces had taken position, Ramos Arizpe sent another letter to López, denouncing his actions and calling on him to convoke a meeting of the commission elected by the junta of March 6–7 together with the members of the Municipal Council and to depart at once.[64] López did as suggested, and the Saltillo Municipal Council informed Ramos Arizpe and Llano that López had promised to begin his departure at three o'clock that day.[65] He did leave, and, on the invitation of the Municipal Council, Lemus and his troops entered Saltillo.[66]

On the following day, March 14, 1823, Saltillo held a mass meeting at which the municipal, ecclesiastical, and military officials took the oath of allegiance to the Plan of Casa Mata. The two additional articles added at Monterrey were also adopted in Saltillo.[67]

Nuevo Santander adhered to the Plan of Casa Mata on April 9, when its Provincial Deputation declared at the same time that it would act as the supreme governing junta for the province until the national Congress could meet.[68] On the same day, the province of Tabasco through its Political Chief, José Antonio Rincón, also announced adherence.[69]

By April 9, all of the Eastern Interior Provinces except Texas had joined in support of the Plan of Casa Mata. López, on March 10, had sent the governor at San Antonio by special messenger a copy of the act of his adherence to the Plan and the proceedings at Monterrey, Saltillo, and

Monclova.[70] On receiving this communication on March 21, the governor, the Municipal Council of San Antonio de Béxar, the ecclesiastical officials, the heads of the army, and others met and reaffirmed allegiance to Iturbide.[71] La Bahía del Espíritu Santo took similar action. Some twenty-odd days later, according to the governing council of Texas, government papers arrived that gave the Municipal Council of San Antonio sufficient light on political events in the country to adhere to the Plan of Casa Mata on April 15, in accord with the measures adopted and transmitted to it by the Provincial Deputation of Puebla.[72]

That the Provincial Deputation of the province of México located in the capital of the empire would make an open admission of adherence to the Plan of Casa Mata could hardly have been expected; but it did take steps to further the Plan after having received it together with a letter from Echávarri, dated February 1, 1823. The reason for issuing the Plan was thus explained:

> The ruin toward which the country was moving with gigantic strides, because of the lack of a national representative body, attracted my attention and that of the other officers of this army. We discussed at length the best way to save the country from the many-rooted evils and agreed unanimously to that in the attached copy of the act that I have the honor of sending to that most excellent Deputation, never doubting that all will receive your approval and that you will assist in the prompt establishment of Congress to constitute us under wise laws that will make our country happy. Please do me the kindness of replying. . . .[73]

Just when this letter was delivered to that Provincial Deputation has not been verified, but it was probably on February 8, for on that date one of Echávarri's officers, José Infamón, delivered the Plan of Casa Mata to Iturbide.[74] It is logical to suppose that either he or someone accompanying him brought the letter to that Provincial Deputation. It certainly was delivered prior to February 25, for on that date the Provincial Deputation sent it to the Minister of Domestic and Foreign Affairs to be relayed to Iturbide.[75]

News of the Plan had already reached Mexico City. Rumors concerning it had been circulating since February 2, when Carlos María Bustamante wrote in his diary: "News concerning Echávarri is very pleasing, as it is said to be certain that he has agreed with the government of Veracruz and has recognized substantially the Plan of Veracruz."[76] On February 8, copies of the supplement to the *Diario de Veracruz* of February 2, carrying Echávarri's letter transmitting the Plan of Casa Mata to the local Municipal Council and a modified version of the Plan, reached Mexico City.[77] This news arrived while Iturbide was on his way to one of the belated bullfights in honor of his coronation.[78]

On the following day, Iturbide canceled his plans to leave for Puebla to take command of the army. Instead, a special session of the Junta Nacional Instituyente was held that afternoon (February 9),[79] at which time the Plan sent by Echávarri was read. Iturbide assured the body of prompt and effective action on his part and of the support of all but some two thousand men in the army. Some members wanted to discuss the Plan and act at once, but Iturbide recommended the appointment of a committee to deliberate before proposing action. Mariano Mendiola, Toribio González, the Marqués de Rayas, Francisco Argandar, and Juan Nepomuceno Mier y Altamirano were named to the committee.[80]

On the same day, Iturbide drew up a manifesto to the people in which he gave a rather confused idea of what had happened at Casa Mata. He said the commission, which, according to Article 7, was to be dispatched immediately to place the Plan in his hand, had not arrived.[81] He reiterated his promise to act only for the good of the country and to use peaceful methods in conciliating and rewinning the erring and misinformed members of the army. This document was issued on February 10 and appeared in the *Gaceta* on the following day.[82]

On February 10, Iturbide decided to send a commission to treat with Echávarri, to which he named Pedro Celestino Negrete, Mariano Nicolás Robles, Juan José Espinosa de los Monteros, Ramón Esteban Martínez de los Ríos and Carlos García.[83] They arrived in Jalapa on February 17.[84]

Meanwhile, in Mexico City the committee appointed by Iturbide to render an opinion on the Plan of Casa Mata bitterly denounced it. Some of the deputies present in the Junta Nacional Instituyente thought the wording of the report needed softening; one even suggested that the dissolved Congress should be reinstalled; but the majority voted to accept the committee report.[85] It appeared in the *Gaceta del gobierno imperial de México* of February 20 and 22.

Not long after having sent Iturbide the communication from Echávarri, the Provincial Deputation of México received word that Puebla had adopted the plan of Casa Mata in full. It sent that letter to Iturbide, on February 26, with a copy of its reply, which read:

> In the name of humanity, this Deputation extends to your Excellency [the Provincial Deputation of Puebla] due thanks for the zealous care with which you are trying to avoid the evils consequent to civil war and the dismemberment of society. You may be sure that the constant desire of this Deputation and of the majority of the people that compose its province is directed toward the reunion of a national Congress elected with complete liberty and in conformity with the sane and recognized principles of public law and that in order to realize it [the reunion of Congress] this Deputation will make use of every means that prudence dictates and the laws permit. México, February 26, 1823.

[signed:] José Benito Guerra, José Alejo Alegría, Dr. José María Mora, José Florentino Conejo, Francisco Javier de Heras.[86]

To Echávarri went a brief note stating that he could gather from the copy of the communication to the Puebla body the feelings and inclinations of the Provincial Deputation of México.

There was nothing in any of these communications to offend Iturbide and his government. The letters merely repeated the sentiments that Iturbide had been insisting were his. On March 1, however, the Provincial Deputation addressed a letter to him in which it urged, as the only possible remedy for the situation, the immediate restoration of the dissolved Congress so that it might either draw up a Constitution or convoke a new assembly to do so.[87] In another communication the Provincial Deputation of México objected "to Iturbide's order to arm the city rabble" and warned that "he himself would be held responsible for the anarchy and havoc sure to result."[88]

Thus, with the adoption of the Plan of Casa Mata within six weeks by almost every province,[89] Mexico was soon broken up into provinces or states, all adhering to the Plan. Each Provincial Deputation on adhering to it assumed complete control of provincial affairs and declared itself independent of the existing national government under Iturbide. This did not mean, however, that each province intended to set itself up as a sovereign, independent nation. On the contrary, all recognized themselves as parts of the Mexican nation. The Plan of Casa Mata had made, however, no provision for the establishment of a national government, perhaps because the framers did not foresee such a necessity or because they thought any such provision incompatible with Article 11, which declared that the position of the emperor should be decided by the national representation. Whatever the reason, as a result of the acceptance of the Plan, Mexico was soon faced with the problem of having no recognized national government. The rebelling provinces were well aware of this condition and at once began to take steps to remedy it.

The Provincial Deputation of Michoacán named José Mariano Michelena as its representative to consult with representatives of the intendancies of Guanajuato and Querétaro on a national government composed of deputies from each of the provinces.[90]

The Puebla Deputation followed a similar course. As early as March 4, it had sent communications to the Provincial Deputations and Municipal Councils throughout Mexico proposing that representatives meet in Puebla to confer on the problems of naming a provisional national government and reestablishing the old Congress or convoking a new one.[91] Those army officials who had reached Puebla by that date concurred in the proposed plan of having two representatives from each province come to Puebla to consider means of establishing a provisional national government and a Congress.[92]

The Puebla proposals caused confusion in the provinces of Michoacán, Querétaro, Guanajuato, and San Luis Potosí for a brief period. Those intendancies were proceeding along the lines of the Michoacán suggestion when the Puebla proposal posed the problem of whether the representatives should go to Puebla or should get together at some place within their own boundaries.[93] By March 12, Michelena recommended that representatives of those four provinces meet in Querétaro to decide whether to go to Puebla.[94] The Provincial Deputation of Guanajuato had elected representatives to meet in Querétaro,[95] when it, apparently, received some communication from the Eastern Interior Provinces and decided to send its representatives there. Fearing that this change in a meeting place would cause needless delay, Michelena urged the Provincial Deputation of Querétaro to send messages to those of Michoacán, Guanajuato, San Luis Potosí, the Eastern Interior Provinces, and others, asking them to agree on Querétaro as a temporary meeting place at least. In the meantime, he was going to Puebla to learn what was happening there.[96] Ten days later, he was advised no meeting had been held. The letter he received suggests the existent confusion.[97] Michelena, named as one of Michoacán's representatives for a meeting in Querétaro, was taking part in conferences at Puebla, participated in by army officials, former deputies to the dissolved Congress, and representatives named by various Provincial Deputations in conformity with Puebla's proposal of March 4. Some question appears to have been raised concerning the presence of representatives of the Provincial Deputation at those meetings; Michelena tendered his resignation as a representative and revealed in the letter that he was the one who had first proposed the assembling of provincial representatives to take steps toward the reestablishment of a national government. The Provincial Deputation of Michoacán refused to accept his resignation and requested him to keep it informed of all developments.[98]

The latent ambiguity of the Plan of Casa Mata also confused Iturbide. He did not seem to think at first that the Plan of Casa Mata was directed against him and sent a commission to confer with the leaders of the revolt. The members of the Junta Nacional Instituyente appear to have taken a more realistic attitude toward the Plan. They favored strong measures, but Iturbide decided on a wait and see policy.

Iturbide's commissioners arrived at Puebla on February 13. From there they sent a communication to Echávarri stating their purpose to make manifest to the leaders of the Plan of Casa Mata that the "constant resolution of His Majesty had been and remained that the government should be a limited constitutional monarchy and at the earliest possible moment the corresponding convocation for the meeting of the Congreso Nacional Instituyente should be issued." At the same time, the commission pointed out that the beneficent sentiments of His Majesty were in accord with the enlightened and liberal principles believed to have influenced the proclamation of the Plan of Casa Mata.[99]

At Tepeyahualco, the commissioners received Echávarri's reply saying that at a meeting of the representatives of the army on February 15 a deputation of generals and other officers had been unanimously designated to confer with the commissioners at Perote. This decision was reversed the same day, and the commissioners were advised to proceed to Jalapa to treat directly with the army's spokesmen.

The commission arrived in Jalapa on February 17 and immediately conferred with the General Council of War. The Plan of Casa Mata was read. Negrete, spokesman for the commissioners, said that the emperor was in complete accord with the installation of a sovereign Congress and that an agreement could be reached quickly if the conference was ready to enter into a discussion of the articles of the Plan in order to modify the part that appeared to hurt the nation, especially that referring to the convocation of Congress. Gregorio Arana immediately opposed any change whatever in the Plan without the presence of representatives of Guadalupe Victoria's forces at El Puente and Santa Anna's forces at Veracruz. Manuel E. Hernández opposed making any change without previously "hearing the voice of the nation through the medium of the Provincial Deputations." After a lengthy discussion, the majority voted to await the arrival of representatives from El Puente and from the Provincial Deputation of Veracruz.[100]

On the following day, however, at a council of war, it was decided that Echávarri and part of his force should proceed to Puebla. The commissioners thereupon urged another conference in order that some decision on the most important points might be reached, even though the representatives from El Puente and Veracruz had not arrived. At a conference on February 20, opposition to any action arose. José M. Portilla said that "since the Council of War could not make laws for the country, it was necessary to await the assembling of the representatives of all the Provincial Deputations that had adhered to the Plan in order to know what the public wanted, for the army should sustain public opinion." Others felt Portillo's suggestion to be dangerous. Arana again opposed any action. It was finally resolved that (1) if the country thought it best, the convocation should be in accord with that in practice in Spain, (2) the line of demarcation between Iturbide's and Echávarri's forces should be discussed in Puebla, and (3) upon the approval of this action by the emperor, the expenses of the army should be paid by the government, the roads opened to commerce, and free communication established with the metropolis.[101]

In accord with the second resolution passed, a line of demarcation between Iturbide's and Echávarri's forces was agreed upon, on February 25. The fifth and final article of that agreement, that the four preceding were to be in force until Iturbide had made known his adherence to the Plan of Casa Mata, showed clearly, however, that the commissioners had completely failed to effect any compromise in regard to the Plan.[102]

On February 26, Iturbide called a special secret session of the Junta Nacional Instituyente at which he presented the report of his commissioners and asked its views. He informed it that the rebelling army of Casa Mata wanted a Congress convoked in accord with the Spanish Constitution, the army to be paid from the national treasury, and the demarcation of a line across which neither the rebelling troops nor the government should pass. According to Bustamante, Iturbide assured the junta that his commissioners had come to an agreement with the Echávarri forces in that Congress should be convoked according to the Spanish Constitution and that it should have absolute freedom to decide in favor of whatever form of government it pleased. Iturbide added that, as for himself and his house, he was renouncing his rights; but that he would oppose the establishment of a republic, because a limited monarchy should always be demanded.[103] The matter was referred to a committee composed of Mariano Mendiola, José Miguel Guridi y Alcocer, Manuel López de la Plata, José María Bocanegra, José Vicente Orantes, Antonio José Valdés, and Agustín Iriarte.

The committee reported on the same day (1) that the plan for the convoking of Congress drawn up by the Junta Nacional Instituyente should be sent by means of commissioners to the General Council of War of the revolting forces so that their leaders could see that the bases of the election plan already drawn up were more liberal than those of the Spanish Constitution and those decreed by the Sovereign Provisional Governing Junta and that no person or group had more right to claim to be the voice of the provinces than the Junta Nacional Instituyente, composed as it was of subjects who merited the confidence of the provinces. (2) Should objections that they could not overcome be raised by the General Council of War, it should name its own commissioners to explain the objections to the Junta Nacional Instituyente and to take part in its discussion so that the best interest of the nation might be forwarded through the adoption of the election law set forth in the Spanish Constitution or drawn up by either the Junta Nacional Instituyente or the Sovereign Provisional Governing Junta or formed from the three. (3) The line of demarcation should be left to the prudence and knowledge of the emperor. (4) All other questions such as payment of the army, provisions for free communication and commerce with the capital, and the administration of taxes—consequences of the existing state of war and the manner in which the country should be governed until the installation of Congress—should be postponed until after the call for elections had been issued. The committee report was adopted.[104]

The day after Iturbide's commissioners, minus Negrete and García, returned to the capital on February 27, they made two reports to Iturbide, one giving an account of the official conferences and the agreements reached, and the other the conclusions formed by the commission from the sessions and also from official conversations with Echávarri and his supporters. In this they explained why they had ceased to press for a variation of Article 2 of the Plan of Casa Mata, the most objectionable to Iturbide and the one they had been specifically instructed to have changed.[105] Iturbide had repeatedly insisted that he was in complete agreement with the Plan insofar as it called for the prompt installation of Congress and that the Junta Nacional Instituyente, instructed by him to prepare a plan for the convocation of such a body, had rushed it to completion and he had ordered it published on February 25.[106] Martínez de los Ríos, one of his commissioners, had proposed in the discussions with Echávarri and his supporters that, in order to make Article 2 acceptable, the Spanish plan for the election of deputies, with the modification of one deputy for every thirty thousand inhabitants, take its place.[107] In suggesting the modification he had pointed out that such a change had been considered by the committee of the Junta Nacional Instituyente working on the project and thus had introduced the fact that the Junta Nacional Instituyente had a plan for the calling of Congress.

Upon finding the mood of Echávarri and his advisers unfavorable, Iturbide's commissioners decided not to urge a change in Article 2, for in their unofficial report to Iturbide they said:

> Since our principal purpose was to convince the junta [of Echávarri and his advisers] of them [the admittedly serious defects of the plan used in the calling of the first Congress and proposed in Article 2 of the Plan of Casa Mata], we thought it best not to press the matter further, especially as we observed the willingness of the junta to change the article if the people thought the adoption of the Spanish plan for the election of members to the Cortes to be more just. And of course we proposed to make all of this known to Your Majesty in order that, informed of the spirit with which the army worked to pacify the opinion of those who insisted on the reinstallation of the former Congress, you might decide on the most direct method to relieve at once the anxiety that the conservation of the representative system and its prompt organization has caused you.

The commissioners then recommended the reinstallation of the dissolved Congress as the quickest and most effective way out of the dilemma. Since immediate action was imperative, the recalling of the old Congress would avoid the inevitable delay of the Spanish plan, the opposition to any other plan that might arise, and the not remote divergence of opinion that might develop in the provinces by some wanting one form and others another. They advised Iturbide that by such action he would be freed of the imputation of compulsion in the matter. And while he might be charged with admitting guilt for having dissolved Congress in the first place or with weakness in restoring it, they did not believe he would permit that kind of criticism to keep him from doing what was best for the country.[108]

The Provincial Deputation of México also recommended on March 1 that Iturbide reinstall the old Congress so that it could complete the work for which it had been first installed or convoke a new one, while provisionally exercising the legislative functions in urgent cases. The Deputation warned Iturbide that only such a measure on his part could save the country from complete anarchy.[109] Iturbide in agreement with his Council of State recalled Congress on March 4. In his proclamation, he said that he had worked for its reform, believing that such was the will of the people, but since they desired that the old body resume its session, he was so decreeing.[110]

By this action, Iturbide effectively aborted the Plan of Casa Mata, which had definitely called for the election of a new Congress and not the restoration of the old one. It might have satisfied the intendancies and Provincial Deputations if the old restored Congress had immediately called for the election of a new Congress as the Plan of Casa Mata had proposed. However, it did not begin work on an election law immediately. On the contrary, as we shall see in the next chapter, the old restored Congress did everything it could to maintain itself in power.

The first gathering of the reconvened Congress, referred to by Carlos María Bustamante as the Junta Nacional Instituyente,[111] because most of the fifty-three deputies attending had been members of that body, took place on March 7, 1823. Tomás Alamán pointed out that its authority was in grave doubt;[112] that almost all the deputies then present had composed the Junta Nacional Instituyente, which did not enjoy national support; and that his province of Guanajuato had adopted the Plan of Casa Mata, which provided that a new Congress be convoked. He argued, therefore, that it was necessary at least to await the arrival of the majority of the deputies and the responses of the provinces to the decree calling for the reassembling of the old Constituent Congress.[113] Lorenzo de Zavala, José Antonio Valdés, Fernández de Córdova, and José Joaquín Herrera all concurred with Tomás Alamán that the number of deputies present was not sufficient for Congress to resume its sessions.

José Valle, Iturbide's recently appointed Minister of Domestic and Foreign Affairs, said that Alamán's argument was beside the point, that only forty or fifty members were needed, and that sessions should begin at once. Even after Iturbide's plea for immediate action, the body adjourned until the following day.

Not until nearly three weeks later, on March 29, did the reassembled body declare itself in session. In the intervening weeks, various attempts to pronounce it in session had been made, but each time deputies had arisen to question the authority of the gathering. Miguel Muñóz, on March 10, told the assembled deputies: "From the acts of the provinces complete adherence to Echávarri's plan is evident; hence this Congress is not wanted but rather the calling of a new one. We should pass no measure because we are not deputies, since our authority has been annulled. Although we may be reelected, at present, there is no Congress." And on the same day, Melchor Múzquiz stated that, since the provinces that had withdrawn from the national government wanted a new Congress, the reassembled deputies should occupy themselves solely in issuing the call for it.[114] Bustamante, Valle, and others held that Congress could declare itself legally installed, that the reestablishment was what the people wanted and was not contrary to the Plan of Casa Mata; but still the deputies could not agree.

Meanwhile, Iturbide's proclamation recalling the old body had reached the provinces. The leaders of the rebelling forces were then still in Puebla. There a junta, composed of representatives of the army, the Political Chief of the province of Puebla, members of its Provincial Deputation, deputies of the dissolved Congress then in Puebla, three parish priests, and three representatives of the Municipal Council, on March 7, issued a broadside in which it refused to recognize the recalled Congress because it did not enjoy complete liberty and called for each of the other Provincial Deputations to send two representatives to meet in Puebla to determine the best manner of reestablishing the national representation.[115]

Two days later, the same junta resolved that the titular government of Mexico as well as that of each of the intendancies or the provinces be informed that the so-called Congress was not recognized, nor would it be obeyed, because it was not national. It was not and could not be free under the government that had reconvened it, and it included deputies who had been proscribed by the nation, because they had not displayed true firmness of character. The Iturbide government should evacuate the capital in order that a free Congress might be installed or allow the deputies to leave to assemble where they might choose.[116]

On March 3, the reassembled deputies to the restored Congress heard the report of a committee appointed ten days earlier to study the correspondence between the government and the rebel forces and the provinces adhering to the Plan of Casa Mata and to recommend action by that body. It stated that (1) the Constituent Congress had not been legally dissolved and was as legitimate as it had been on its day of installation; (2) when the deputies named to compose it were reassembled, they would have the authority necessary for legislative acts and could exercise legislative functions; (3) only that body could issue a legitimate call for a new Congress; and (4) a committee should be sent to Puebla to make known to the army leaders and the authorities gathered there what Congress and the government had done and intended to do and to convince them that Congress could function with absolute liberty and that its recognition and support was the only way to save the country from anarchy.

In regard to the first three points, the deputies decided that no action was necessary; the fourth was approved, as was a proposal that the Provincial Deputation of México be asked to appoint one of its members to accompany the congressional committee, to add weight to the delegation. Rafael Mangino and Manuel Sánchez de Tagle were appointed to represent Congress and José Florentino Conejo, to represent the Provincial Deputation of México.[117]

On their arrival in Puebla with Bravo and Negrete, whom they met en route, a junta composed of the same membership as the former Puebla juntas was called; but neither any representative of other Provincial Deputations nor Michelena was present, as stated by Lucas Alamán, Bustamante, and Banegas Galván.[118] At the session on March 15, the commissioners explained that, since the authority of the reestablished Congress was unquestionable, their only purpose in coming was to let the military leaders and the governmental bodies of Puebla know that it enjoyed complete liberty. They insisted that, if a new assembly was to be called, it could be convoked only by the old one. After lengthy discussion, it was resolved by the junta that, should the necessary number of deputies assemble, the army and the junta would recognize the illegally dissolved Congress and obey it, if convinced that it was functioning in complete freedom.

When the commissioners asked what measures or conditions would furnish proof of such freedom, some suggested that the body leave Mexico City; some, that the liberating army occupy the capital; and others, that the executive power be embodied in a Regency; but no agreement was reached.[119]

The commissioners on March 16 made known their failure to convince the Puebla junta that Congress had the desired freedom of action, but implied that there was to be another meeting to be reported later.[120] No further mention of the commissioners is recorded in the congressional minutes. Mangino and Sánchez de Tagle returned to take part in that body, but no further reference was made to the Puebla junta.

Unsuccessful efforts to have Congress in session continued. After Iturbide abdicated on March 19, leaving it to designate an executive power, the restored Congress still took no action; some of the deputies, among them Bustamante, argued that the number present was insufficient. He contended that under the laws of the Cortes (still in force), in the absence of the Political Chief or intendant, the members of the Provincial Deputations in the order of their election were to assume the executive office, as had been done in the provinces no longer recognizing Iturbide, and that the province of México could and should do the same. Other deputies agreed that, since Iturbide's government was only governing the intendancy of México, its administration should, on his resignation, devolve upon the Political Chief of México or his alternate.[121]

All this discussion reveals is that Mexico had broken up into independent intendancies or provinces, each of which assumed complete control within its bounds. The Political Chief had become the provincial executive and the Provincial Deputation, or a junta brought into existence by it, had assumed the legislative functions of the government of the provinces or intendancies in all but a few provinces or intendancies by the middle of March 1823. While the province of México had not done so, because Iturbide was there, its deputies were recommending this step. As Sánchez de Tagle said, no central government actually existed.[122]

The liberating army entered Mexico City on March 26, and with it came many of the former congressional deputies. With 103 deputies present, Congress declared itself in legitimate session on March 29, recognized the termination of the executive power under the empire and the nullification of the Plan of Iguala and the Treaty of Córdoba, and named a committee to designate a provisional executive power.

The disintegration of the national government in Mexico City was further emphasized in the course of the debate relative to the publication and circulation of a proclamation announcing the reestablishment of Congress. When it was proposed that the Political Chief of the province of México issue the declaration, the objection was offered that his authority was restricted to the province or intendancy of México and did not authorize him to circulate a manifesto of the Congress nationally. Manuel Mier y Terán said that only the national government should circulate such a document. But there was no national executive power and the provinces recognized none but that of their respective Political Chiefs.[123] In reality, from this date until the promulgation of the Constitution of 1824, most of the provinces or intendancies of Mexico carried on their government independently and obeyed the decrees of the national government only when they chose to do so. The national government no longer had the power to force the provinces or intendancies to accept its decrees.

SIX

Attitude of the Provincial Deputations toward a New Congress

The reestablishment of the Congress did not end the confused problem of a national government for Mexico. At first it seemed a happy solution, and many provinces addressed congratulations to the reestablished body and to the executive agency it set up. Since the Plan of Casa Mata had stipulated a new Congress, most of the intendancies and Provincial Deputations expected it to be called promptly. Besides, the people wanted new representatives: fifty-three members of the reconvened body had, through their membership in Iturbide's Junta Nacional Instituyente, won the mistrust and disfavor of many provincials and leaders of the provinces, others had taken an active part in proclaiming Iturbide emperor, and all the deputies of the first Constituent Congress had been elected under a law that was now unacceptable to many of the provinces.

The reassembled deputies, however, were divided on the question of calling a new Congress, some maintaining that they had been elected to draw up a new Constitution and that their term of office did not expire until the document had been completed, others agreeing with the provinces on the calling of a new constituent assembly. The conflict between the restored Congress and the provinces furthered the disintegration of the national government and played into the hands of those supporting federalism in Mexico.

The proposal of Valentín Gómez Farías, on April 2, 1823, that a new Congress be convoked and a committee appointed to draft and present an electoral law within eight days was seconded by Melchor Múzquiz; a committee, composed of Mariano Herrera, Javier and Carlos María Bustamante, Francisco Sánchez de Tagle, Toribio González, Tomás Beltranena, and Valentín Gómez Farías, was named to study and render an opinion on it.[1]

At that time, there were representatives of the Provincial Deputations of Oaxaca, Zacatecas, San Luis Potosí, Guanajuato, Michoacán, Guadalajara, and Querétaro present in Mexico City, who had been named commissioners in compliance with the call sent out by Puebla in March, but who had returned to the capital when members of the old restored Congress reconvened in order to keep their respective Provincial Deputations informed of events. On the night of April 4, they all testified before the congressional committee,[2] a majority of which favored a new convocation, and insisted that the provinces that they represented demanded a new Congress.[3]

Gómez Farías was even more specific. He said that, since five to seven members of the committee were in favor of a new assembly and the commissioners unanimously demanded it, he anticipated a favorable report.[4]

To his surprise, when the committee presented its findings on April 14, 1823, it had been so influenced by the arguments of Sánchez de Tagle and Carlos María Bustamante that it recommended instead that (1) a new Congress to constitute the nation should not be convoked; (2) the existing Congress, while the constitutional committee was drafting a Constitution, should proceed with the organization of the treasury, the army, the administration of justice, and so forth; and (3) when the completed constitutional draft came up for discussion, the question of its ratification should be left to a future Congress.[5]

Herrera, Sánchez de Tagle, and Javier and Carlos María Bustamante were the only committee members who signed the report without reservations. Beltranena and González said that they subscribed on condition that Article 3 provided that, upon the completion of the draft of a Constitution and the approval of the part relative to holding elections for a new Congress empowered to approve the Constitution, the new Congress should be convoked immediately. González added a postscript to the effect that he would offer further comment during debates in Congress but that his constituents wanted a new assembly.[6]

Carlos María Bustamante, even though he had signed the report without reservations, prepared and read his personal vote on the matter. Although this had been written to be presented at the committee's meeting on April 4 and much of the argument had been incorporated into the official committee report, he concluded by asking that (1) Congress await the reaction of the provinces, (2) the provinces be instructed to have their active deputies take their seats in the restored assembly, (3) the provinces enlarge the powers of the deputies to include the drafting and accepting of a Constitution, (4) the provinces accept the resignation of those deputies whose political belief had caused them to deviate from the will of their constituents (each accused deputy retaining the right, however, to plead his case before Congress), (5) in the elections of deputies to fill such vacated seats the letter and spirit of the first electoral law be fully observed, and, finally, (6) the committee's report and Bustamante's opinion be printed and circulated and journalists be allowed to express their opinion before Congress proceeded to the discussion of the committee's recommendations.[7] Gómez Farías did not sign the report but promised to present his opinion at an early date. The restored Congress took no action on the committee's report other than to order it printed and circulated before proceeding to the discussion of its recommendations.[8]

It appears that some of the deputies, hoping this report would set the misled provinces straight, cause reason to triumph, and bring a favorable reaction from the provinces in regard to the recommendations it embodied,[9] had copies sent to the leading organizations in the provinces and asked for their reaction to it. Servando Mier, on April 23, sent a copy of the "eloquent" report to the Municipal Council of Monterrey with instructions that everybody be permitted to read it.[10] In a letter to his friend José Bernardino Cantú on June 2, Mier expressed surprise that Cantú had offered no comments on the "sound" report sent to the Municipal Council with instructions to pass it on to the Provincial Deputation of Monterrey.[11]

Juan Ignacio Godoy said that, as a special representative of the Provincial Deputation of Guanajuato as well as a deputy to Congress, he had reported to his Provincial Deputation on the action taken, had sent it a copy of the report, and had asked for further instruction on the subject.[12] Godoy, himself clearly in favor of a new Congress, said it was very easy to foresee that the circulation of the report among the provinces would become a boomerang that would frighten its own authors; and he added, "That is exactly what has happened."[13]

Some Provincial Deputations whose deputies had appealed for instructions even prior to the circulation of the committee report expressed themselves promptly. The Deputation of Nuevo León, Coahuila, and Texas, which, on April 1, had named Servando Mier and Melchor Múzquiz as its representatives to the Puebla junta and instructed them in regard to the calling of a new Congress and the establishment of a provisional national government,[14] on April 12 received word that both had taken their seats in the reassembled body, that Múzquiz had seconded the Gómez Farías proposal of April 2 that a new assembly be convoked and a committee appointed to draft the electoral law, and that both suggested provisional recognition of Congress until a new one could be called and desired further instructions. Two days later, at a joint meeting of the Provincial Deputation, the Municipal Council of Monterrey, the acting commandant, city officials, members of the clergy, and prominent citizens to consider the matter, the Plan of Casa Mata as adopted by Monterrey on March 6 and the instructions sent to their commissioner were read. Ramos Arizpe then recommended that, although acceptance of the old Congress was contrary to the Plan outlined in those documents, limited recognition be approved, to the extent only of its serving as a medium for the prompt calling of a new Congress. Following review by him and others of the events preceding its convocation and explanations of the shortcomings of the electoral law under which it had been chosen, provisional and conditional recognition of it and the Supreme Executive Power was voted.[15]

When the congressional committee report was made public on April 14, the provincial commissioners who had either taken their seats as deputies or remained in the capital to keep their Deputations informed of events transpiring did more than express their surprise. They addressed a forceful statement to Congress on April 18, in which they, as representatives of the intendancies and provinces of Guadalajara, Michoacán, Oaxaca, Zacatecas, Guanajuato, Querétaro, and San Luis Potosí, demanded a new Congress to frame the Constitution. They pointed out the weakness of the electoral law under which the deputies to the reassembled body had been named and asserted that changed conditions in the country demanded changed instructions. They also made clear that only with the understanding that Congress would limit its efforts to the prompt issuance of a new law of convocation in keeping with the changed conditions of the country had congratulations been extended to that body.[16]

The Provincial Deputation of Puebla in a similar memorial, dated April 23, 1823, pointed out that it had repeatedly disapproved the edict of convocation of November 17, 1821, by which the Constituent Congress had been reduced to a body to draw up special regulations and the apportionment of deputies had been based not on the population but on the number of districts in a province. Now, under the Plan of Casa Mata, all the provinces, each independent and recognizing no superior authority, awaited the calling of a new Congress, and each reserved to itself the indisputable rights (1) of reviewing, examining, and ratifying the Constitution or not and (2) of recalling its deputies if they failed to carry out the will of the province. Union of the provinces could be achieved only through the election of new deputies, with each province determining the number to be elected.[17]

Gómez Farías, as a member of the Congressional Committee on the Convocation of a New Congress, in his minority report, read on April 19, reminded the deputies that the speed with which Provincial Deputations and Municipal Councils, bodies most representative of the people, had accepted the Plan of Casa Mata, which called for a new Congress, indicated definitively what the majority of the people wanted. He pointed out that Spain, under similar circumstances in 1820, had called a new Cortes and not reinstalled that dissolved in 1814; he quoted at length from Francisco Martínez Marina, the distinguished Spanish political scientist, to show that the powers of the deputies were not absolute and irrevocable and called on his fellow deputies to heed the voice of the nation and call a new constituent assembly.[18]

Congress ordered the Gómez Farías report printed and circulated, but took no step toward either convoking a new assembly or naming a committee to draw up a Constitution. Nevertheless, both subjects were kept constantly before the body. Repeated proposals that a committee be appointed to draft a Constitution were merely referred to committee.[19]

When Bocanegra asked, on May 14, that the constitutional principles known to be the will of the nation be promptly prepared and published, a new committee, composed of José Valle, Servando Mier, José María Jiménez, Juan de Dios Mayorga, Francisco María Lombardo y García, José Mariano Marín, Lorenzo de Zavala, Javier Bustamante, Bocanegra, and Gómez Farías, was named to study the matter.[20]

According to Servando Mier, he had handpicked these individuals in advance to form a Constitution, and they had been working on one since about April 28.[21] On May 21, Congress voted that a new assembly be convoked immediately and that the plan or "Bases for a Federative Republic," which had been entrusted to Servando Mier's committee, should be printed and circulated at once.[22]

The plan or bases was not discussed, Servando Mier said, because "the provinces began to scream that we [the Congress] lacked the power to frame a Constitution for the nation."[23] But long before May 16, as has been shown, the provinces had been telling Congress in no uncertain terms that it had no such authority. They continued to do so and to resist the Congress actively.

The arrival in Guadalajara of the congressional committee's report recommending the deferment of a new Congress propelled the Provincial Deputation into action. At a special session on May 9, that body,[24] when the decree of April 23 relative to the recognition of the existing government was read,[25] resolved to suspend its execution, to demand a new constituent assembly, and to publicize that Guadalajara did not recognize the existing body except as temporary and convoking. With representatives from the Municipal Council of Guadalajara present on May 12, the Provincial Deputation voted to send its views to Congress and to the Supreme Executive Power and to print and circulate them.[26] At the same time, it was decided that, until a reply was received, all decrees and orders issued by either would be suspended and the Provincial Deputation would be the highest authority in the province and the last court of appeal.[27] A lengthy manifesto, embodying all points discussed and a scathing reply to the congressional committee report, was at once issued.[28]

The commissioners from Zacatecas, Arrieta and Vélez, were present at the April 4 hearing in the reassembled Congress and signed the protest of April 18 against the committee's report. The Zacatecas Provincial Deputation further confirmed the desire of the people of Zacatecas for a new Congress by approving Gómez Farías' minority report and addressing a statement of its approval to Congress.[29] Then, like Guadalajara, it resorted to action by issuing, on June 18, a statement that henceforth the restored

Congress would be recognized only as a convoking body, and orders issued by it or the Supreme Executive Power would be subject to approval of the Provincial Deputation of Zacatecas.[30]

News of the reinstallation of the dissolved Congress and the establishment of the Supreme Executive Power reached Mérida, Yucatán, in the latter part of April; on April 25, the Provincial Deputation took up the matter of recognition of each. After lengthy discussion, it was decided to recognize the national government under three conditions: (1) its prompt convocation of a new Congress and the immediate dissolution of the old one, (2) the continuation of Bravo, Victoria, and Negrete as members of the Supreme Executive Power, and (3) nonintervention of the national government in filling offices until the Constitution had been framed.[31] Yucatán never modified that resolution. Its Provincial Deputation and the province as a whole looked upon itself as independent and set about organizing its government without instructions from Mexico City.

What happened in the province of Oaxaca during the latter part of April and the month of May has not been learned. Its commissioner, after participating in the congressional hearing of April 4 and the signing of the protest of April 18, returned to Oaxaca. By June 1, the province had become so distrustful of the national government that it declared complete independence from Mexico City and at once began to set up an independent provincial government.

Michoacán had taken early steps toward establishing a national government when it called together representatives of Michoacán, Guanajuato, Querétaro, and San Luis Potosí and named Michelena and Martín García to attend such a meeting. Michelena was later named an alternate to the Supreme Executive Power, but García continued to represent Michoacán and, in that capacity, took part in the April 4 meeting of the congressional hearing and signed the protest of April 18.

After some of Michoacán's deputies in the restored Congress asked their Provincial Deputation, on April 23, for further instructions as to a new Congress,[32] it replied on May 7 that the will of the people had been demonstrated repeatedly in the clearest and most positive terms and that its own position had been made known to the restored Congress through its commissioner, who, with those of six other provinces, had clearly and forcefully presented its decision that a new assembly was imperative. The Provincial Deputation pointed out that as early as February 25 it had issued a proclamation asking for a Constituent Congress with full authority. On March 8, in a manifesto, it had repeated the demand and explained why this was necessary. In promoting the formation of a national government, it had instructed its commissioners and also those sent to Puebla to demand the prompt convocation of a new Congress. The people of the intendancy of Michoacán, fully informed of all those actions, had then given conclusive evidence of their approval. Their attitude had also been clearly shown on receipt of news of the reestablishment of the old Congress, when the Provincial Deputation stated that it would not recognize any body that did not enjoy complete liberty to deliberate and that was not composed of members worthy of the trust of the province and did not have complete authority to act. Michoacán's stand had been approved not only by all that province but also by other similar bodies that had issued the same instructions to their commissioners. The Michoacán body, therefore, had no doubt that the desire of the entire country was that a new assembly be convoked. It warned its deputies that failure to heed the expressed will of the intendancy would bring disaster to the country and informed them of three resolutions that it had adopted: (1) demanding a new Congress with full powers to constitute the nation, (2) approving and supporting the statements of its own and other commissioners before the congressional committee on April 4 and in the written protest of April 18, and (3) instructing its deputies to make known to the restored Congress the well-founded suspicion that it would not be recognized as a body to draw up a Constitution for the nation.[33]

The Provincial Deputation of Guanajuato took similar steps when informed of the action of the restored Congress relative to a new one and asked for further instructions. The Deputation held a meeting on April 30 to decide whether the existing body should call a new assembly, but no record of its action has been found.[34] Subsequent statements indicate that the calling of a new Congress was favored. In response to a request from Lucas Alamán, Minister of Domestic Affairs, on May 10, for a report on public opinion on the matter, Domingo Chico, Political Chief of the province, reported that replies from all but two of the Municipal Councils of the province showed a majority for a new Congress.[35] About May 22, at a general meeting of the Provincial Deputation and the other official bodies, it was resolved that the restored Congress should be told of the grave risk that would face the intendancy of Guanajuato if the decree convoking the new assembly was delayed longer.[36] Pedro Otero, Commandant-General, wrote on May 23 to Morán, commander-in-chief of the Liberating Army, that public opinion unanimously demanded a new Congress and urged him to instruct the supreme government to secure the prompt issuance of the convocation for a new body in order to calm public agitation.[37]

News of the congressional decree of May 21 that Congress would issue a call as quickly as possible reached Guanajuato by regular mail on Saturday, May 24,[38] serving to calm the unrest and to preserve the peace and unity of the province.[39]

Alamán, in his report of May 30 on the disturbances in the provinces of Guanajuato, Querétaro, and Michoacán during that month, said that peace had been reestablished in all, but that the restored Congress should issue the new electoral law immediately in order to persuade the people that its promise was made in good faith.[40]

Full details of the steps taken by the Provincial Deputation of Querétaro have not been located, but it did express itself on the matter. Its commissioner, Anastacio Ochoa, took part with the others in Mexico City on April 4 and 18, and its Provincial Deputation likewise asked, on May 16, for the views of the Municipal Councils on the congressional committee report of April 12. Querétaro, with lengthy arguments, disapproved that report and also the *Voto particular* of Bustamante.[41] That the Provincial Deputation did demand a new Congress is clear from its statement on May 20, 1823, to its deputy, Dr. Félix de Osores, that it had, in its representation, expressed itself as favoring a call for a new assembly but not in terms disrespectful of the existing Congress.[42] Respect for the established authorities was promised in both communications.

Sometime before June 11, nonetheless, the Provincial Deputation of Querétaro, in response to a suggestion from that of Valladolid, had named a commissioner to meet there with others from Michoacán, Guanajuato, and San Luis Potosí to discuss joint action in regard to a call for a new Congress and the establishment of a federal republic.[43] Its patience sorely taxed by congressional delay in issuing the convocation, on June 11 and 12 the Deputation held a joint meeting with the Municipal Council of Querétaro and the Commandant-General to consider the anarchy threatening the country, which was directly traceable to this delay. Of the ten resolutions adopted, three emphasized the urgent need for a new Congress.[44]

The Provincial Deputation of San Luis Potosí, after its commissioners had participated in the committee meeting of April 4, had signed the protest of April 18 and had returned.[45] Subsequently, the Provincial Deputation of San Luis Potosí had replied to Congress in regard to the congressional report, for on June 15 the *Aguila mexicana* ran an advertisement for the Alejandro Valdés bookstore offering for sale printed copies of the *Vote of the Province of San Luis Potosí in Favor of the Necessity for a New Call for Elections to Congress to Remove the Many Mistakes Incurred by the Committee of the Sovereign Congress When It Tried to Prove the Contrary.*[46] During May, both the Provincial Deputation of San Luis Postosí and its Political Chief, José Ildefonso Díaz de León, had received communications from Guadalajara inviting that province to join with Guadalajara in openly favoring and promoting the establishment of a federal republic. On May 25, the members of the Provincial Deputation, the Municipal Council, the treasury, clergymen, a large number of prominent citizens, and Dr. Tomás Vargas and Antonio López de Santa Anna met to consider what action should be taken.[47] Santa Anna declared that he was ready to protect the province with the division under his command and that he would support whatever program the province adopted. With Vargas, Lic. Victor Rafael Márquez,

Antonio López de Santa Anna,
General and President of Mexico,
1833–1835. Undated photograph,
Genaro García Collection.

Lt. Col. Pedro Valdéz, and Lt. Tomás Requeña representing the citizens, it was voted that a vigorous representation in favor of a new Congress be presented to the restored Congress; but, until a reply was received from the national government, San Luis Potosí would not follow Guadalajara's lead in refusing to obey the national government. When the congressional decree of May 21 arrived three days later, the minutes of the meeting were published with a statement that the arrival of the decree showed the wisdom of the action taken.[48]

The attitude and activities of the provinces had caused the restored Congress to issue the decree of May 21, and the vote on this decree reflected the feeling of the provinces toward that body. Seventy-one members voted in favor of the recommendation to call a new Congress and thirty-three against. Six out of nine Michoacán deputies present voted in the affirmative; all of those present from Veracruz, Guadalajara, Zacatecas, Querétaro, and San Luis Potosí voted for it; and those from Guanajuato voted four to one against. A third of all the negative votes came from the province of México.[49]

Congress then appointed, on the same day, a committee composed of Bonifacio Fernández, José Valle, Carlos María Bustamante, Prisciliano Sánchez, and Francisco García, to work on the election plans,[50] but not until June 9 was the bill convoking a new Congress read for the first time. The provinces in the meantime had grown progressively more impatient, especially since the restored Congress had on the same day, May 21, 1823, voted that the "Bases of a Federative Republic," which had been drawn up by an unofficially appointed congressional committee,[51] be printed at once and distributed. That action tended to increase the mounting irritation of the provinces and to encourage the rapidly growing suspicion of bad faith on the part of the restored Congress, because many provinces were irrevocably opposed to the restored Congress having anything to do with producing the Constitution.[52]

During this period of the restored Congress's failure to face up to the issue of calling a new Congress as specified in the Plan of Casa Mata, the issue at hand had broadened from provincial power as embodied in the Provincial Deputations to national power embodied first in the emperor, then in the Supreme Executive Power, a creature of the restored Congress, and finally and most importantly in the restored Constituent Congress itself, which satisfied neither the monarchists still existing in Mexico nor the republicans there.

SEVEN

Evolution of the Pioneer State Legislatures

While the restored Congress dallied during the spring of 1823, several of the provinces (Nueva Galicia with its capital at Guadalajara, which is often cited as the province of Guadalajara, Oaxaca, Yucatán, and Zacatecas) began to take steps to establish independent state governments; and others declared their intention to do so. One of the first to set up its own state government was Nueva Galicia with its capital at Guadalajara. As early as April, the establishment of a provincial Congress was being discussed, and on April 6 a manifesto signed by "El Cuerpo de Liberales" (the Liberal Group) of Guadalajara, Nueva Galicia, recommended the prompt "installation of our provincial Congress," close alliance with other provinces in foreign affairs, and absolute independence from the rest of the country in regard to provincial matters.[1] At the meeting of the Provincial Deputation of Guadalajara on May 9, which informed the recalled national Congress that Guadalajara favored a new one, the Provincial Deputation of Guadalajara advised the national government that it had decided on a federal representative government.[2]

During the special session of May 12, the Guadalajaran Provincial Deputation deliberated on measures to make a federal republic operative in case the national Congress did not convoke a new Congress, temporarily suspended the execution of all decrees and orders issued by the national government, and made itself, with three members from the Municipal Council, the supreme authority in the province and the final court of appeal. It also published its actions as an official order to the city of Guadalajara and province of Nueva Galicia,[3] informing all other Provincial Deputations in the country of the steps taken and encouraging them to join in the establishment of a general federation. On the same day, it also issued a lengthy manifesto, stating that New Galicia favored a confederation of provinces like that of Pennsylvania, New Jersey, and New York, with each enjoying popular representative government.[4]

Its Political Chief, Luis Quintanar, also issued a statement to the Political Chiefs and governors of the other provinces in which he showed that

Luis Quintanar, General. Lithograph, from Manuel Rivera Cambas, *Los gobernantes de México* (Mexico City: Imprenta de J. M. Aguilar Ortiz, 1873).

congressional disregard of public opinion had forced the Provincial Deputation of Guadalajara to urge the election of a new Congress and the establishment of a federal government. In order to repel any attempt at aggression from without that might result from this official stand, he had ordered his troops to guard the frontiers of the province, but he wanted Guadalajara's position known in order to forestall any attempt to misinform the leaders and inhabitants of other provinces.[5]

Also on May 12, Quintanar informed the national Supreme Executive Power of Guadalajara's resolution and his intention to carry it out, ordering troops to the frontiers in order to prevent aggression and suspending the remission of funds to Mexico. He then informed the people of the province of his action.[6] And in a circular apparently addressed to the political leaders of the municipalities and of the provinces, he explained the advantages of the federal over the central form of government. The circular concluded with the assurance that should the reader, in accord with the community that he represented, see fit to declare in favor of the federal form as the most perfect formulated by a political scientist, he should do so without fear of violence on the part of the existing national Congress.[7]

The Provincial Deputation continued to work for the establishment of a federal government. Its acts as well as its proclamations and those by the Political Chief were all broadcast in printed form to the four corners of the country, as is evidenced by the existence of many of them in the municipal and state archives throughout Mexico. Quintanar himself made it a practice to send at least two copies of each document concerning events in Guadalajara to all the principal Municipal Councils and to all Political Chiefs and Provincial Deputations.[8]

After further discussion of the establishment of a federal government in Mexico on May 27 and 30, the Provincial Deputation of Guadalajara on June 5 issued a statement of its principles, which it had meanwhile ascertained were in complete agreement with those of other provinces of the nation. It expressed regret, however, that the newspapers of Mexico City had interpreted its actions as inimical to the general welfare of the country. The Provincial Deputation therefore resolved:

1. For the present and until the general national Congress of the federated states of Mexico meets, the capital of Mexico shall be recognized as the center of the union of all of them.

2. Likewise the present national Congress and the Supreme Executive Power shall be recognized, it being understood that the existing national Congress has only the character of a convoking body.

3. The law of convocation and the other general ones that may be issued by the existing national Congress as *mere regulations* shall be punctually obeyed.

4. All orders of the national Supreme Executive Power that are directed to the general well-being of the States of the Mexican Nation shall also be obeyed.

5. Those orders that have to do solely with the state of Jalisco shall be suspended, if not acceptable to the state.

6. All present employees of this state of whatever class and rank shall continue in their positions as long as, in the judgment of the state, they are considered worthy of them.

7. No new positions whatever shall be created in this state, nor shall vacant positions be filled by the national Supreme Executive Power except on the nomination of the state itself.

8. The nomination shall be restricted to natives of this state or to residents of it for seven or more years and shall be made according to the regulations for the provisional government of this state, which shall be published as soon as possible.

9. These measures shall be communicated to the national Congress and government in Mexico City and shall be printed and circulated to all other states of the nation and to the towns of this state.[9]

On the following day, Quintanar sent six copies of these minutes to the Minister of Foreign and Domestic Affairs in order that the national Supreme Executive Power might know explicitly that the Provincial Deputation of Guadalajara in the province of Nueva Galicia was acting with just and honest intentions and trying to avoid a break on its part and that the Provincial Deputation did not have selfish designs, as had been implied in Mexico City.[10]

Members of the Provincial Deputation, convinced that the time to govern themselves and to set up a state government had arrived, in a special session on June 16, adopted and addressed to the "inhabitants of the free state of Jalisco" a plan of provisional government for the "new state." Its twenty articles read:

Art. 1. The province known at present as Guadalajara shall in the future be called the free state of Jalisco.

Art. 2. Its territory, at present, is formed of the twenty-eight districts that make up the intendancy of Nueva Galicia, to wit: Guadalajara, Acaponeta, Ahucatlan, Autlan, Barca, Colima, Cuquio, Compostela, Colotlan, with that of Nayarit and the *corregimiento* of Bolanos, Etzatlan, Hostotipauillo, Lagos Mascota, Real de San Sebastián, San Blas, Santa María del Oro, Sayula, Sentispac, Tomatlan, Tala, Tepatitlan, Tepic, Talljomulco, Tequila, Tonalan, Tuzcacuesco, Zapotlan el Grande, and Zapopan.

Art. 3. The state of Jalisco is free, independent, and sovereign within itself and it shall recognize no other relationships with other states or provinces but those of brotherhood and confederation.

Art. 4. Its religion as always shall be the Roman Apostolic Catholic religion with tolerance of no other.

Art. 5. Its government shall be popular and representative.

Art. 6. Therefore, the state has the right to make its own Constitution and to frame, in union with other states that confederate with it, the general relations of all of them.

Art. 7. All the inhabitants of the state have the right to vote in the elections of its representatives who are to form the provincial Constituent Congress.

Art. 8. All inhabitants of the state enjoy the inalienable rights of liberty, security, equality, and property, and the state should guarantee them.

Art. 9. In return the inhabitants are under obligation to respect and obey the established authorities, and to contribute to the upkeep of the state at the time and in the manner it may order.

Art. 10. In this state the three powers, legislative, executive, and judicial, shall never be vested in a single person or body, nor shall two of the powers be combined.

Art. 11. Until the provincial Constituent Congress is established, the legislative power shall be vested in the Provincial Deputation.

Art. 12. Its functions shall be restricted to the framing of a convocation of the provincial Congress and dictating of provincial regulations that the observance of existing laws may require.

Art. 13. The executive power of the state shall reside in the acting Political Chief, who in the future shall be called governor of the state of Jalisco.

Art. 14. The executive power shall preserve the internal and foreign order of the state and have command of the army.

Art. 15. To the executive power, in accord with the Provincial Deputation, belongs the nomination of the employees of the state spoken of in Article 7 of the official order of June 5, which shall be observed in all its parts.

Art. 16. The judicial power of the state shall be exercised by the authorities established at the present. The Audiencia shall be the court of highest appeal.

Art. 17. The Municipal Councils and other bodies and authorities, civil as well as military and ecclesiastical, shall continue to exercise the functions delegated to them.

Art. 18. The state shall be governed by the Spanish Constitution and the existing laws, in anything that is not in conflict with the present plan.

Art. 19. This plan shall be communicated to all the authorities and corporations of the state in order that it may be observed.

Art. 20. Any official or person of any class who refuses to observe this plan shall ask not later than three days after its promulgation for his passport to leave the state in the time fixed by the government.[11]

The minutes of the special session were published as an official order on June 21, accompanied by a lengthy proclamation by Quintanar, in which he reviewed political events since 1821. He said that the Mexican people had wanted a republic from the very beginning of independence but that their wishes had been thwarted first by the Plan of Iguala and later by Iturbide's desire to become emperor. Quick to realize the usurpation of their natural rights, the people had overthrown the tyrant; then the provinces had to oppose the orders of a second tyrant, the restored national Congress. As a result, there was no national Congress, the authority of the deputies having been annulled by their constituents. There was, therefore, no national government in Mexico; the nation had reverted to its natural state; consequently, the respective Provincial Deputations, whose members were popularly elected, were fully authorized by the people to designate the course to be followed. The Provincial Deputation of Guadalajara, acting on those principles and desiring that the people elect their own representatives to the provincial Constituent Congress, would therefore limit its activities to issuing a call for the election and such regulations as would not admit of delay.[12]

With this manifesto and the June 16 minutes of the Provincial Deputation, Quintanar sent to all the Provincial Deputations throughout Mexico and to the Municipal Council of each provincial capital, on June 23, circulars containing the plan for the provincial government of the state of Jalisco, which had been solemnly installed on June 22, 1823. He added that Jalisco wished to unite in the closest bonds of fraternity and confederation with the new states that other provinces might form and asked that the political leaders make known to their constituents that the provisional government of the state of Jalisco was in operation.[13]

The orders and decrees that the national government of Mexico continued to forward to Quintanar and the Provincial Deputation of Guadalajara were either accepted, modified, or rejected by that body. When the decree of June 17 setting forth the electoral law governing the election of deputies to the national Constituent Congress was received on June 25, it was referred to the committee earlier appointed by the Provincial Deputation, which had drawn up an electoral law for the calling of the provincial Constituent Congress. The committee recommended on June 27 that the national law be faithfully obeyed, but with the specific understanding that the Mexican nation was to be a popular, representative, federal government in accord with the general will manifested by Jalisco on June 5. The recommendation continued:

Art. 1. The deputies that shall be named in this state to the national Mexican Constituent Congress shall constitute the great Anahuac nation under the system of a federal republic in conformity with the general and uniform will of the country.

Art. 2. Consequently, they shall proceed immediately to lay down the basis for the general federation of the Mexican states and to form their general Constitution and their authority shall be restricted solely to this function.

Art. 3. The basis for federation and the general Constitution of the federated states shall not be promulgated as law until it has been ratified by the provincial Congresses of the states themselves.

Art. 4. Since in a federal system of government each federated state can have only one vote in the federated Congress, in order to avoid useless expense to this state, three regular deputies and as many alternates to the national body shall be elected in it.

Art. 5. These deputies shall be subject to recall by the provincial Congress according to the terms set by it as soon as it is installed.

Art. 6. On the day following the election of deputies to the national Congress, fifteen regular deputies and five alternates shall be named to form the provincial Constituent Congress of this state.

Art. 7. The members of the Constituent Congress must be over twenty-five years of age, natives of the state or residents of it for seven years, whether laymen or clergymen; however, not more than three clergymen may be named deputies and only one clergyman may be named an alternate.

Art. 8. As soon as the deputies of the provincial Congress have been elected, they shall be informed at once so that they may come immediately to this capital so that the state Congress can be installed.

Art. 9. This installation shall take place as soon as two-thirds of the deputies have arrived; the form of the installation shall be stated in a special decree relative to that point.

Art. 10. Once the Congress is installed, the present Provincial Deputation shall be dissolved and the Congress shall determine how and by whom the functions assigned to the Provincial Deputation shall be performed.

Art. 11. The provincial Congress shall be charged principally with the formation of a state Constitution under the system of a popular, representative, federal government, which has been pronounced so decisively and firmly by all communities of the state itself.

Art. 12. Each member of the provincial Congress except civil employees, soldiers, and clergymen shall be compensated at the rate of one hundred and fifty pesos a month and one peso a league for traveling expenses; if the civil employees, soldiers, and clergymen have an income smaller than that to be given the other deputies, they shall be paid the difference.

The recommendation of the committee was adopted in full by the Provincial Deputation and sent to Governor Quintanar for publication.[14]

In order that all might know what the state of Jalisco was doing, the entire proceedings of the meeting, together with the national electoral law and an order that the interpretations made by the Provincial Deputation be strictly followed, were published by Quintanar as an official order on July 1 and circulated.[15]

A program for the installation of the Constituent Congress of Jalisco was adopted by the Provincial Deputation and made public on September 3.[16] By September 10, the electoral process had been completed and deputies elected, with September 14 designated as the date for their installation.[17] The Jaliscan Congress was duly installed, with Quintanar making the congratulatory speech. The days of September 14, 15, and 16 were then given over to the long-desired event. All business houses were closed, the city was decorated and lighted, and parades and concerts were held in the afternoon and a serenade each night in the principal plaza.[18] Regular sessions of the Jaliscan State Congress began on September 18, and the first decree declared the dissolution of the Provincial Deputation, whose functions were henceforth to be those of the state Congress, to which the archives of the dissolved body as well as the money in its treasury were transferred.[19] The first Legislature of the state of Jalisco was in existence.

While Nueva Galicia was the first province of Mexico whose Provincial Deputation declared its intention of setting up a provincial Congress, Oaxaca was the first to convert itself into a federal state, beginning shortly after the intendancy adopted the Plan of Casa Mata. Members of the provisional governing junta of nineteen were elected on February 24, at a joint session of the Provincial Deputation and the Municipal Council of Oaxaca City with Nicolás Bravo presiding. Installed with great rejoicing ten days later, this junta assumed control of the government of the province of Oaxaca and, for a time, took the place of the Provincial Deputation.[20] The establishment of such a body, even provisionally, tended toward the formation of a federal republic, for which the country, in the opinion of Carlos María Bustamante, was not ready.[21] Its existence was brief, however, for it was dissolved sometime in April and the Provincial Deputation was reestablished.[22] Records and accounts of the activities of that restored body have not been found. The contents of its orders are not known, but it seems to have caused a movement in Oaxaca against the national restored Congress.[23] In commenting on the Provincial Deputations in Mexico, Bustamante, on May 2, 1821, said that they, like that of Oaxaca, were becoming the stepmothers of the nation instead of its support, for unable to govern their own provinces they wanted to rule the whole country.[24]

Details of the events occurring in the province of Oaxaca during the latter part of April and the month of May are not clear. But apparently the Oaxacan province was not pleased with the acts of the national restored Congress and was trying to exert pressure on it. By June 1, confidence in it had declined to such an extent that the Oaxacan Provincial Deputation decided to declare complete independence from Mexico City. On that date, at a meeting of its Provincial Deputation, Antonio León, the Political Chief, said that at its last meeting it had been agreed that a special meeting be called when necessary and that such an occasion had arisen.[25] A committee from the Oaxacan Municipal Council reported that the people wanted a federal republic and that a large part of those assembled at a gathering in the city favored secession from the capital of Mexico and the establishment of a federal state. After consultation with municipal and military officials, the Deputation, together with representatives of other local bodies, voted unanimously to declare absolute separation from the national government of Mexico City.

A committee composed of representatives from the Provincial Deputation, the Municipal Council, and the army on the next day presented a plan for the establishment of a provisional government for the province of Oaxaca.[26] According to this, Oaxaca was to profess only one religion, that of the Roman Catholic Church. Sovereignty was to be exercised exclusively by the province of Oaxaca under a federal system through a provincial Congress established on the basis of liberty, equality, property, and security. The members of Congress were to be named by district elections in the manner stated in the convocation. Until the Congress met, the command of the army was to reside in the Commandant-General of the province; all other affairs were to be handled by the superior governing junta.[27] This body was to limit itself to passing essential regulations and provisions and not to make promotions or fill offices except provisionally in the most urgent cases. As soon as more than half the deputies arrived, the Congress was to begin functioning and the junta was to be dissolved. All existing laws not contrary to a federal system were to be valid until the provincial Congress decreed otherwise. Orders from the national government in Mexico City were not to be recognized, and Oaxaca's deputies to the national Congress were to be recalled. The governing junta was to take any necessary measures in case of extraordinary events.

There was to be a provisional council of war, named by the junta and composed of three military officials, not members of it. The Commandant-General was to take no steps without the majority approval of the council of war, which was to keep the governing junta informed of all military decisions. The Oaxacan province, which had no extraterritorial ambitions, was to limit its military force to that sufficient, in the opinion of the council of war, to preserve order within the province and to withstand aggression from without. It was not anticipated that those provinces that had not yet pronounced for a federal system of government would commit hostilities against Oaxaca. Should that occur, such a province would be considered an enemy. In the face of such action, the province of Oaxaca reserved its rights and would always demand them in the general Congress of the nation. Declared enemies of the federal system within Oaxaca, if proven guilty, were to be exiled from the province.[28]

The plan was immediately adopted and the call for elections issued shortly thereafter. Obviously elections were held promptly,[29] for on July 6, 1823, the provisional Congress of the free state of Oaxaca was formally installed, decreed the cessation of the provincial governing junta, and assumed the responsibilities of the former Provincial Deputation of Oaxaca.[30] The conversion of that body from an advisory council to a provincial Congress had been consummated in Oaxaca.[31]

Yucatán was the second province to establish a Constituent Congress after adherence to the Plan of Casa Mata. On March 4, 1823, the Yucatecan Provincial Deputation had assumed complete control of the government of that intendancy. Since some of its members did not think that body should exercise executive and military authority as well as legislative functions,[32] a five-member provisional popularly elective body with functions designated by the Provincial Deputation together with representatives of the Municipal Council of Mérida, the clergy, and the army was established; elections were ordered to begin on April 27 in the parishes and to be completed in the capital of the province on May 18, 1823.[33]

After General Melchor Alvarez, the Captain-General and Political Chief, who had been named by Emperor Iturbide, retired to Champoton, not wishing to become involved in the events transpiring, Pedro Bolio y Torrecilla, in accord with the Spanish Constitution of 1812, became the Political Chief, and the Yucatecan Provincial Deputation began to study the problem of providing the intendancy with a commandant. Actually, from the time of its adhesion to the Plan of Casa Mata, the Yucatecan Provincial Deputation, considering its province free, had directed all of its affairs. After it appointed José Segundo Carvajal Captain-General of the province on May 26, Alvarez informed the Deputation that he wanted to resume his duties, but he was told that he would have to appeal to the provisional administrative junta, which was to be installed shortly.[34]

By the end of May, the Yucatecan Provincial Deputation was taking definite steps toward converting the province into a federal state. At a special session, on May 29, it heard petitions from a large number of citizens, officials, and soldiers, asking that Yucatán proclaim its intention to form a part of the Mexican nation only under a federal system, which would permit it to draw up its own Constitution and to make laws that were considered best for the province. To the national government should be delegated the right to make treaties, declare war, and direct matters of interest to the nation as a whole, as well as to name diplomatic officials, army officers from brigadier up, and church officials from bishop up. The nomination of all other provincial authorities was reserved to the Yucatán "Senate," and the state government was given the responsibility of providing its part of the national expenses.[35] The Yucatecan Provincial Deputation, in order to sound out public opinion, called in representatives from municipal and ecclesiastical bodies, the army, and all of the provincial electors chosen to elect the members of the provisional administrative junta, most of whom were in Mérida at that time. All voted to adopt the measures set forth in the petitions and also to elect the provisional junta or executive body of five members to govern the Yucatecan province until a state Constituent Congress could be elected and installed. Tiburcio López, Pablo Lanz, Francisco Facio, Simón Ortega, and Raymundo Pérez were immediately named to the junta.[36]

The Yucatecan Provincial Deputation, together with the provincial electors and the representatives of the various provincial and municipal bodies in Mérida, instructed the junta: (1) to exercise the executive functions formerly exercised by the Provincial Deputation under the Spanish Constitution of 1812 and the decrees of the Spanish Cortes insofar as they were not contrary to a republican form of government and were in accord with the needs of the province; (2) to call a popular election at which deputies to the provincial Congress were to be elected on the basis of one deputy for every twenty-five thousand inhabitants (the provincial electors chosen were to meet in Mérida on August 1, 1823, to name the deputies); and (3) to dissolve immediately following the installation of the provincial Congress.[37]

The members of the junta were installed at Mérida on May 30, 1823, and an account of the establishment was distributed throughout the province of Yucatán. All the province approved; even Campeche, which had been objecting to the activities of the Yucatecan Provincial Deputation, sanctioned the federal plan.[38] The junta, on June 6, 1823, issued the call for the election of deputies to the provincial Constituent Congress.[39] The municipal elections were held on June 29; the district elections, on July 13; and the provincial elections, on July 27.[40]

On August 20, the Constituent Congress of Yucatán was installed with great rejoicing;[41] it began at once to draw up laws and a Constitution for the state of Yucatán.[42]

Zacatecas was the fourth Mexican intendancy to set itself up as a "free" state. One of the strongest and most insistent voices speaking in the national restored Congress for a new one and for provincial autonomy was that of the Zacatecan deputy, Valentín Gómez Farías. In his *Voto particular* (Personal Vote) of April 19, he had supported the conversion of Provincial Deputations into true provincial Congresses and expressed the desire of the provinces for autonomy in regard to their provincial affairs.[43] In other words, Gómez Farías favored "states' rights." That he was speaking for his province is evidenced by the fact that the Zacatecan Provincial Deputation upon receipt of the printed copy of his *Voto particular* not only approved of it but also addressed a statement of its approval to the national restored Congress.[44] Zacatecas, like its neighbor Nueva Galicia with its capital at Guadalajara, was tired of importuning the reluctant restored national Congress. The Zacatecan Provincial Deputation with the assistance of two members of the Municipal Council of Zacatecas City on June 18, 1823, agreed upon a provisional form of government;[45] on July 12, it issued the plan for a provisional government of the free state of Zacatecas until the state Constituent Congress met. Both the provisional plan of government issued on June 18 and the plan for the convocation contained substantially the same measures as the plan of Nueva Galicia issued at Guadalajara on June 5 and 16. Three provisions of the Zacatecas plan should be noticed, however: (1) the state of Zacatecas was defined as having eight districts: Aguascalientes, Fresnillo, Juchipila, Mazapil, Nieves, Pinos, Sombrereta, and Zacatecas; (2) the maintenance of internal order and exterior relations of the state and other functions of the executive power were to reside in a provisional governing junta composed of the acting Political Chief, Domingo Velásquez; the Commandant-General, Pedro de Iriarte; and the local commandant, Juan Paredo, with Pedro Ramírez and Manuel de Abreu serving as alternates when necessary; and (3) in spite of the provisions of Article 16 of the law of June 17 issued by the national restored Congress in Mexico City and convoking the new national Congress, the Zacatecan Provincial Deputation was not to be renewed in the coming elections but was to continue exercising its functions until the installation of the Zacatecan Constituent Congress, which should determine the future of the Deputation.[46]

As was to be expected, the independent action of the province of Nueva Galicia with its Provincial Deputation acting at its capital at Guadalajara and of the Zacatecan Provincial Deputation disturbed the national restored Congress. As early as May, there had been talk of sending troops under Gen. Pedro Celestino Negrete to subdue Guadalajara,[47] but the national government finally decided to send both General Negrete and Nicolás Bravo to subdue the two provinces, because they had refused to accept the decree of June 17 convoking the new Constituent Congress of the nation.[48] The troops left for Guadalajara, Nueva Galicia, on July 5, 1823.[49]

The Provincial Deputations of both Guadalajara and Zacatecas had announced that they would permit no aggression from without, and both were fully informed of the forces being sent against them and cooperated in their plans for resistance. On receipt of an order from the national Supreme Executive Power to aid the troops under Negrete and Bravo in every possible way, whose object "it was said" was to protect the province of San Luis Potosí, the intendant of Zacatecas reported the matter to the Zacatecan Provincial Deputation, which immediately notified both generals not only that the movement of national troops was unnecessary but that not a single national soldier would be allowed to enter the state. The Zacatecan Provincial Deputation also reminded Bravo that he had said upon his departure from Mexico City that the purpose of his expedition was to eliminate the opposition to the federal system that some of them had adopted. It continued that in the province of Zacatecas there was no such opposition, for its promulgation had been received with great public approval. The province of Zacatecas, therefore, did not need any troops from without to preserve order or to remove opposition, nor did it have any means to aid an unnecessary and unwanted army.[50]

A copy of this letter to the two generals was sent at once to the Provincial Deputation of Guadalajara with a statement that the causes of the two free states were one and that they must work together and assist each other in every possible way. Zacatecas thanked Guadalajara for the copy of the plan for provisions of a state government as well as the changes it had made in the national electoral law and advised that it had adopted almost the same measures.[51] The two provinces then prepared to resist the approaching national armies with force, if necessary. Fortunately, a clash was avoided by Bravo's halting his troops at Irapuato and agreeing to a conference at Lagos with representatives from both provinces. The Provincial Deputation of Guadalajara named Gen. Luis Quintanar, Pedro Vélez, and Juan Cayetano Portugal to represent that state, and Quintanar issued a manifesto to the "free state of Jalisco," on July 18, informing its people of the purpose of the meeting.[52] The Provincial Deputation of Zacatecas named Pedro de Iriarte, Juan José Román, and Santos Vélez as its representatives. Bravo himself did not attend the meetings, but appointed José Domínguez and Mariano Villarrutia to represent him. Later he sent Juan Domínguez to join in the conference.[53]

When the sessions opened, on August 8, 1823, Bravo's commissioners stated that, although the states of Jalisco and Zacatecas had both recognized the national Congress and the Supreme Executive Power as the center of the nation and had offered to obey the orders emanating from the two bodies insofar as those orders contributed to the well-being of the nation, they had not complied with the orders from the national government, but had made changes in the electoral law that rendered it ineffective. If the two states did not wish to obstruct the meeting of the newly called Congress and to embroil the country in the worst kind of anarchy, they must comply completely with the electoral law and obey the orders of the national government. The representatives of Jalisco and Zacatecas replied that as the two states had proclaimed in favor of federalism before offering to obey the electoral law they could not subject themselves to any parts of the electoral law contrary to the federal system. They maintained that the additions they had made to the law pertained only to their respective states, did not concern in any way the nation as a whole, and did not impede the assembling of a new Congress. They said, furthermore, that all orders issued by the national government for the good of the nation had been observed. The meeting adjourned until the following day so Bravo's commissioners could report to him and get further instructions.

At the second conference the representatives of the states of Zacatecas and Jalisco reaffirmed their willingness to recognize and obey the national government in everything pertaining to the welfare of the nation as a whole, to contribute their part to the support of the national expenses, and to use their resources and forces to sustain its independence and liberty. They maintained their right, however, to reject any orders injurious to their respective state's right or pertaining solely to their internal affairs. They defended their right to establish the provincial Congress they had already called and to instruct their deputies to the national Congress as they saw fit. They asserted, furthermore, that the rules for the provisional government of the states issued by Jalisco on June 18 and by Zacatecas on July 12, 1823, would continue in force, until changed by law by the states' Congresses or by the newly called national Congress. Those participating in the conferences agreed to all the above-stated points. They were duly set forth in twelve articles to which all present subscribed.

When that document reached Bravo, he eliminated all that Zacatecas and Jalisco demanded as their rights, called for the execution of all orders that had been or would be issued by the national government, and returned it to the commissioners on August 12. They then met at Lagos on August 14 with the representatives of Jalisco and Zacatecas, who refused to accept any significant change made by Bravo. His commissioners reported that they had done all they could to obtain the adoption of his revisions, admitted that Jalisco and Zacatecas had some sound basis for their action, and recommended that he accept the agreement as finally revised, differing but slightly from the agreement of August 9. Bravo must have realized that further conferences were useless, for, on August 18, he informed his commissioners that he could not approve the agreement but that he had forwarded it to the national government. He instructed his commissioners so to inform the states' representatives and then returned to Irapuato to await further instructions from Mexico City.[54]

This attempted display of arms on the part of the national government to force Jalisco and Zacatecas to submission had aroused considerable agitation throughout the country. Prisciliano Sánchez, deputy from Guadalajara, Gómez Farías, and Francisco García had all protested in the restored Congress itself against such action and had pointed out that both Oaxaca and Yucatán had gone much further in establishing state governments. Such action on the part of the national government would result, they stated, in the various provinces arming themselves for defense. Finally complete anarchy would result.[55] José María Covarrubias, speaking in Congress on August 1, also warned that armed action against Jalisco would start a conflagration too great to control and asked for reconsideration of the decree that gave the government the power to use armed force.[56] Bustamante wrote in his diary on August 4 that the deputies from Jalisco, by having their proposals published and circulated even before they had been admitted for discussion, were trying to undermine the government in its plan for action against that province.[57]

On August 15, Congress met in special session at the request of the Supreme Executive Power. Four of the ministers attended the session, at which Lucas Alamán reported on the Lagos conference and on the persistence of Jalisco and Zacatecas in their old demands. There was some debate over what procedure should be followed. Bustamante said that the government should first render its opinion on the matter; that, in turn, should be referred to a congressional committee, which should make recommendations to Congress. The body voted, however, to refer the whole matter to a special committee, which recommended the following day that, since no decision on the Jalisco affair could yet be rendered, the government should be authorized to settle it and the request of the Provincial Deputation of Guadalajara that the past be forgotten should be granted.[58]

A short time later Bravo, on instructions from the government, retired with his forces to Celaya, and Quintanar, shortly afterward, returned to Guadalajara. The provinces of Jalisco and Zacatecas proceeded with the establishment of their state governments. Jalisco, as has been stated, installed its Congress on September 14; Zacatecas, the fourth state to do so, installed its on October 19, 1823,[59] and on that date its Provincial Deputation ceased to exist.

These four provinces of Oaxaca, Yucatán, Nueva Galicia (with its Provincial Deputation sitting at Guadalajara and frequently referred to as the province of Guadalajara), and Zacatecas were the pioneer state governments. They dared to face down the old restored national Congress and the national government of Mexico as provided by the Plan of Casa Mata of February 1, 1823. They declared their complete independence in internal provincial affairs and elected and established their own state Congresses through their Provincial Deputations while still under the control of the Spanish Constitution of 1812.

EIGHT

Establishment of Other State Legislatures

The policy of the province of Jalisco (or Guadalajara) in broadcasting each event that occurred in that state through copies of printed proclamations, broadsides, official orders, and minutes of the meetings of its Provincial Deputation sent posthaste to every part of Mexico soon aroused the citizens of other provinces, if they had not already been aroused. As early as May 23, 1823, Pedro Otero, in writing from Guadalajara to the Marqués de Vivanco concerning the influence of this printed material, said that Quintanar was urging Guanajuato to follow in Guadalajara's steps, that the material was in the hands of everyone, and that its persuasive arguments had increased the desire for reform of the national representation in the province of Guanajuato. Many of the people there, Otero said, would already have followed Guadalajara if they had not recognized that he was handling the matter most judiciously.[1]

Most of the provinces of Mexico, from the date of their adherence to the Plan of Casa Mata, apparently considered themselves independent provinces or states. They felt a need for and wanted a national government; but they believed that they had the inalienable right either to join it or, if it did not meet with their approval, to stay out of it. In other words, the provinces, considering themselves independent, believed that the national government should consider their ideas rather than that they should conform to the ideas of the restored Congress, a body that they recognized only as provisionally expedient.

The almost spontaneous reaction of the provinces upon receiving the congressional Committee Report on the Convocation of a New Congress indicates the unanimity of opinion among them. Guadalajara appears to have been the first in making an overt move, but the speed with which others took such steps indicated that they were working along similar lines prior to learning of the actions of Guadalajara. Correspondence of men of the day supports this belief. Bustamante wrote on April 17, 1823, that vendors were then selling on the streets of Mexico City a printed item entitled "La República de Guadalajara."

Four days later, he wrote that a junta had been formed in Monterrey, composed of members from Coahuila, Texas, Nuevo Santander, and Nuevo León, and that those four provinces appeared to be aspiring to a "federation with México."[2] Servando Mier, on April 23, in a letter to the Municipal Council of Monterrey, also referred to the wish of the four Eastern Interior Provinces to become "a sovereign confederate state of the Mexican Republic." He added that the steps being taken by the province would inevitably lead to this, but that he hoped it would not happen for ten years, by which time the provinces would possess the prerequisites of sovereign states.[3] Stephen F. Austin, writing from Saltillo, Coahuila, on May 10, said Ramos Arizpe, then in Saltillo, had informed him that the principal provinces of the nation, among them Oaxaca, Guadalajara, Guatemala, Guanajuato, and the Eastern Interior Provinces, had declared in favor of a confederated republic very similar to that of the United States and that he thought the majority of the members of Congress favored it.[4]

Bustamante, on May 12, wrote that Guadalajara was daily becoming more agitated, because unscrupulous men had convinced those good people that they should be governed under a federated republic. It is rather evident, therefore, that, by May 1823, the idea of a federal republic was circulating throughout the country and even being discussed by the deputies of the restored Congress, although some of them were strongly opposed to that form of government, and others, though not opposed to the system, felt that its introduction into Mexico should be delayed.[5] A group of deputies (José Valle, Servando Mier, José Mariano Marín, Lorenzo de Zavala, Javier Bustamante, José María García, José María Bocanegra, and Valentín Gómez Farías), as noted, in the last days of April had begun to work on a draft of a Constitution.[6] And on May 21, Congress announced that the Eastern Interior Provinces had created a supreme junta that had declared itself sovereign and indicated that those provinces wished to confederate with Mexico,[7] and Múzquiz pointed out that Oaxaca had done the same.[8] Ramos Arizpe, who had led the Eastern Interior Provinces to adopt the Plan of Casa Mata and to name him head of its provisional governing junta, had continued to direct affairs in those provinces even after he had relinquished his post as president of the junta on April 1, the date on which the Provincial Deputation was formally reestablished. The Municipal Council of Monterrey wrote to Servando Mier that on April 30 force had been required to prevent the city from separating from the national government, that Ramos Arizpe had installed a new junta of which he was president, and that he was trying to force his ideas upon the Council.[9]

Complete details of the events occurring in the Eastern Interior Provinces between April 1 and May 28 have not been found. That Ramos Arizpe was working toward the establishment of some kind of junta is clear. The Municipal Council of Saltillo on April 10 had sent out instructions to the other municipal bodies of the province inviting them to elect a representative to the junta of the district. On April 30, the Municipal Council of San Nicolás de la Capellanía elected Ramos Arizpe as its representative.[10] Four days later, the junta was installed in Saltillo. It was composed of Ramos Arizpe (president), Agustín de la Viezca, Jesús Ramos, and Rafael Eça y Múzquiz, each of whom had been named by a Municipal Council of the district. The purpose of the junta was to unify opinion in that district with that of Monclova and Monterrey and to see that Coahuila's deputies proceeded to Monterrey. The junta held sessions (ten in all) until May 23, 1823, when they ceased because "the purpose of the body had been realized."[11]

Stephen F. Austin, on May 11, 1823, wrote from Saltillo: "In this quarter there have been some dissensions but they are about to terminate. The Congress is acknowledged and the new system fully adopted, with the condition that these four provinces wish a confederated republic. . . . There still exist some differences of minor importance between this place and Monterrey, but all will unite in supporting the congress and a liberal government."[12]

At midnight on May 26, 1823, the Municipal Council of Saltillo met in special session to hear some citizens of the community who wished to express their ideas concerning the form of government that Mexico was to adopt. City officials and prominent citizens were also invited and a considerable number attended. It was agreed that those present favored a federal republic; but it was decided that it would be best to hold another meeting the next day to which a larger number of people, including the clergy, government officials, prominent citizens, and the Municipal Council of San Esteban de Tlaxcala, would be invited. At that meeting the acts of the previous day were read. Then José León Lobo Guerrero pointed out that besides declaring for a federal republic they should also call attention to the fact that the province of Coahuila did not have a deputy in Congress to speak for it. This suggestion was unanimously approved, as were the following seven resolutions: (1) the supreme executive of the nation should not hold office for life or be able to pass the office to any of his heirs; instead, his term should be limited and the office filled by national election; (2) the executive should be responsible to the country for his actions; (3) the government of the nation should be a federated republic, each province being independent as far as its internal and economic government was concerned; (4) the four Eastern Interior Provinces should form a single state in the Mexican federation; (5) these proposals should be sent to other Municipal Councils and to the Political Chief to be forwarded to the Supreme Executive Power and to Congress, (6) it was hoped that the Political Chief would circulate this manifesto to the Municipal Councils of all other Eastern Interior Provinces; (7) this act and that of the previous night should be recognized as expressing the will of the people of Saltillo and should be sent to the provincial governing junta of Coahuila, to Parras, and to other places in the province. The act was signed by those present, including Ramos Arizpe and José León Lobo Guerrero.[13]

Not satisfied with the public expression in favor of a federated republic, Ramos Arizpe continued his effort to secure an even stronger statement. Meetings to that end were held by the Municipal Council of Saltillo, which called the townspeople of Saltillo and of San Esteban de Tlaxcala together on June 4. At that junta, presided over by José Miguel González, mayor of Saltillo, it was resolved that since the restored Congress had forgotten the reason it was tolerated and was busying itself with matters that exclusively concerned the provincial Congresses, it was absolutely necessary for each province to establish its own government in a permanent form. Each should, therefore, take measures to provide for security and provide for its independence and establish its own internal autonomy. Consequently, the following seven resolutions were unanimously adopted. (1) All the inhabitants of Saltillo and San Esteban de Tlaxcala favored the union of all the Mexican provinces and recognized the Supreme Executive Power and the restored Congress as a body to issue a convocation for a new one to frame the general Constitution of the nation. (2) All legally established authorities in the four provinces were recognized and were to continue in office according to the laws. (3) These four provinces must be granted internal government, independent of other provinces in economic and territorial matters but united with them in regard to general and foreign relations. (4) Felipe de la Garza was to head the government of the province and (5) to exercise the executive power with the title of Governor-General of the four provinces until the meeting of the provincial Congress. (6) He was authorized to issue without delay a convocation for a Congress composed of deputies of the four united Eastern Interior Provinces to frame a Constitution of a single state made up of the four of them. (7) The adoption of these proposals was to be made known to de la Garza, as Political Chief of the provinces, and to the governing junta of Coahuila, who, it was hoped, would cooperate actively and efficiently in bringing them to prompt fulfillment.[14] Servando Mier, in speaking of this action by Saltillo, credited Ramos Arizpe with being responsible for it and added that all the province of Coahuila and Nuevo Santander, as well as the towns of Pilon and Cerralvo, had adopted it.[15]

Although Nuevo León did not adopt such a strong program as Coahuila, it did also take a stand in favor of a federated republic on June 5. The Provincial Deputation, with Felipe de la Garza,[16] the Political Chief, presiding, held an open forum with members of the Monterrey Municipal Council and ecclesiastical chapter, the rector and professors of the college, government employees, and prominent citizens present. The purpose of the meeting was to consider, in view of the occurrences in New Galicia, the May 21 decree just received and the question of a new Congress. Furthermore, since the pronouncements of Saltillo, Pilon, and Cerralvo and the agitation in other places might produce friction and disturbances, a formal statement in regard to the form of government and the methods by which it should be established was highly desirable in order to unite opinion in all four provinces. After lengthy discussion, those assembled voted in favor of a federal republic and of informing the national government of that decision.[17]

De la Garza replied, on June 8, 1823, to Saltillo's proposal that he take the lead as executive of the Eastern Interior Provinces. He said that the Provincial Deputation at its meeting three days earlier had resolved to declare formally that these provinces (1) had adopted the federal form of government, under which they would compose one or more free, sovereign, independent states as they themselves might agree, and with the other provinces would compose the Mexican nation in accord with the federal Constitution then being drafted; (2) had recognized the existing Congress solely as a body to convoke the new one and to perform such other functions as did not conflict with the federal system; (3) had recognized the Supreme Executive Power, under the same conditions, as the provisional government of the nation; and (4) had determined that, since the welfare of the provinces demanded prompt, efficacious measures, their government would at present devote itself exclusively to that object. De la Garza added that another session of the provincial body would be held that same day to deal with the last point; and at that time the proposals of Saltillo would be kept in mind and whatever measures were adopted would, he was sure, receive the support of all the provinces.[18]

No account of the meeting or the measures adopted by the Provincial Deputation on June 8 has been found. A legislative junta of the three provinces was authorized as the sovereign body to dictate the laws for the provinces; to the national Congress was delegated the power to pass only laws of general interest. A circular to that effect was sent out to the three provinces,[19] as was also the "plan for the new basis for the constitution of those provinces," which was written in Topo and ordered printed with great urgency by de la Garza.[20] The Provincial Deputation named de la Garza Political Chief of those provinces.

The province of Nuevo Santander began consideration of a public statement in favor of federalism on June 7, and ten days later its Provincial Deputation formally voted in favor of a federal republic.[21] Servando Mier said that that province declared itself sovereign and did not even deign to inform the national government of its actions.[22]

The activities in the Eastern Interior Provinces, all of which Servando Mier and Bustamante attributed to the influence of Ramos Arizpe,[23] had a pronounced effect upon the national Congress. Servando Mier proposed that provincial Congresses with broadest powers be installed at once in accord with the project of a Constitution, which had been ordered published; the Minister of Justice and Ecclesiastical Affairs, in a secret session of June 25, proposed that Congress adopt a provisional federal pact between the national government and the provinces; and, in order to dissipate Ramos Arizpe's influence in those provinces, Congress, as has been stated, voted to establish a Provincial Deputation in each of the Eastern Interior Provinces.[24]

These four provinces never declared their intention to separate from the Mexican nation. In all their communications they insisted that they would support it in every possible way. They simply proposed to proceed with the establishment of a provincial or state government as a part of the federal republic. But when the decree of June 19 convoking the new Congress was received, they announced that the measures toward setting up the state government had been suspended and that they would await the actions of the future Congress.[25]

The Provincial Deputation of Querétaro was by no means so specific. In a letter of May 20 to its deputy, Félix de Osores, it again instructed him to use every means possible to see that the province got the territory belonging to it, "because the federal system so required." It is quite evident, therefore, that the establishment of a federal republic in Mexico was then considered by the province to be a foregone conclusion. Furthermore, its Provincial Deputation stated in the minutes of its June 11 and 12 meetings that all the people had manifested their preference for a federal republic and that even the existing Congress adhered to the system only because such was the will of the people.[26] Since its delay in convoking the new Congress had brought the whole country to the verge of anarchy, the Provincial Deputation of Querétaro resolved not to recognize Congress except as a convoking body and approved the pronouncement of Celaya and San Miguel el Grande in favor of a federal republic and their nomination of Brigadier Miguel Barragán as commander-in-chief and of Brigadier Luis Cortazar as second in command of the armed forces of the province, which would be placed at the disposal of the Provincial Deputations of Guanajuato and Michoacán if needed by them to retain order. The army would be supported by the three provinces in question; and the squadrons of the sixth regiment, stationed at that time in Querétaro but belonging to the province of México, would be permitted to remain where they were or return to México. These articles were not to become effective until approved by the Provincial Deputations of Michoacán and Guanajuato.[27]

The decree on June 17, convoking the new Congress, was received by Querétaro with rejoicing and its provisions accepted in full; with it in hand, the Provincial Deputation hoped to be able to keep the province calm.[28] That body did not appreciate, however, the reprimand it received from the Minister of Domestic Affairs in his communication of June 18 and 27, in regard to Querétaro's actions of June 11 and 12. And its Provincial Deputation issued in reply a lengthy manifesto in which it charged Congress with responsibility for all the disturbances that had occurred. The provinces, after having used in vain every means to convince Congress of the need for a new one, had decided to obtain their demand at any cost. Having realized their powers, Jalisco (Guadalajara), Nuevo León, Oaxaca, Campeche, Zacatecas, and others had then withdrawn from the national government and begun working for the establishment of a federal republic. While there was still hope that a new convocation would calm the widespread anarchy, the Provincial Deputation of Michoacán had invited that of Querétaro to send commissioners to meet with those of its own province and those of Guanajuato and San Luis Potosí to agree on the wisest precautionary measures and on the best method of forcing Congress to call for a new one promptly. Commissioners had been named and hopes were high concerning the effectiveness of such a conference when news was received of the unexpected *Pronunciamiento* (Pronouncement) of Santa Anna and of the actions of the garrisons of Celaya and San Miguel el Grande. The only solution possible under the circumstances had been for the Provincial Deputation to head the movement in order to direct its energy into useful and peaceful channels and thus to disarm the enemies of the country who were attempting to use the cry "liberty and federalism" for their own purposes. The Provincial Deputation of Querétaro concluded by stating that all it had done had been for the good of the nation as a whole, and it felt, therefore, that its actions should be so recognized.[29] To a similar communication addressed to the Supreme Executive Power on July 15, Alamán replied that the national government recognized that Querétaro had worked for the good of the country.[30]

The province of Guanajuato also favored a federal republic. So wrote Otero, the commandant, on May 23, 1823, when informing Morán of the communications received from the province of Jalisco. Since receiving the congressional decree of May 21, he had, however, been able to keep the province quiet.[31] Cortazar, the Political Chief, had replied to Jalisco that there was no reason to fear that the national government of Mexico would decide for any other than a federal form.[32]

When the decree of June 17 reached Guanajuato by special messenger on the night of June 22, it was welcomed by loud ringing of church bells and a manifesto from Cortazar to the people. He said that he, like them, was convinced that a federal republic would promote the happiness of the province; the work of laying the foundation for it should be entrusted, however, to the Constituent Congress that had been called. As a means of unifying the ideas and feelings of the province, he had, in accord with

Otero, ordered that the watchword in reply to "Who goes there?" should be "The federal republic."[33]

Sometime between May 7 and the early days of June of that year, Michoacán had decided on the advisability of a conference between commissioners from its Provincial Deputation and those of San Luis Potosí, Guanajuato, and Querétaro, and correspondence to that end had been initiated. The purpose was to work out a uniform program to be followed by the four provinces for their mutual protection against the dangers threatened by the dilatory actions of the reassembled Congress. As already stated, one of the commissioners from the province of San Luis Potosí had met with the Provincial Deputation of Michoacán on May 7, and it is possible that the idea of concerted action stemmed from that meeting. Unified action was, however, not a new idea to the four. They had followed it after adopting the Plan of Casa Mata, and it had been the practice of their Provincial Deputations for some time to keep one another informed of ongoing activities.

Events in the province of San Luis Potosí delayed the proposed conference somewhat but, in the opinion of the four provinces, increased the necessity for holding it. Santa Anna, as has been stated, had reached San Luis Potosí under difficult circumstances, and his difficulties increased when Díaz de León, the Political Chief, informed him that it was impossible to supply the horses and mules requested. The Political Chief complained, too, that Santa Anna's highhanded method of confiscating equipment was antagonizing all the province and asked for the return of the police wagons borrowed from the San Luis Potosí Municipal Council. Santa Anna countered by informing the Provincial Deputation that the chief's lack of energy was the only reason that equipment had not been provided, but the provincial body defended the Political Chief. Santa Anna's troops continued to stir up the people, and one of his officers attempted to arouse them to declare a federal republic. Although the Political Chief, the Provincial Deputation, and other official bodies favored that form of government, they felt the proclamation was at that time unnecessary and inadvisable; Díaz de León so informed Santa Anna and again demanded, on June 3, the return of the borrowed wagons.[34]

On the same day Santa Anna's troops, equipped for battle, marched to the main plaza, where an officer ordered the reading of Santa Anna's proclamation in which he adhered to a federal republic. An officer then asked the provisional garrison to form ranks to hear the proclamation. After hearing it, the entire garrison refused to join the movement; instead it took up positions in two church towers and on a convent roof and declared it would resist any aggression on Santa Anna's part. The whole city was alarmed; many families left their homes for safer regions. People in the neighboring villages armed themselves the best they could and joined the garrison in shouting death to Santa Anna and his troops. Santa Anna appeared personally, but in vain, before the garrison in an attempt to win it over. By nightfall he circulated a plan in which he declared himself with his army "Protector of the Federation of the Provinces."[35]

None of the official government bodies of the province supported him. A resident of San Luis Potosí wrote on June 11 that the Provincial Deputation, the Municipal Council, and the citizens of the province had all refused to take part, and that all army officers who had refused had been exiled from the province by Santa Anna.[36] The editors of *Aguila mexicana* said that reliable sources in San Luis Potosí had reported that the authorities there had not accepted the plan but had been silenced through fear of the forces at Santa Anna's command.[37] Later actions of the Provincial Deputation also tend to confirm the belief that it did not approve the plan or any of Santa Anna's actions.

The national government, concerned with the disturbances in San Luis Potosí caused by Santa Anna's troops, named Brigadier Gabriel de Armijo as commandant of the province.[38] He set out from Mexico City on May 31 for the interior.[39] When Santa Anna learned that Armijo was approaching, he sent a copy of his plan of June 5 to Armijo and warned him not to enter the province until he had given evidence of absolute adherence to it.[40] Armijo replied that neither he nor any of his men could deny obedience to the legally constituted authorities and that he had transmitted to them Santa Anna's communication and would withhold comment until he received a reply.[41]

Soon thereafter Armijo sent the parish priest of Valle de San Francisco, Col. José Martínez Chavarro, and Francisco Antonio de los Reyes to Santa Anna with five proposals that they urged him to accept.[42] Instead he rejected them and attempted to secure an interview with Armijo.[43] On the afternoon of June 15, they conferred for over three hours, but no agreement was reached. On the following day, Armijo advised Santa Anna of his intention to march to the Hacienda de Pardo. When Armijo reached the ranch about midnight, Santa Anna's forces opened fire. To avoid bloodshed, Armijo withdrew a short distance and reported the whole affair to the Minister of Domestic Affairs.

Santa Anna then returned to San Luis Potosí and explained to the Provincial Deputation and the Municipal Council, on June 19, why he had left. He asserted that he had a much larger force, but Armijo was conscripting and arming citizens who were unaware of his true motives, and, unless he was forced to desist, civil war was inevitable. Santa Anna proposed that the Provincial Deputation take measures to prevent the outbreak of hostilities. Ignacio Rayón suggested that Armijo be asked to withdraw from the province and to revoke the orders he had issued, but the majority of the members of the Provincial Deputation who spoke recommended that Santa Anna leave and that Armijo be permitted to hold the office to which the national government had appointed him. To avoid imminent hostilities, several members suggested that a committee from the Provincial Deputation and the Municipal Council act as mediators between the two.

The attitude of the two bodies toward Santa Anna was clearly indicated at the meeting. Apolinario Aspeita said that if Santa Anna recognized the national government, there was no cause for dissension between him and Armijo; if he did not recognize it or the Provincial Deputation, he was an enemy to liberty. José Joaquín Garate also censured Santa Anna for not having recognized any authority, characterized his actions in the province as most unwelcome, and recommended that he leave. Santa Anna then replied that his failure to recognize any authority was due to his haste in drafting his plan and that he actually had recognized the existing national government by his letter transmitting it for approval; finally, he offered to accept the decision of the commissioners of the four provinces and to serve under the man named to command their army.

The Provincial Deputation then named José Antonio Becerra and Rafael Villalobos commissioners to transmit to Armijo the proposal that (1) until he received a reply from the provinces trying to form a federation and from the Supreme Executive Power, he take a position wherever he chose; (2) Santa Anna and his forces should remain in the city of San Luis Potosí, but as soon as Armijo accepted these proposals, Santa Anna would recognize him publicly as the Commandant-General, whose orders were to be obeyed; (3) neither commander should open hostilities without first informing the Provincial Deputation; (4) that body would send commissioners to a meeting of the four provinces to discuss joint efforts in favor of federalism and to name a head of the armed forces of the four provinces, whom Santa Anna had promised he would obey. He, with all others present, signed these resolutions.[44]

Armijo agreed on June 21 to these proposals on seven conditions: (1) until the representatives of the provinces and the generals called to meet at Celaya had adopted a plan of action, no citizen of the city of San Luis Potosí should be arrested or tried except by regularly constituted authorities; (2) Santa Anna's troops might either remain temporarily under him or join Armijo's command, but in any case Armijo was to be recognized by all as the Commandant-General; (3) his troops should be given preference in using national funds; (4) his future orders enlisting the recognition and support of the entire province were to be energetically executed but were not to be considered hostile by Santa Anna, and all details of the agreement would be faithfully observed; (5) Armijo would keep his troops within the region between "real de los Pozos" (Pozos) and the Zavala Hacienda; (6) all measures would be temporary and would bind both alike to acceptance of the decisions of the junta of Celaya; (7) copies of the proposals of the Provincial Deputation and these conditions would be drawn up and signed by the Provincial Deputation, the Political Chief, the generals Armijo and Santa Anna and their secretaries, and a copy would be retained by each general.[45]

Santa Anna notified the Provincial Deputation on June 25 that he had refused to accept Armijo's conditions and had notified him to withdraw from the province within twenty-four hours or suffer the consequences. Armijo might remain in Querétaro or elsewhere until the federation compacts of the four provinces had been concluded. When the general to command the army of the four provinces had been elected, Santa Anna would with pleasure obey Armijo's orders, as he had already promised, or would retire his troops to whatever point he deemed best. Santa Anna concluded that if Armijo did not leave the province at once, he would throw all his resources against him.[46]

The members of the Provincial Deputation of San Luis Potosí forcefully informed Santa Anna that he was breaking his agreement to await the decisions of the conference of Celaya and that his proposed action could serve no good purpose and was in defiance of the national government, which the province recognized. They informed him that the electoral law convening the new Congress had arrived by special messenger the night before. This fact they felt should cause him to accept further mediation, which they offered. If Santa Anna still refused to consider, the Provincial Deputation would be silent until it could speak again with reason and justice and be heard. The Deputation also sent a similar appeal for further mediation to Armijo.[47]

Santa Anna did not heed the reply of the Provincial Deputation. Instead, on the same day, June 24, he marched out of the city with the purpose of surprising Armijo, who, however, eluded him and approached San Luis Potosí from a different direction. On June 27, Armijo stopped a short distance away and sent word to the Provincial Deputation that he would enter the city if the body thought it wise. Wishing to avoid fighting within the city and fearing vengeance from Santa Anna for having admitted Armijo, the Deputation recommended that he take quarters at Los Ranchos, a league away, which he did. Santa Anna passed through San Luis Potosí, on June 28, in pursuit of Armijo, who again eluded him. When Santa Anna then returned to San Luis Potosí, the Provincial Deputation fled to San Miguel Mesquitic, about three leagues distant, and, from there, did what it could to help the province and the city.[48] Santa Anna's soldiers, according to a letter from a resident to the editors of *Aguila mexicana,* proceeded to rob, insult, and bayonet at will. The Municipal Council of San Luis Potosí protested; to which Santa Anna replied that the insulting and abusive attitude of the people toward him and his soldiers had forced them to such actions.[49]

The meeting of the representatives of the generals of the four provinces was held in Celaya, on July 1, 1823. Those present were Otero, commandant of Guanajuato, Luis Cortazar, commandant of Querétaro, José María del Toro, representing Santa Anna, Barragán, commandant of Michoacán and also representing Armijo, and José María Márquez of San Luis Potosí, as secretary. Barragán presided. Four resolutions were adopted and signed by all present: (1) the Supreme Executive Power was recognized as the highest national authority; (2) the assembled troops were to support the resolutions adopted; (3) the commissioners of the four Provincial Deputations were to be informed in order that they might begin their sessions immediately; and (4) Barragán was named commander-in-chief of the troops resident in the four provinces.[50]

Santa Anna, realizing that the role he had been playing in San Luis Potosí had brought him to the brink of disaster, chose to make as graceful an exit as possible. On July 1, he reported to the restored Congress and the Supreme Executive Power that the disturbances in those provinces and sinister reports had caused him to delay his march to Mexico City and to proclaim his plan of June 5. Time had now vindicated Congress: the call for elections had been issued and Congress was working for a federal republic. He, therefore, did not delay an instant in making known to it that he and his soldiers were entirely satisfied. Should it wish further rejoicing in the country, it should at once approve the proposals of the six deputies to Congress of June 12.[51] He concluded that time would justify his actions.[52] In his communication to the Supreme Executive Power he said that he had learned with pleasure of the long-desired call for the elections of deputies to a new Congress, the suspension of hostilities against Guadalajara, Jalisco, and the fact that Congress was working on the basis of establishing a federal republic. He and his men, elated to see their desire fulfilled and the purpose of the plan of June 5 realized, were at once suspending their military operations. They had decided voluntarily to manifest to the nation that, satisfied with the upright intention of the Supreme Executive Power, they gladly desisted from carrying out the plan, thus giving the lie to those who maliciously had informed Santa Anna to the contrary. As proof of his respect for Congress, he would dissolve the army under his command as soon as ordered by the national government and with only the troops of the province would proceed to Mexico City.[53]

Santa Anna left San Luis Potosí on July 10, 1823, and Armijo entered the city shortly thereafter, as did members of the Provincial Deputation and others who had taken flight. While in San Miguel Mesquitic the Provincial Deputation had continued its work and had, in union with the Municipal Council of San Luis Potosí, named two commissioners, Tomás Vargas and

Juan José Domínguez, to meet with commissioners from the other three Provincial Deputations at Celaya, to discuss the procedure most likely to prevent further disorder and reestablish public tranquillity.[54]

These commissioners with Martín García de Carrasquedo of Michoacán, Joaquín de Oteyza and Vicente Lino Sotelo of Querétaro, and Benigno Bustamante of Guanajuato began their conferences in Celaya on July 10, with the purpose of consolidating public opinion in order to prevent anarchy. Since the government had issued the call for elections, it could not object to the meeting, especially since Barragán, the Provincial Deputations of Querétaro and Michoacán, and perhaps the other two had informed the national government that its purpose was not the union of the four provinces or withdrawal from the national government but rather the pooling of their resources for the benefit of the country as a whole.

At the second session the commissioners adopted seven resolutions, including (1) recognition of the Supreme Executive Power, (2) approval of the establishment of a federal republic, (3) adherence to the decree calling a new Congress, (4) validation of the articles adopted at the meeting of the generals on July 1 in Celaya, (5) recognition of Barragán as Commandant-General of the four provinces subject to the national government and (6) of his patriotic zeal, and (7) suspension of measures for the pacification of San Luis Potosí to avoid interference with any orders of the national government.[55]

The national government from its first knowledge of the meeting of Celaya had looked upon it with disfavor and so expressed itself to the initiator, the Provincial Deputation of Michoacán.[56] The Supreme Executive Power on July 5 ordered the commissioners recalled and the junta dissolved, as was done on July 11.[57]

Veracruz, México, and Tabasco made no appeals to Congress in regard to a body to succeed it, but Veracruz and México did express themselves on the matter of a federal republic.

The Provincial Deputation of Veracruz welcomed the news of the reestablishment of the "august Constituent Congress" with a proclamation to the people under its jurisdiction;[58] when it learned of Santa Anna's action in San Luis Potosí, it informed the national government of its complete confidence and support and issued a circular letter to that effect to the citizens of the province.[59]

After Congress had named a committee to study the matter of forming a committee to draw up the bases of a federal republic, the Provincial Deputation of Veracruz, on June 20, 1823, informed its constituents that while that matter should be left to the new national legislative body the Deputation recognized the advantages of the federal system and agreed with the country as a whole that it was the best. With complete faith in the national government, it would await and obey the resolutions of the present Congress in regard to that matter.[60]

On August 16, 1823, the Veracruz body, in a lengthy reply to Guadalajara's communication of July 18 relative to its pronouncement of a federal republic, stated that each province, rather than considering itself independent, should consider the good of the whole country. What was to be achieved by some provinces declaring themselves independent in order to form federations with others? Would not this feed the fires of discord? No one denied the right of the provinces to decide what form of government would best contribute to their progress and prosperity; recognizing that right, all had publicly favored a federal republic. Some provinces had unfortunately overstepped themselves in establishing a federal government without consulting the national government or waiting for it to act.[61]

The province of México, on July 19, 1823, also replied to the June 24 and July 1 communications from Guadalajara, Jalisco, stating that the Provincial Deputation of México favored federalism. The geographical position of the Mexican nation, the great extent of its provinces, the difficulties of communication, the diversity of its climates and products—all demanded federation. Experience had demonstrated the necessity of provincial Congresses and a more exact and uniform distribution of governmental functions. The idea of federalism, however, did not necessarily exclude centralism; the two could coexist in the same country with complete harmony. Provincial affairs should be directed by the provinces through their executives, Congresses, and courts; national interests, by the national government. The difference between central and federal republics consisted in the division of powers of the government. In a central republic all power was preserved for the central authority; whereas in a federal republic only matters of national interest were entrusted to the supreme powers and those of provincial interests were reserved for the provincial government. On all these points the Provincial Deputation of México was in complete agreement with that of Guadalajara, Jalisco, but not with the measures Guadalajara had taken to establish the state and national government, for the essence of federalism was that national affairs were to be settled by the national Congress and only provincial ones were to be locally handled. The province of México also objected to Guadalajara's proposal that each state elect only one deputy to the national Congress, who should be subject to recall by the state at any time, and to the view that the national Constitution should not be valid until ratified by the provincial Congresses. Instead, the province of México urged that Guadalajara accept the decree of convocation, elect trustworthy deputies, and work through them for the good of the nation.[62]

When Congress, on June 17, finally issued the electoral law convening the new Constituent Congress, most of the provinces accepted the decree and set about preparing for the election. All were willing to wait for a new Congress to draw up the plan of the federal republic before the establishment of state governments and the framing of state constitutions except Guadalajara (now under the name of Jalisco), Zacatecas, Oaxaca, and Yucatán, which refused to abolish their state Congresses but did inform the national government that they would not adopt their state Constitutions until after the new Congress had laid down the fundamentals of the national federal government.

By this time the provinces felt they no longer had anything to fear from the national government. They could now send to Congress men who wanted a federal republic and would write a federal Constitution, for it was generally recognized even by the restored Congress that it was the only form of government that would hold the country together and prevent complete anarchy.

Further evidence that the national government recognized the demand for a federal form of government came to light in a secret session of Congress, when the Minister of Justice, on June 25, 1823, informed it that the government—convinced that in the federated system, toward which the states were manifestly moving, each state should enjoy equal organizations and duties as far as possible—recommended that Congress consider the establishment in each province of a Legislature or provincial Congress composed of thirteen members elected by plurality of votes of the electoral council that was to name deputies to the future national Congress. Until then the provincial Legislature should be composed of actual members of the Provincial Deputations plus additional members to make the total thirteen, these additional ones to be named by the former electoral councils to be reconvened in the provincial capitals for that purpose. The president of each should be elected by a plurality of votes each month, and the functions of said bodies should be (1) to watch scrupulously over the administration of the public funds, exercising the power to suspend inefficient officials; (2) to perform all the functions of the Provincial Deputation under existing laws; and (3) to present to the executives the list of candidates for all political, financial, and judicial offices, except those of the higher courts (Audiencias), and to remove employees from office only through legal procedures.[63]

Since Servando Mier had proposed a week earlier that provincial Congresses with the broadest powers in accord with the basis be installed immediately, a plan he said many deputies and the administration favored, he was elated when the preceding recommendation was made. Even Bustamante supported the idea, saying that, when the revolution was inevitable, the government itself should direct it.[64]

Although the committee to which the matter was referred recommended that the membership of the existing Provincial Deputations be enlarged and that their powers be increased in accord with the suggestions made, Congress approved, by decree of July 11, the name "Provincial Deputations" and the enlargement of their powers but rejected increased membership.[65] Bustamante said that Congress, shortly to be succeeded by a new one, with only the powers to convoke a new body and without authority to exercise functions pertaining exclusively to a constituent assembly, found itself in serious difficulty over the matter of increasing the powers of the Provincial Deputations in order to transform them into provincial Congresses, especially since they had abused the authority given them under the Spanish Constitution.[66]

According to the electoral law of June 17, 1823, the membership of the Provincial Deputations was to be completely renewed, but present deputies were eligible for reelection. Deputies were to be elected to the Provincial Deputations of Chiapas, Chihuahua, Coahuila, Durango, Jalisco, Guanajuato, México, Michoacán, Nuevo León, Nuevo México, Nuevo Santander, Oaxaca, Puebla, Querétaro, San Luis Potosí, Sinaloa, Sonora, Tabasco, Texas, Tlaxcala, Veracruz, Yucatán, and Zacatecas. All but Jalisco, Zacatecas, Yucatán, Oaxaca, and Chiapas elected deputies to their respective bodies. Of these, the first four, which had already transformed the Deputations into State Legislatures, saw no necessity for electing deputies to an extinct body.

The province of Chiapas presented a special problem. Prior to 1821, it had been part of the Captaincy-General of Guatemala, but then had declared itself independent of Guatemala and later joined the Mexican empire, as did Guatemala. After the Plan of Casa Mata, Guatemala with the approval of the restored Congress withdrew from the Mexican nation. It had not withdrawn by June 17, but the possibility of such action was recognized, for Article 10 of the decree of that date stated that, if the province of Guatemala remained a part of Mexico, it should, for the purpose of the election, use the latest censuses, and Article 11 included Chiapas in the listing of provinces of Guatemala.[67] Guatemala's withdrawal was formally recognized by the Mexican Congress on July 1.[68]

Servando Mier, at that time, warned Congress that the statements used in debates and the reasons given for the recognition of Guatemalan independence were dangerous ones, because other provinces of Mexico would be in a position to offer the same reasons. He pointed out that all the Interior Provinces had at times enjoyed a government separate from that of Mexico.[69]

Chiapas proved to be the province that considered itself independent and free to decide what it should do. When Vicente Filisola invited it to join an independent Guatemala and Nicolás Bravo invited it to remain a part of Mexico and to join those supporting the Plan of Casa Mata,

Chiapas decided to adopt a policy of watchful waiting. When news of Iturbide's abdication reached there on April 5, the Municipal Council of Tuxtla asked Commandant Farrera to call a junta of representatives of the province. The Political Chief, Luis Antonio García, convoked a meeting of the Provincial Deputation, the Municipal Council, the principal citizens of the capital, and other officials for April 8.[70]

At the meeting it was decided that each of the twelve districts of the province should elect a deputy to represent it in the provincial junta.[71] Elections were held and on June 4 the junta, with ten deputies present, was formally installed by the Political Chief and its authority recognized by the entire province. In its sessions of June 7 and 9, the junta transformed itself into a supreme provisional junta and declared the province independent of both Guatemala and Mexico. It left the door to Mexico ajar, however, by declaring that, if it should readopt the Plan of Iguala, Chiapas would consider itself a part of Mexico.[72] In acknowledging receipt of the declaration of the junta of Chiapas of its right to become an independent state or to join with either Guatemala or Mexico, Alamán, on July 9, 1823, stated that Mexico would welcome with pleasure a decision on the part of Chiapas to continue as a member of the Mexican nation.[73]

From that time until September 1824, Chiapas wavered on the matter of remaining an independent state, joining Guatemala, or joining Mexico. The junta at first leaned toward Guatemala, and the Provincial Deputation toward Mexico. It, therefore, dissolved the junta only later to recall it. At times the junta exercised complete authority in Chiapas Libre; at times officials from Guatemala or Mexico acted as Political Chiefs of the province. Both countries employed force and diplomacy in wooing Chiapas. The supreme governing junta, on December 16, 1823, issued a call for each district to vote on whether it wished to form a part of Guatemala or Mexico. Some voted and reported, some did not. On March 24, 1824, the junta again called for a vote, but not until September did it officially announce a three-fourths majority of votes in favor of joining Mexico.[74] Two days later, a solemn proclamation was issued by the "free state" of Chiapas announcing federation with the Mexican nation.[75]

Even after this proclamation, some dissatisfaction was manifested by Guatemalan partisans, but resistance ceased toward the middle of November 1824, with the arrival of the Mexican Constitution of October 4, 1824, which listed Chiapas among the states of the Mexican confederation. The junta on October 25, 1824, informed the Mexican Congress that elections had been called for deputies to both the national Congress and the state constituent assembly;[76] and on January 5, 1825, the Constituent Congress of the state of Chiapas was formally installed with a membership of Eustaquio Zebadua, Joaquín Gutiérrez de Arce, Juan María Balboa, Francisco Guillén, Juan José Domínguez, Manuel Saturnino Osuna, Cayetano

Blanco, Pedro Coroña, Manuel Escandón, Juan Crisomotomo Robles, and Mariano Rojas.[77] This accomplished, the junta of Chiapas ceased to exist.

Meanwhile the new Constituent Congress of Mexico had been installed on November 7, 1823; Ramos Arizpe, representing the province of Coahuila, was one of its most influential members. As early as November 1, 1823, Bustamante stated that the preparatory sessions of Congress promised nothing good, because Ramos Arizpe of Coahuila and Jesús Huerta of Guadalajara had been named to pass on the deputies' credentials and both of them were known as straight federalists.[78] Both were also appointed, on November 10, with Manuel Argüelles, Rafael Mangino, and Tomás Vargas to the committee to draft a Constitution for the consideration of Congress;[79] Ramos Arizpe was named chairman.

When Pablo de la Llave, Minister of Justice, on November 14, urged Congress to express itself on the system of government to be established, Ramos Arizpe, as chairman, promised the draft of the Constitution would be ready by November 17, 1823.

It has been inferred by Eugene C. Barker and William Archibald Whatley that Ramos Arizpe's *Acta constitucional* offered on November 20 was influenced by Stephen F. Austin's plan for a federal Constitution.[80] Ramos Arizpe met Austin in Saltillo for the first time between May 8 and 10. Austin left that city for Monterrey on the morning of May 11, while Ramos Arizpe remained in Saltillo until after June 5.[81] That the two men discussed the matter of a federal republic is very likely, for it was the subject then being discussed throughout Mexico. It is possible that Austin then conceived the idea of drawing up the "Plan of a Federal Constitution." This he showed to Ramos Arizpe for his comments when he next saw him; Ramos Arizpe did write his comments on the document and recommended that it be published. However, too much significance should not be given to this act, for the drafting and publishing of plans for a federal republic were being encouraged in Guadalajara, Oaxaca, and other provinces as a means to promote the establishment of a federal republic. It is difficult to believe that forty-eight-year-old Ramos Arizpe with his background, experience, and convictions, who had participated actively in the making of the Spanish Constitution of 1812, would be greatly influenced by thirty-year-old Austin.[82]

The evidence presented to indicate that Ramos Arizpe's *Acta constitucional* resembled Austin's "Plan" is even less acceptable. Austin's "Plan" was a poorly organized composite of the Spanish Constitution of 1812 and the United States Constitution. Ramos Arizpe's *Acta*, on the other hand, was a well-organized offering modeled on the Spanish Constitution and varied from it only when "the federal republic idea compelled change."[83] The parallelism between the Spanish Constitution and Ramos Arizpe's *Acta* is clear through clause after clause, not only setting forth the same ideas but also employing the same words.[84] In fact entire articles were borrowed, not surprisingly, verbatim from the Spanish Constitution.[85]

Ramos Arizpe, furthermore, was well acquainted with the Constitution of the United States of America long before he met Austin.[86] A careful study of his *Acta* reveals its differences in organization, terminology, and phrasing from the United States Constitution. Furthermore, the *Acta* contained a number of articles and ideas not contained in either the Spanish Constitution or the United States Constitution. Those articles were produced by problems indigenous to Mexico at that time.

Ramos Arizpe presented the *Acta* on November 20.[87] It stated that the states of the confederation were (1) Chiapas, (2) Guanajuato, (3) the Western Interior State composed of the provinces of Sonora, Sinaloa, and the two Californias, (4) the Northern Interior State composed of the provinces of Chihuahua, Durango, and New Mexico, (5) the Eastern Interior State composed of the provinces of Coahuila, Nuevo León, Texas, and Nuevo Santander, (6) México, (7) Michoacán, (8) Oaxaca, (9) Puebla de los Angeles with Tlaxcala, (10) Querétaro, (11) San Luis Potosí, (12) Tabasco, (13) Veracruz, (14) Jalisco, (15) Yucatán, and (16) Zacatecas.[88] The designation of states in Article 7, except in the case of Querétaro and Tabasco, was apparently made on the basis of the former intendancies and coincided with the plan proposed by Ramos Arizpe and Michelena in 1820 and 1821 in Spain, where they argued for Provincial Deputations in each intendancy in Mexico and specifically for three in the Interior Provinces: one at Arispe for the provinces of Sonora, Sinaloa, and the Californias; one at Durango for the provinces of Chihuahua, Durango, and New Mexico; and one for the Eastern Interior Provinces. As has been shown, the establishment of Provincial Deputations in each of the Interior Provinces did not occur until 1822 and 1823, Coahuila, Texas, Nuevo León, Sonora, Sinaloa, Chihuahua, and Durango all having established individual Provincial Deputations for the first time after the election of September 1823. The division of the Interior Provinces into three large political states or provinces had long been one of Ramos Arizpe's pet schemes. It is not surprising, therefore, that he tried to make it a part of the Constitution.

Article 5 of the *Acta constitucional,* which provided that the integral parts of the Mexican Republic were independent, free, and sovereign states, was approved on December 19.[89] Only seven deputies voted against the provision for independent free states; five were from the province of México, one, from Veracruz; and one, from Puebla. Twenty-five voted against the provision that the states were sovereign; of those, twelve were from México; six, from Puebla; two, from Michoacán; and one each, from Veracruz, Chihuahua, Sinaloa, Querétaro, and Sonora.[90]

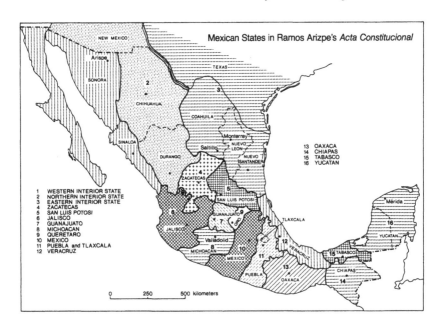

Discussion on Article 7 began on December 20, it having been agreed that Chiapas, the Eastern and Western Interior Provinces, and Tabasco would not be discussed at that time. On the same day, Congress approved (1) Guanajuato, (2) México, and (3) Michoacán, as states; and on the following day it approved (4) Oaxaca and (5) Puebla, but no decision was reached in regard to Tlaxcala's forming a part of that state. The Tlaxcala problem was referred back to the Constitutional Committee. During the next two days, approval was given to statehood for (6) Querétaro, (7) San Luis Potosí, (8) Veracruz, (9) Jalisco, (10) Yucatán, and (11) Zacatecas.[91]

Although from the beginning of the session of the new Constituent Congress the Provincial Deputations had been referred to as provincial Congresses,[92] they had not been officially so designated and their powers were still officially limited to those granted by the Spanish Constitution and the decrees of the past Mexican Congress. The provinces wanted broader powers and so instructed their deputies. Santos Vélez of Zacatecas proposed on December 26 that the Constitutional Committee be ordered to present as soon as possible the law referred to in Article 27 so that those provinces that had been declared states could proceed at once to establish their individual Legislatures, if they had not already done so.[93]

Carlos María Bustamante proposed on December 29 that the states be declared at liberty to establish their provincial Congresses and that the new plan for their formation presented by the Constitutional Committee be printed and circulated at once.[94] Discussion began on the plan the same day, but it was referred back to the committee.

The revised plan was presented to Congress on January 5, 1824, and discussion continued until January 8. During that time, an attempt to declare the already established Legislatures of Oaxaca, Yucatán, Zacatecas, and Jalisco null and void failed. The plan, as finally adopted, instructed the states of Guanajuato, México, Michoacán, Puebla, Querétaro, San Luis Potosí, and Veracruz to proceed to establish their State Legislatures, to be composed of eleven to twenty-one deputies. The Provincial Deputation in each state was to designate the number of deputies and alternates to be elected. Elections were to be held in accordance with the electoral law of June 17, 1823.[95]

Elections were held promptly in the states of México, San Luis Potosí, Guanajuato, Michoacán, Puebla, Veracruz, and Querétaro. Notice of the installation of Querétaro's Legislature on February 17 was read in Congress on February 23.[96] México reported the installation of its Legislature on March 2; and Guanajuato, on March 25.[97] Puebla's constituent Legislature held its first session on March 19, 1824; news of the installation of that of Michoacán on April 6 was read to Congress on April 13; the San Luis Potosí Legislature was installed and issued its first decree on April 21; and the Veracruz body was installed on May 9.[98]

Meanwhile, discussion in Congress had continued in regard to other provinces of Mexico to be designated as states. The creation of the Western Interior State (composed of Sonora and Sinaloa) and the Northern Interior State (composed of Chihuahua, Durango, and New Mexico) was approved on January 10, 1824.[99] Tlaxcala was declared a state on January 20, 1824.[100] Nine days later, Tabasco and Nuevo Santander, with the name of Tamaulipas, were each declared states, while Nuevo León, Coahuila, and Texas were declared a single state to be known as the Eastern Interior State.[101]

Instructions to these new states to hold elections for their constituent Legislatures were approved shortly thereafter. Those for the Eastern Interior State, the Western Interior State, and the Northern Interior State passed on February 4 and for Tabasco, Tamaulipas, and Tlaxcala, on February 7.[102]

Two of these newly recognized states, Tabasco and Tamaulipas, proceeded to hold their elections and to install their respective Legislatures; Tabasco, on May 3 and Tamaulipas, on July 7.[103]

Strong protests against the measures taken in regard to the Interior Provinces were offered almost immediately. From the resulting debates it appears that these states were erected on the basis of earlier military, political, and financial division of the region into three commandancies of the Eastern, Western, and Northern Interior Provinces and the intendancies of

Arispe, Durango, and Saltillo.[104] Doubtless such a division would have been acceptable to those provinces in 1814 or even in 1820 and 1821, but not so in 1824 after they had some taste of managing their own affairs through Provincial Deputations. Even in 1824, however, the Eastern Interior State might have endured if Tamaulipas had not demanded and obtained statehood; but as soon as this happened, Nuevo León began to clamor for similar status.

Servando Mier proposed on January 29 that, if the four Eastern Interior Provinces were not to be one state, Nuevo León be declared a state, and Coahuila and Texas form one or two states as they preferred.[105] Although his proposal was unsuccessful on that day, he continued to offer it and was supported by petitions from the Political Chief, the Provincial Deputation, and other governmental bodies of Nuevo León.[106] As a result, on May 7, 1824, Nuevo León was declared a state and instructed to convoke its Legislature and the state of Coahuila and Texas was to do likewise, it being understood that Texas was to inform the national government as soon as it felt in a position to form a separate state.[107]

Opposition to the creation of a Northern Interior State also began early. Francisco Antonio de Elorriaga, one of Durango's deputies, proposed on February 23, 1824, that Durango be declared a state. He was supported by various governmental authorities of that province.[108] As a result of the arguments offered, Congress on May 22 voted Durango a free and independent state.[109]

The next question that arose was whether to unite Chihuahua and New Mexico into one state. Congress finally voted on July 5, 1824, that Chihuahua should be a state and New Mexico should be a territory; the decree to that effect was approved on the following day.[110]

Although Tlaxcala was declared a territory and instructed to establish its Legislature, it did not do so, for some of the municipalities and officials of that province wanted it erected into a state, some wanted it joined to Puebla, and others wanted it made a territory. Congress, deluged with petitions and proposals from all factions, finally voted, on November 24, 1824, that Tlaxcala should have the status of a territory in the Mexican Federation.[111]

Statehood having finally been acquired, the Provincial Deputations of each province saw to the holding of elections and to the installation of constituent Legislatures. Durango's Legislature was installed on June 30, 1824;[112] Nuevo León's on August 1;[113] that of Coahuila and Texas on August 15;[114] Chihuahua's on September 8;[115] and that of the Western Interior State on September 12, 1824;[116] and as already recounted, Chiapas became a state in the Mexican Republic in September 1824 and installed its Legislature on January 5, 1825.

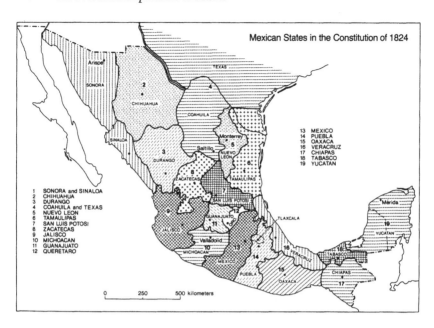

The Installation of State Constituent Congresses in Mexico

Name	Date of installation	Date declared state
Oaxaca	July 1, 1823	December 21, 1823
Yucatán	August 20, 1823	December 23, 1823
Jalisco	September 14, 1823	December 23, 1823
Zacatecas	October 19, 1823	December 23, 1823
Querétaro	February 17, 1824	December 23, 1823
México	March 2, 1824	December 20, 1823
Puebla	March 19, 1824	December 21, 1823
Guanajuato	March 25, 1825	December 20, 1823
Michoacán	April 6, 1824	December 22, 1823
San Luis Potosí	April 21, 1824	December 22, 1823
Tabasco	May 3, 1824	February 7, 1824
Tamaulipas	May 7, 1824	February 7, 1824
Veracruz	May 9, 1824	December 22, 1823
Nuevo León	August 1, 1824	May 7, 1824
Coahuila and Texas	August 15, 1824	May 7, 1824
Chihuahua	September 8, 1824	July 6, 1824
Durango	June 30, 1824	May 22, 1824
Western Interior State	September 12, 1824	January 10, 1824
Chiapas	January 5, 1825	September 1824

With the installation of the State Legislatures, the Provincial Deputations turned over their archives and passed out of existence. They had served their purpose. They had laid the foundation for state government; boundaries between provinces had been largely established; statistical information on the provinces had been compiled; political districts had been set; the various resources and problems of the states had been brought to light; as members of the Provincial Deputations, men had been trained to understand and direct provincial or state affairs; the people had been awakened to citizenship through the numerous elections held annually in the parishes to elect deputies for the various positions in the municipalities, Cortes, or Provincial Deputations and enlightened politically in preparation for a new system; and the provinces, largely through their Provincial Deputations, had demanded statehood and a federal system and obtained it. More important, the Mexican provinces in becoming states retained their desire and will to fight for a unified national government rather than become small nations as happened with the provinces of Central America.

Furthermore, the struggle for provincial autonomy, which began at least with the creation of the provincial juntas in Spain (with the Napoleonic invasion in 1808) and grew, with the bid for provincial autonomy in the Spanish American viceregal areas (in the periods 1808–1814 and 1820–1821), to the Spanish Cortes and among the Mexican deputies serving in it, had made it possible for the restored Provincial Deputation of New Spain to play a significant role in the quick success of the movement for independence under the Plan of Iguala and the overthrow of the Iturbide empire under the Plan of Casa Mata. The Plan of Casa Mata made it possible for intendancies and provinces to take control of their areas through their Provincial Deputations and to bring a new system of government to Mexico. They turned over their archives to their successors, the State Legislatures, which replaced them. The work of the Provincial Deputations was well done!

Deputies in Mexican Provincial Deputations Elected According to Spanish Constitution of 1812

1813–1814

Provincial Deputation of the Eastern Interior Provinces
Capital: Monterrey, Nuevo León
Installed on March 21, 1814

Deputies (and province represented)
 Bernardino Cantú, Nuevo León
 Dr. José León Lobo Guerrero, Nuevo León
 José Melchor Sánchez Navarro, Coahuila
 Francisco Antonio Gutiérrez, Coahuila
 Ylarión Gutiérrez, Nuevo Santander
 Pedro Paredes, Nuevo Santander
 Pedro Manuel del Llano, Texas
Source: Libro de actas de las juntas electorales de parroquía, de partido, y de provincia, ms., Archivo General del Gobierno del Estado de Nuevo León, año de 1814, no. 2, in 1814, legajo no. 1.

Provincial Deputation of Guatemala
Capital: Guatemala City
Installed on September 2, 1813

Deputies
 Eulogio Corea, Chiapas
 Manuel José Pavón, Guatemala
 Mariano García Reyes, Guatemala
 José María Pérez, Guatemala
 Bruno Medina, Honduras
 Dr. José María Delgado, El Salvador
 Dr. José Simeón Cañas, El Salvador
Source: Mario Rodríguez, *The Cádiz Experiment in Central America 1808–1826*, p. 117.

Provincial Deputation of Nueva Galicia (New Galicia)
Capital: Guadalajara
Installed on September 20, 1813

Deputies
  José Simeón de Uría, Guadalajara
  Juan Manuel Caballero, Guadalajara
  Tomás Ignacio Villaseñor, Guadalajara
  José Chafino, Guadalajara
  Conde de Santa-Ana, Zacatecas
  Jacinto Martínez, Zacatecas
  Rafael Riestro, Zacatecas
Alternates
  Toribio González, Guadalajara
  Benito Antonio Vélez, Guadalajara
  Felipe Chavarina, Zacatecas
Sources: *Diario de México,* October 23, 1813; "Aviso del resultado de las elecciones de diputados a Cortes y a la diputación provincial en Zacatecas," in Alba, *La constitución de 1812 en la Nueva España,* I, 180.

Provincial Deputation of New Spain
Capital: Mexico City
Installed: July 13, 1814

Deputies
  José Angel Gazano, México
  Juan Bautista Lobo, México
  (none found elected), Michoacán
  (none found elected), Oaxaca
  Dr. Francisco Pablo Vásquez, Puebla
  Col. Pedro Acevedo y Calderón, Querétaro
  Lic. José Daza y Artazo, Tlaxcala
  Dr. Antonio Manuel Couto y Ibea, Veracruz
Alternates
  Lic. Ignacio García Illueca, México
  Juan Nepomuceno de Otero, Puebla
Sources: *Diario de Mexico,* March 16, 1814; Lista de los señores vocales de la diputación provincial nombrados por la junta electoral de esta provincia de la Puebla de los Angeles, signed by Ramón Díaz de Ortega, Puebla, June 18, 1814, ms., AGNM, Ramo de Historia, vol. 445; Miguel Sandoval to Calleja, May 18, 1814, in Alba, *La constitución de 1812 en la Nueva España,* I, 48; José de Quevedo, governor of the province of Veracruz, to Calleja, Veracruz, March 18, 1814, ms., AGNM, Ramo de Historia, vol. 445.

Provincial Deputation of San Luis Potosí
Capital: San Luis Potosí

Said to have been installed, but much searching for names of deputies elected and any action taken has proven fruitless.

Provincial Deputation of Western Interior Provinces
Capital: Durango

Said to have been established, but much searching for data has proven fruitless so far.

Provincial Deputation of Yucatán
Capital: Mérida
Installed on April 23, 1813

Deputies
  Juan José Duarte, Yucatán
  Ignacio Rivas, Yucatán
  Diego de Hore, Yucatán
  Manuel Pacheco, Yucatán
  José María Ruz, Yucatán
  Manuel Pacheco, of Tihosuco
  Francisco de Paula Villegas, Campeche
  Andrés de Ibarra, Campeche
Alternates
  José Joaquín Pinto
  Francisco Ortiz
  José Francisco de Cicero
Source: Manuel A. Lanz, *Compendio de historia de Campeche*, p. 505.

Deputies in Mexican Provincial Deputations, 1820–1821

Provincial Deputation of Chiapas (declared independence of Guatemala and of Spain and had not yet joined Mexico)
Capital: Ciudad Real
Elected and installed in mid-1821

Deputies
  Juan Nepomuceno Batres
  Manuel Ignacio Escarra
  José Anselmo de Lara
  Francisco Guillén
  José Liño García

José Vivis
Pedro José Solórzano
Alternates: Names not given
Source: Manuel B. Trens, *Historia de Chiapas desde los tiempos más remotos hasta el gobierno de general Carlos A. Vidal,* p. 215.

Provincial Deputation of the Eastern Interior Provinces
Capital: Monterrey, Nuevo León
Elected on October 3, 1820
Installed on November 20, 1820

Deputies
    Dr. José León Lobo Guerrero, Coahuila
    Mauricio Alcocer, Coahuila
    Dr. Fermín de Sada, Nuevo León
    Santos de Uribe, Nuevo León
    Dr. Eustaquio Fernández de Lara, Nuevo Santander
    Don Manuel de la Torre, Nuevo Santander
    Don Ambrosio María de Aldasoro, Texas
Alternates
    Lt. Col. Juan Fermín de Juanicoteña, Coahuila
    José Antonio Rodríguez Gómez, Nuevo Santander
    José Ignacio de Arizpe, Nuevo León
Source: *Noticioso general* 7, no. 754, October 27, 1820, p. 1.

Elected to the Provincial Deputation of the Eastern Interior Provinces on March 13, 1821:
    Dr. Bernardino Cantú, Nuevo León
    Don José Melchor Sánchez Navarro, Coahuila
    Dr. José María Gutiérrez de Lara, Nuevo Santander (later Tamaulipas)
    Br. José Vivero, Texas
Alternates
    Curate José Ignacio Sánchez Návarro, Coahuila
    Capt. José Antonio Quintero, Nuevo Santander
Source: *Noticioso general* 8, no. 50, April 25, 1821.

Provincial Deputation of Nueva Galicia (New Galicia)
Capital: Guadalajara
Elected on August 28, 1820
Installed on September 12, 1820

Deputies
    Dr. Toribio González, Guadalajara
    Juan Manuel Caballero, Guadalajara
    Dr. José Miguel Gordoa, Guadalajara
    Matías Vergara, Guadalajara

Lic. Rafael Dionisio Riestro, Zacatecas
Lic. José María García Rojas, Zacatecas
Lic. José Crispín Velarde, Zacatecas
Alternates
  Jose García, Guadalajara
  Alfonso Sánchez Leñero, Guadalajara
  Agustín de Iriarte, priest of Totachie, Zacatecas
Sources: *Noticioso general* 7, no. 738, September 20, 1820, pp. 1–2; D.P., *Actas de* . . .
Nueva España, I, 157.

Provincial Deputation of Nueva España (New Spain)
Capital: Mexico City
Installed on September 30, 1820

Deputies
  Dr. José Miguel Guridi y Alcocer, Tlaxcala
  Don José María Fagoaga, México
  Don Juan Bautista Lobo, Veracruz
  Lic. Juan Wenceslao de la Barquera, Querétaro
  Don Patricio Furlong (installed October 17, 1820), Puebla
  Lic. Francisco Ignacio Mimiaga (installed October 7, 1820), Oaxaca
  Lic. Juan José Pastor Morales (installed November 25, 1820), Michoacán
Alternates
  José Ignacio García Illueca, México
  José Dionisio Leal, Puebla
  Dr. José Mariano Amable y Urbina, Oaxaca
  Captain-General & Political Chief Juan Ruiz de Apodaca
  Intendant Ramón Gutiérrez del Mazo
Source: D.P., *Actas* . . . *de Nueva España,* I, 83–84, 86, 93–94, 128.

Provincial Deputation of San Luis Potosí
Capital: San Luis Potosí
Installed on November 17, 1820

Deputies
  Marqués de San Juan de Rayas, Guanajuato
  Don Mariano Marmolejo, Guanajuato
  Lic. José María Semper [or Septien?], Guanajuato
  Don José María Núñez de la Torre, Guanajuato
  (name presently not found), San Luis Potosí
  (name presently not found), San Luis Potosí
Alternates
  Don José María Fernández Herrera, Guanajuato
  Don Andrés Pérez Soto, Guanajuato

Lic. Victor Rafael Márquez, San Luis Potosí
Intendant Fernando Pérez de Marañon, presiding officer
Source: "San Luis Potosí, 23 diciembre 1821," in *Noticioso general* 7, no. 741, September 27, 1820, p. 2.

Provincial Deputation of the Western Interior Provinces
Capital: Durango
Elected October 7, 1820
Installed on November 26, 1820

Deputies
  (name not found), Durango
  (name not found), Durango
  (name not found), Chihuahua
  (name not found), Chihuahua
  Juan José Ruíz de Bustamante, New Mexico
  Lorenzo Gutiérrez, New Mexico
Alternates
  Santiago Ortiz, New Mexico
Source: *Noticioso general* 7, no. 761, November 13, 1820, p. 2.

Provincial Deputation of Sonora and Sinaloa

Stated to have been installed and functioning but no names or dates known.
Source: D.P., *Actas . . . de Nueva España*, I, 157.

Provincial Deputation of Yucatán
Capital: Mérida
Probably elected in September 1820
Installation date not ascertained

Deputies
  Fray Miguel de Castro y Araoz, president, not given, probably Yucatán
  Diego de Hore, not given, probably Yucatán
  José María Ruz, not given, probably Yucatán
  Francisco Paula Villegas, not given, probably Yucatán
  Vicente María Velázquez, not given, probably Yucatán
  Jose Eduardo Peña, not given, probably Yucatán
  with Lorenzo de Zavala, as secretary
Source: *Noticioso general* 7, no. 746, October 9, 1820.

Elections in February 1822
for 1822–1823

(Elected to the Provincial Deputations of Mexico in 1822–1823 according to the electoral law issued in November 1821 by the Junta Provisional Gubernativa)

Provincial Deputation of Chiapas
Capital: Ciudad Real

Chiapas at this period was independent of Guatemala and of Mexico

Provincial Deputation of the Eastern Interior Provinces

Apparently did not install a Provincial Deputation for reasons explained in chapter 4

Provincial Deputation of Guadalajara (Nueva Galicia)
Capital: Guadalajara

Deputies
  Dr. Pedro Vélez
  Dr. Juan Cayetano Portugal, *cura* of Zapopen
  Sr. José Chafino
  José Casal
  Dr. Jesús Huerta, *cura* of Atotenilco
  Lt. José María Narvaez
  Dr. José María Gil
Alternates
  Sr. Domingo González Maxemin
  Urbano S. Ramón
  Presbyter Buenaventura Guareña
Source: *Gaceta imperial de México* 1, no. 63, February 7, 1822, p. 495; *El sol* 1, no. 21, February 13, 1822, p. 4; *Noticioso general* 9, no. 17, February 17, 1822, p. 3.

Provincial Deputation of Guanajuato
Capital: Guanajuato

Deputies
   Marqués de San Juan de Rayas (Don José Mariano Sardanete)
   Col. Domingo Chico
   Lic. José María Bezzanilla
   Lt. Col. Salvador Conde
   Matías López Arias
   José María Herrera
   Lic. Carlos Montes de Oça
Alternates
   Bachiller Ignacio Obregón
   Sr. Francisco Tresguerras
   Lic. Ignacio Ayala
Sources: a broadside entitled *Lista de los señores diputados por la provincia de Guana-juato para las cortes constituyentes de México* (México: [1822]); *Gaceta imperial de México* 1, no. 62, February 5, 1822, p. 489; *El sol* 1, no. 19, February 6, 1822, p. 80; *Noticioso general* 9, no. 161, February 6, 1822, p. 80.

Provincial Deputation of México
Capital: Mexico City and later Toluca

Deputies
   Don Manuel de Heras Soto, México
   Don José María Valdivielso, México
   Lic. Benito José Guerra, México
   Dr. José Luis María Mora, México
   Lic. José Florentino Conejo, México
   Don Francisco Javier de Heras, México
   Field Marshal Luis Quintanar, Querétaro
Alternates
   Don Antonio Icaza
   Dr. José Vicente Sánchez
   Lic. Mariano Tamáriz
Sources: *Noticioso general* 9, no. 13, January 30, 1822, p. 3; broadside entitled *Lista de los señores diputados para las cortes constituyentes de este imperio mexicano que se han nombrado en las provincias de Veracruz, Querétaro, y Tlaxcala; Gaceta imperial de México* 1, no. 63, February 7, 1822, p. 492; *El sol* 1 no. 20, February 9, 1822, p. 4; Charles W. Macune, Jr., *El estado de México y la federación mexicana, 1823–1835,* p. 193.

Actually, the Provincial Deputation for the provinces of México and Querétaro served from March 5, 1822, to August 3, 1823, but because of depletion of members through the withdrawal in 1823 of José María Valdivielso, the Marqués de San Miguel de Aguayo, Field Marshal Luis Quintanar, Manuel de Heras Soto, the Conde de Casa Heras, and Dr. José Vicente Sánchez, due to illness or promotion outside México, their replacement was necessary. A junta of the remaining members of the Provincial Deputation plus members of the Mexico City Municipal Council replaced them with Francisco Fagoaga, the Marqués de Apartado, Brig. Gen. Manuel Gómez Pedraza, and Jacobo de Villarrutia, and alternate Lic. José María Jáuregui. They served with the others elected in January 1822, from August 4, 1822, to September 22, 1823.

Source: Macune, *El estado de México y la federación mexicana*, p. 194.

Provincial Deputation of Michoacán (sometimes given as Valladolid de Michoacán)
Capital: Valladolid (later known as Morelia)
Body installed February 1, 1822

Deputies
 Dr. José Díaz de Hortega
 Lic. José María Ortiz Izquierda
 Don Juan de Lejarza
 Dr. Juan José de Michelena
 Capt. Francisco Amarillo
 Lic. Manuel Diego Solórzano
 Major Sergeant Pedro Villaseñor
 Secretary Juan de Lejarza
 Intendant and Political Chief Ramón Huarte
Source: *Actas de la diputación provincial de Michoacán, 1822–1823*, edited by Xavier Tavera Alfaro, p. 12.

Provincial Deputation of Nuevo México (New Mexico)
Although not awarded a Provincial Deputation, it elected and installed one by April 1822 and reported to Congress on its actions; Congress did award it one on June 18, 1823—see chapter 4)
Capital: Santa Fé
Elected 1822
Installed 1822

Deputies
 Francisco X. Chávez
 Pedro Ignacio Gallegos
 Juan Bautista Virgil
 Juan Estevan Pino
 Agapito Alba
 Manuel Rubí
Alternates
 Juan Rafael Ortiz
 Capt. Bartolomé Baca
Source: Records of the Deputation in Surveyor General's Office in Santa Fe, New Mexico.

Provincial Deputation of Nuevo Santander
Capital: varied between Aguayo and San Carlos

Deputies
   Dr. José María Gutiérrez de Lara, *cura*
   Don Pedro Paredes
   Capt. retired José Manuel de Zozaya
   Don Juan Francisco Gutiérrez
   Don Ignacio Peña
   Don Juan Bautista de la Garza
   Don Lucas de la Garza
Alternates
   Rafael Quintero
   Capt. José Antonio Guzmán
   Don Joaquín Benítez
Source: *Noticioso general* 9, no. 28, March 6, 1822, p. 4; *El sol* 1, no. 22, March 2, 1822, pp. 111–112.

Provincial Deputation of Oaxaca
Capital: Antequera de Oaxaca

Deputies
   Br. Manuel Lucas Almogavar
   Lic. Manuel Nicolás de Bustamante
   Sr. Mariano Flores
   Col. Manuel del Solar Campero
   Nicolás Fernández del Campo
   Lic. Luis Castellanos
   Manuel Domínguez, *cura*
Alternates
   Col. José López Ortigoza
   Br. Lucas Morales Ibañez
   Don José María Ideaquez, provost of San Felipe
Sources: a broadside entitled *Lista de los señores diputados de Antequera en el valle de Oaxaca para México; Gaceta imperial de México* 1, no. 62, February 5, 1822, p. 488; *El sol* 1, no. 19, February 6, 1822, p. 80; *Noticioso general* 9, no. 16, February 6, 1822, p. 3.

Provincial Deputation of Puebla
Capital: Puebla de los Angeles

Deputies
   Dr. José María Oyer (sometimes spelled Oller), *cura* of Tlacotepec
   Dr. Pedro Piñeiro y Osorio
   Col. Miguel del Campo
   Don Joaquín Furlong, R.P.P. del Oratorio
   Capt. Rafael Adorno

Lic. José María Morán
Sr. Manuel Ticier
Alternates
Sr. Pedro Barroso
Sr. Manuel Piñeda
Lt. Col. Juan González
Sources: a broadside entitled: *Lista de los señores diputados por Puebla; Gaceta imperial de México* 1, no. 60, January 31, 1822; *El sol* 1, no. 18, February 2, 1822, p. 76; *Noticioso general* 9, no. 14, February 1, 1822, p. 4.

Provincial Deputation of San Luis Potosí
Capital: San Luis Potosí

Deputies
Capt. José Pulgar
Br. José María Guillén
Br. Mariano Azpeitia
Sr. Francisco García
Lic. Ildefonso Díaz
Capt. Luis Barragán
Sr. Eufrasio Ramos
Alternates
José Antonio Becerra, *cura*
Sr. Rafael Delgado
Sr. Francisco Reyes
Sources: a broadside, *Lista de los señores diputados nombrados por la provincia de San Luis Potosí* (México, 1822); *Noticioso general* 9, no. 20, February 15, 1822, p. 4; *El sol* 1, no. 22, February 16, 1822, p. 92.

Provincial Deputation of Sonora and Sinaloa
Capital: Arispe
Elected: prior to April 5, 1822

Deputies
Obispo Fray Bernardo del Espíritu Santo
Lt. Col. Antonio Narvana
Rafael Morales
Presbyter Manuel Iñigo Ruiz
Don Antonio Almada
Don Manuel Gómez de Herran
Presbyter Salvador Julián Moreno
Alternates
Presbyter José Santiago Domínguez Escobosa
Presbyter Juan Elías González
Presbyter Salvador Salido
Source: *Noticioso general* 9, no. 41, April 5, 1822, p. 4.

Provincial Deputation of Tabasco
No information found as to exactly when it was awarded the right to become a
province—as early as August 1822 the proposal for its creation was offered in Congress;
but no definite action had been taken prior to the creation of the Junta National
Instituyente in late 1822, which may have approved such action; it was functioning
by late April 1823
Capital: San Juan Bautista de Villahermoso

Deputies
D. José Antonio Rincón, Political Chief, president
Antonio Sierra
Lorenzo Ortega
José Puich
Nicanor Hernández Bayona
Pedro López
José María Cabral
Ignacio Prado
Juan Esteban Campos, secretary
Sources: *Gaceta del gobierno supremo de México,* June 3, 1823; Manuel Mestre
Ghizliazza, *Documentos y datos para la historia de Tabasco,* I, 124, 134–135.

Provincial Deputation of Tlaxcala
Capital: Tlaxcala

Deputies
Sr. Juan Nepomuceno Aragón
Sr. Pedro Celada y Gómez
Antonio Casal
Sr. Juan Bautista Blazquez
Sr. José Vicente Grajales
Sr. Lorenzo Pozo
Sr. Mariano Romero
Alternates
Sr. Juan José Iturbe
Sr. Francisco Muñoz
Sr. Manuel Bernal
Sources: *Lista de los señores diputados para las cortes constituyentes de este imperio mexi-*
cano que se ha nombrado en las provincias de Veracruz, Querétaro, y Tlaxcala; Gaceta
imperial de México I, no. 63, February 7, 1822, p. 494; *El sol* I, no. 21, February 13,
1822, pp. 3–4; *Noticioso general* 9, no. 17, February 8, 1822, p. 2.

Provincial Deputation of Veracruz
Capital: Veracruz

Deputies
Sr. Francisco Arrillaga
Sr. Manuel Antonio Cabada

Sr. Manuel López Sobreviñas
Sr. José María Quiros
Sr. José Antonio Sastre, *cura* of Veracruz
Sr. José María Aguilar
Sr. José Xavier Olazábal
Alternates
  Sr. Pedro del Paso y Troncoso
  Lic. José María Serrano
  Sr. Manuel Mendoza
Sources: a broadside entitled *Lista de los señores diputados para las cortes constituyentes de este imperio mexicano que se han nombrado en las provincias de Veracruz, Querétaro, y Tlaxcala; Gaceta imperial de México* 1, no. 63, February 7, 1822, pp. 493–494; *El sol* 1, no. 20, February 9, 1822, p. 84; *Noticioso general* 9, no. 16, February 6, 1822, p. 4.

Provincial Deputation of the Western Interior Provinces (Nueva Vizcaya including Durango, Chihuahua, and New Mexico)
Capital: Durango
Election: date not found
Installed: date not found

Deputies
  Felipe Ramos
  Simón de Ochoa
  José Francisco del Fierro
  José Agustín Gamia
  José Miguel de Escontría
  Miguel Pérez Gavilán
  Miguel de Zubiría, secretary
  Juan Navarro, Political Chief and intendant
Alternates: names not given
Source: Provincial Deputation of Durango to José Antonio de Echávarri, Durango, March 10, 1823, in *Noticioso general* 10, no. 42, April 7, 1823, pp. 1–2.

Provincial Deputation of Yucatán
Capital: Mérida
Elected: date not found but probably in February 1822
Installed: date not found but probably in February 1822

Deputies
  Pedro Almeida
  José Joaquín Torres
  Pedro José Guzmán
  Basilio María Argaiz
  Juan José Espeso
  Pablo Moreno
  Pedro Pablo de Paz

Melchor Alvarez, Political Chief
Pedro Bolio, intendant
Source: "Libertad de Yucatán," in *Gaceta del gobierno de México* 1, no. 49, April 12, 1823, pp. 184–186.

Provincial Deputation of Zacatecas
Capital: Zacatecas

Deputies
    Lic. Domingo Velásquez
    Dr. Mariano de Iriarte
    Don Juan Vélez
    Don Ignacio Miranda
    Dr. Luis Gordoa
    Dr. Juan José Román
    Don José María Elías
Alternates
    Presbyter José María Berreuco
    Don José Francisco Arrieta
    Don Juan Bautista Martínez
Sources: *El ayuntamiento de Zacatecas acompaña a su oficio de 24 de enero último las listas de los individuales electos diputados a cortes y vocales para la diputación provincial; Noticioso general* 9, no. 20, February 15, 1822, p. 1; *El sol* 1, no. 22, February 16, 1822, p. 95.

September 1823 Elections

(Provincial deputies elected to Provincial Deputations in September 1823, according to law issued on June 17, 1823, by the restored Constituent Congress)

Provincial Deputation of Chiapas
Capital: Ciudad Real
Elected and installed about September 18, 1823

Deputies
    Luis Antonio García
    José Manuel López
    Mariano José Suárez
    Juan de Velasco y Martínez
    Gregorio Suasnavar
    Mariano Montes de Oça
    Seventh member's name not given, nor those of alternates.
Source: Manuel B. Trens, *Historia de Chiapas desde los tiempos más remotos hasta el gobierno del general Carlos A. Vidal*, pp. 252–253.

Provincial Deputation of Chihuahua
Capital: Chihuahua

Deputies
    Col. José Ignacio Urquidi
    José Ignacio Ochoa
    Mariano Horcasitas
    Mariano del Prado
    Estevan Aguirre
    Francisco Loya
    José María Echevarría
Alternates
    José María Irigoyen
    Joaquín José Escarsega
    José Miguel Salas Valdéz
Source: *Gaceta del gobierno supremo de México* 2, no. 47, September 30, 1823, p. 213.

Provincial Deputation of Coahuila (awarded by Congress on August 18, 1823)
Capital: Saltillo
Elected on October 8, 1823

Deputies
   Lic. Rafael Eça y Múzquiz
   Br. Francisco Fuentes
   Lic. Juan Vicente Campos
   Capt. Félix Malo
   José Melchor Sánchez Navarro
   Agustín de la Garza
   Capt. José María Viezca
Alternates
   Victor Blanco
   Joaquín de Arce
   Lt. Col. Mariano Varela
Sources: *Gaceta del gobierno supremo de México* 2, no. 47, September 30, 1823, p. 213;
Aguila mexicana no. 174, October 5, 1823, p. 627; *El sol* no. 106, September 28, 1823,
p. 624.

Provincial Deputation of Durango
Capital: Durango

Deputies
   Gaspar Periera
   Br. Diego García Celis
   Esteban del Campo
   Br. Juan Mansonera
   Br. Vicente Elizalde
   Magistral José Ignacio Iturrivarría
   Lic. Juan José Escovar
Alternates
   Lic. Miguel Molina
   Miguel Alcalde
   Santiago Baca y Ortiz
Source: *Gaceta del gobierno supremo de México* 2, September 30, 1823, p. 213.

Guadalajara had changed its name officially to the state of Xalisco or Jalisco by this date
and elected a state Constituent Congress to draw up its state Constitution
Capital: Guadalajara

Deputies
   Prisciliano Sánchez
   Pedro Vélez
   Dr. José María Gil
   Lic. Antonio Méndez
   Field Marshal Anastasio Bustamante

Dr. José Miguel Gordoa
Dr. Esteban Huerta
José María Castillo Portugal
Dr. Juan Nepomuceno Cumplido
Urbano Sanromán
Lic. Vicente Ríos
Manuel Cervantes
Santiago Guzmán
Ignacio Navarrete
Alternates
Dr. Diego Aranda
José Ignacio Cañedo
Justo Corro
Esteban Arechiga
Lic. Rafael Mendoza
Source: *Aguila mexicana* no. 158, September 19, 1823, p. 578.

Provincial Deputation of Guanajuato
Capital: Guanajuato
Elected in September 1823

Deputies
Lic. José María Esquivel y Savago
Presbyter José Joaquín Azpilqueta
Presbyter Manuel Onda
Luis Gonzaga de la Canal
Manuel Ruíz de Chávez
Alternates
Ignacio Gutiérrez
Miguel González Núñez
José María Hidalgo y Castilla
Sources: *Aguila mexicana* no. 151, September 12, 1823; *Gaceta del gobierno supremo de México* 2, no. 45, September 27, 1823, p. 210; *El sol* no. 91, September 13, 1823, p. 354.

Provincial Deputation of México
Capital: Mexico City

Deputies
José Ignacio Alvarez
Sergeant-Major of Engineers Ignacio Echandía
Lic. Benito José Guerra
Dr. José Francisco Guerra
Lic. Pedro Martínez de Castro
Antonio Velasco de la Torre
Lic. Predo Verdigo
Alternates
José María Ballesteros López

Col. José Joaquín Calvo
Juan Pérez Gálvez
They served from September 23 to December 31, 1823.
Sources: *Gaceta del gobierno supremo de México* 2, no. 35, September 9, 1823, p. 160;
El sol no. 87, September 9, 1823, p. 348; Macune, *El estado de México y la federación mexicana*, p. 194.

Provincial Deputation of Michoacán
Capital: Valladolid

Deputies
  Juan José Martínez de Lejarza
  Dr. Angel Mariano Morales
  Lic. Francisco Menocal
  Basilio Velasco
  Lic. José Antonio Castro
  Antonio Manzo de Cevallos
  Manuel Cháves
Alternates
  Lic. Isidro Huarte
  Juan José Pastor Morales
  Joaquín Paulín
Sources: *Gaceta del gobierno supremo de México* 2, no. 43, September 23, 1823, p. 200;
Aguila mexicana no. 152, September 13, 1823, p. 562; *El sol* no. 92, September 14, 1823, p. 368.

Provincial Deputation of New Mexico
Capital: Santa Fé
Elected: date unknown
Installed: date unknown

Deputies
  Antonio Ortiz
  Pedro García
  Jesús Francisco Baca
  Mariano de la Peña
  Jesús Francisco Ortiz
  Pedro Jesús Perea
  Jesús García de la Mora
Alternates
  Jesús Antonio Chávez
  Pedro Bautista Pino
  Juan Rafael Ortiz
Source: Richard V. Baquera, "Paso del Norte and Chihuahua: Revolution and Constitutionalists," M.A. thesis.

Provincial Deputation of Nuevo Reyno de León (awarded by Congress on August 18, 1823)
Capital: Monterrey

Deputies
  Eusebio Gutiérrez
  Andrés Sobrevilla
  Juan José de la Garza
  Bernardino Güimbarda
  Joaquín García
  Pedro de la Garza
  Pedro González
Alternates
  Francisco Mier
  José María Cárdenas
  Pablo Calabazos
Sources: *Aguila mexicana* no. 174, October 5, 1823, p. 637; *El sol* no. 106, September 28, 1823, p. 637, and no. 108, September 30, 1823, p. 432.

Provincial Deputation of Nuevo Santander
Capital: varied between San Carlos and Aguayo during this period

Deputies
  Juan Francisco Gutiérrez
  José Lino Perea
  Ignacio Peña
  Lucas Fernández de Aguayo
  Pedro Rodríguez
  Juan Espiridón Polito
  Cayetano Girón
Alternates
  José Honorato de la Garza (also given as Galarza)
  Feliciano Ortiz Rodríguez
  Manuel Prieto
Sources: *Aguila mexicana* no. 174, October 5, 1823, p. 637; *El sol* no. 105, September 27, 1823, p. 420.

Oaxaca did not elect a Provincial Deputation, for it had already elected a Constituent
Congress to draw up its state Constitution
Capital: Oaxaca
Elected in July(?) 1823
Installed probably in August 1823

Deputies
  José López Ortigoza
  Pedro José de la Vega
  José Esperón
  Manuel Megía

Manuel Sáenz de Enciso
Ignacio de Goytia
Manuel Francisco Domínguez
Francisco Matey
José Mariano González
Juan Ferra
Joaquín Guerrero
Florencio Castillo
José Manuel Ordoño
José María Unda
Source: *Colección de constituciones de los estados unidos mexicanos*, II, 249.

Provincial Deputation of Puebla
Capital: Puebla de los Angeles

Deputies
   José de Oller, *cura* de Talcotepec
   Vázquez Aldaña
   Hilario Olagüibel
   José Doncel de la Torre
   Manuel Romero
   Sebastián Mier
   Antonio Vera
Alternates
   Capt. Juan Osio
   Isidro Pérez Toledano
   Col. Antonio Flon
Source: *Gaceta del gobierno supremo de México* 2, no. 37, September 13, 1823, p. 170.

Provincial Deputation of Querétaro (awarded by Congress after August 1, 1822)
Capital: Querétaro

Deputies
   Dr. Joaquín de Oteyza
   Tomás López de Ecala
   Lt. Col. Manuel Samaniego
   Lic. Martín Rodríguez García
   Ramón Cobarrubias
   Ramón Cevallos
   Lt. Col. Juan Pastor
Alternates
   Bachiller Felipe Ochoa
   Lt. Col. Mariano Zubieta
   Eusebio Camacho
Sources: *Gaceta del gobierno supremo de México* 2, no. 45, September 25, 1823, p. 206; *Aguila mexicana* no. 152, September 13, 1823, p. 562; *El sol* no. 92, September 14, 1823, p. 368.

Provincial Deputation of San Luis Potosí
Capital: San Luis Potosí

Deputies
  Lic. Ignacio Lozano
  Juan García Diego
  Eufrasio Ramos
  José María Guillén
  Macario Guerrero
  Mariano Escandón
  Marcelino Martínez
Alternates
  Lorenzo Obregón
  Rafael Maldonado
  Manuel Ortiz de Zarate
Sources: *Gaceta del gobierno supremo de México* 2, no. 13, September 23, 1823, p. 186; *Aguila mexicana* no. 159, September 20, 1823, p. 581; *El sol* no. 106, September 28, 1823, p. 624.

Provincial Deputation of Sinaloa (awarded by Congress on June 18, 1823)
Capital: Culiacán

Deputies were elected but their names were not reported to the newspapers, and much searching of other sources has proven fruitless.

Provincial Deputation of Sonora (awarded by Congress on June 18, 1823)
Capital: Ures

Deputies were elected and the Deputation functioned in 1823 and 1824 for some time, but a search for names has been fruitless.

Provincial Deputation of Tabasco (said to have been awarded in early 1823)

The Deputation was awarded and was active, but names have not been found.

Provincial Deputation of Texas (awarded by Congress on August 18, 1823)
Capital: San Antonio de Béxar

Deputies
  José Antonio Saucedo
  José María Zambrano
  Ramón Múzquiz
  Juan José Hernández
  Miguel Arciega
  Baron de Bastrop
  Mariano Rodríguez

Alternates
  José Salinas
  Juan Veramendi
  Gaspar Flores
Source: *Aguila mexicana* no. 223, November 23, 1823, p. 2.

Provincial Deputation of Tlaxcala
Capital: Tlaxcala

Deputies
  Juan Bautista Blazquez
  José Antonio Varela
  José Mariano Romero
  Manuel Bernal
  Lic. Ignacio Amador
  José Vicente González de la Cruz
  Gabriel Illesca
Alternates
  José Mariano García
  Presbyter Antonio Reyes
  Juan Evangelista Alvarado
Source: *Gaceta del gobierno supremo de México* 2, no. 37, September 13, 1823, p. 170.

Provincial Deputation of Veracruz
Capital: Veracruz

Deputies
  Pedro del Paso y Troncoso
  Manuel López de Sobreviñas
  Sebastián Camacho
  Lic. José María Serrano
  Pedro José Echeverría y Mignoni
  Manuel Elguero
  Joaquín de Oropesa
Alternates
  Manuel Serapio Calvo
  Luis Galinié
  Lic. Rafael Argüelles
Sources: *Gaceta del gobierno supremo de México* 2, no. 40, September 16, 1823, p. 186; *Aguila mexicana* no. 156, September 17, 1823, p. 572; *El sol* no. 92, September 14, 1823, p. 368.

Yucatán had by this date declared itself a state and did not elect a Provincial Deputation but rather elected a state Constituent Congress of the Republic of Yucatán to draw up a state Constitution

Capital: Mérida
Elected on July 28, 1823
Installed on August 20, 1823

Deputies
  Francisco Genaro de Cicero
  José Tiburcio López
  José Felipe Estrada
  Eusebio Antonio Villamil
  Pedro José Guzmán
  José Ignacio Cervera
  Perfecto Barranda
  Manuel Milanes
  Pablo Moreno
  Juan de Dios Cosgaya
  Pedro Manuel de Regil
  Agustín López de Llergo
  Pedro Almeida
  Miguel Manuel Errasquín
  José Ignacio Cáceres
  Juan E. Echanove
  Manuel Jiménez
  Pedro José Sousa
  Juan Nepomuceno Rivas
  Manuel León
  José Antonio García
  José María Quiñones
  Joaquín García Rejón
  Miguel Duque Estrada
Alternates
  José Francisco Cicero
  José Felipe Capetillo
  Benito Aznar
  Nicolás Carvallo
  Pablo Oreza
  Juan de Dios Henríquez
  Joaquín Ruíz de León
  Juan Pablo Talavera

Sources: *Aguila mexicana* no. 159, September 20, 1823, p. 581; *El sol,* 2nd epoch, vol. 1, September 27, 1823, p. 407; Juan Francisco Molina Solís, *Historia de Yucatán desde la independencia de España, hasta la época,* 2 vols. (Mérida, 1921), I, 15–16.

Zacatecas did not elect a Deputation in September, for like the provinces of Guadalajara (Jalisco), Oaxaca, Yucatán, and others it had already elected eleven members plus four alternates to a provincial or state Congress to form its provincial or state Constitution
Capital: Zacatecas

Deputies
   Lic. Domingo Velázquez
   Dr. Juan José Román
   Lic. José Miguel Díaz de León
   Juan Bautista de la Torre
   Juan Bautista Martínez
   Pedro Ramírez
   José Francisco de Arrieta
   Presbyter Mariano Fuentes de Sierra
   José María Herrera
   Lic. Miguel Laureano Tobar
   Lic. Ignacio Gutiérrez de Velasco
Alternates
   Domingo del Castillo
   Eusebio Gutiérrez de Velasco
   Lic. José María García Rojas
   Antonio Eugenio Gordoa
Sources: *Gaceta del gobierno supremo de México* 2, no. 40, September 16, 1823, p. 186; *Aguila mexicana* no. 156, September 17, 1823, p. 567; *El sol* no. 96, September 18, 1823, p. 384.

Notes

Introduction

1. For a good summary explanation of the Commandancy-General of the Interior Provinces, see the work of María del Carmen Velázquez, "La comandancia general de las Provincias Internas," *Historia mexicana* 28, no. 2 (October–December 1977): 160–177; see also Douglas Alan Washburn, "Institutional Change and Political Development: The Interior Provinces in Late Colonial New Spain," a detailed study of those two institutions—the Commandancy-General and the intendancy system—in those provinces.

2. Ibid., pp. 41ff.; Lillian Estelle Fisher, *Political Administration in the Spanish American Colonies*, pp. 39–43, 275, 299–300; Lillian Estelle Fisher, *The Intendant System in Spanish America*, 97–331; C. H. Haring, *The Spanish Empire in America*, pp. 144–145, 176; Luis Navarro García, *Intendencias en Indias*, pp. 7–16, 24ff.

3. Later named Morelia, Michoacán.

4. Washburn, "Institutional Change and Political Development," pp. 20ff.; Fisher, *The Intendant System in Spanish America*, pp. 97–331; Navarro García, *Intendencias en Indias*, pp. 53–71ff.

5. Navarro García, *Intendencias en Indias*, pp. 53–71ff.; Fisher, *The Intendant System in Spanish America*; Isabel Gutiérrez del Arroyo, "El Nuevo Régimen institucional bajo la real ordenanza de intendente de la Nueva España (1786)," *Historia mexicana* 39, no. 1 (153) (July–December 1989): 89–122.

6. Gabriel H. Lovett, *Napoleon and the Birth of Modern Spain*, I, 1–168; Raymond Carr, *Spain 1808–1939*, pp. 88–91; Timothy E. Anna, *Spain and the Loss of America*, pp. 27–40; Hira de Gortari Rabiela, "Julio–Agosto de 1808: La lealtad mexicana," *Historia mexicana* 39, no. 1 (153) (July–August 1989): 181–203.

7. *Gaceta de México*, April 15, 1809, pp. 325–326; the decree was dated Seville, January 29, 1809; see also Nettie Lee Benson, "The Election of 1809 in New Spain," an article now in preparation for publication in a journal.

8. Benson, "The Election of 1809 in New Spain"; also Archivo General de la Nación de México (hereafter cited as AGNM), Ramo de Historia, vols. 417, 418, and parts of 413.

9. Anna, *Spain and the Loss of America*, pp. 43–63; Charles R. Berry, "The Election of the Mexican Deputies to the Spanish Cortes, 1810–1822," in *Mexico and*

the Spanish Cortes, 1810–1822: Eight Essays, edited with introduction and conclusion by Nettie Lee Benson, pp. 10–28; see also introduction by the editor, pp. 1–7.

10. Spain, Council of the Regency, Decree of February 14, 1810, in *Gaceta del gobierno general de la nación* (Cádiz, Spain), May 18, 1810, pp. 419–420.

11. Ibid.; Berry, "The Election of the Mexican Deputies to the Spanish Cortes, 1810–1822," pp. 10–12; Nettie Lee Benson, "La elección de Ramos Arizpe a las Cortes de Cádiz en 1810," in *Historia mexicana* 33, no. 4 (April–June 1984): 515–539.

12. Berry, "The Election of the Mexican Deputies to the Spanish Cortes, 1810–1822," pp. 10–28.

13. Ibid.; Nettie Lee Benson, "Texas' Failure to Send a Deputy to the Spanish Cortes," in *Southwestern Historical Quarterly* 64, no. 1 (July 1960): 1–12; and Benson, "La elección de Ramos Arizpe a las Cortes de Cádiz en 1810," pp. 515–539.

1. Origin of the Provincial Deputations

1. Spain, Cortes, *Diario de las actas y discusiones de las Cortes, 1811–1813,* II, 70 (December 20, 1810); hereafter cited as *Diario de las Cortes, 1811–1813.*

2. Ibid., IV, 115–116 (March 4, 1811).

3. Ibid., IV, 386–394 (March 28, 1811).

4. Ibid., I, 139 (December 14, 1810).

5. Ibid., II, 68–69 (December 20, 1810).

6. Ibid., II, 69–70 (December 20, 1810).

7. Ibid., IV, 289 (March 21, 1811).

8. Ibid., IX, 373 (October 23, 1811).

9. Miguel Ramos Arizpe, *Memoria que . . . presenta al augusto congreso, sobre el estado natural, político, y civil de su dicha provincia, y las del Nuevo Reyno de León, Nuevo Santander, y los Texas . . . ,* pp. 40–41; Miguel Ramos Arizpe, *Report That Dr. Miguel Ramos de Arizpe . . . Presents to the August Congress on the Natural, Political, and Civil Condition of the Provinces of Coahuila, Nuevo León, Nuevo Santander, and Texas . . . ,* pp. 35–37.

10. "Una junta gubernativa o llámase 'diputación provincial.'"

11. *Diario de las Cortes, 1811–1813,* XI, 5, 48 (December 26 and 30, 1811).

12. Ibid., XI, 238–250 (January 12, 1812).

13. Ibid., XI, 239–245 (January 12, 1812).

14. Ibid., XI, 241 (January 12, 1812).

15. Ibid., XI, 245–246 (January 12, 1812).

16. Ibid., XII, 4–5 (February 10, 1812); 66–67 (April 20, 1812).

17. "And overseas there shall be one Provincial Deputation for each division named in Article 10. In addition there shall be one at Cuzco, in Peru; one at Charcas, in the province of Buenos Aires; one at Quito, in the kingdom of New Granada; one at San Luis Potosí, in New Spain; and one at León of Nicaragua, in the province of Guatemala." This decree was passed on May 1, 1813 (ibid., XIII, 161 162).

18. Cf. Hubert Howe Bancroft (*History of Mexico,* IV, 503), who says that each intendancy could have had a Provincial Deputation (provincial assembly) but that they all united to elect one body for the whole country.

19. It might be added that the Constitution of 1812 thereby recognized a condi-

tion that had long existed, for politically New Galicia, Yucatán, the Eastern Interior Provinces, and the Western Interior Provinces had been virtually independent of the viceroy in practice, if not in theory, for many years.

20. "Instrucción para los ayuntamientos constitucionales, juntas provinciales y gefes políticos superiores, decretada por las Cortes generales y extraordinarias el 23 de junio de 1813," in Juan E. Hernández y Dávalos, *Colección de documentos para la historia de la guerra de independencia de México de 1808 a 1821*, V, 572– 576; *Diario de México*, March 21–March 28, 1814.

21. Mexico, Laws, Statutes, etc., *Colección de los decretos y órdenes de las Cortes de España que se reputan vigentes en la república de los Estados Unidos Mexicanos*, pp. 54–58; Hernández y Dávalos, *Colección de documentos para la historia*, V, 582– 584; Spain, Laws, Statutes, etc., *Colección de decretos y órdenes que han expedido las Cortes desde 25 de setiembre de 1813, . . . hasta el mayo de 1814*, pp. 46–47.

22. Mexico, Laws, Statutes, etc., *Colección de los decretos y órdenes de las Cortes de España que se reputan vigentes en la república*, pp. 35–45.

23. Lucas Alamán, *Historia de Méjico*, V, 33–34; Julio Zarate, *La guerra de independencia*, in *México a través de los siglos*, ed. Vicente Riva Palacio, III, 653.

24. Félix María Calleja to Minister of Grace and Justice, México, August 18, 1814, in Archivo General de Indias, Seville, Spain (hereafter cited as AGI), estante 90, cajón 1, legajo 19, leaf 9; Rafael Alba (ed.), *La constitución de 1812 en la Nueva España*, II, 61–74.

25. Ibid., pp. 74–75.

26. "El Consejo de Estado el 14 de febrero de 1821 manifiesta su parecer sobre el modo y términos, en que se puede espedir el título de gefe superior político de Nueva España al capitán general don Juan O'Donojú," AGI, estante 91, cajón 2, legajo 10.

27. Alamán, *Historia de Méjico*, V, 33–34; Zarate, *La guerra de independencia*, p. 653.

2. Establishment of the Provincial Deputations in Mexico, 1812–1814

1. Spain, Laws, Statutes, etc., *Colección de los decretos y órdenes que han expedido las Cortes generales y extraordinarias (desde setiembre hasta 24 de 1812)*, II, 217–218; *Diario de México*, October 11, 1812.

2. Spain, Laws, Statutes, etc., *Colección de los decretos y órdenes que han expedido las Cortes*, II, 218–219.

3. Ibid., II, 219–220; Nettie Lee Benson, "The Contested Mexican Election of 1812," in *Hispanic American Historical Review* 26 (August 1946): 337; *Diario de México*, October 11–12, 1812.

4. Spain, Laws, Statutes, etc., *Colección de los decretos y órdenes que han expedido las Cortes*, II, 224–226; *Diario de México*, October 12, 1812.

5. "Instrucción conforme a la cual deberán celebrarse en las provincias de ultramar las elecciones de diputados de Cortes para las ordinarias del año próximo de 1813," ms., AGNM, Ramo de Historia, vol. 445, leaves 5–10; "Elecciones para diputados a las Cortes ordinarias de 1813, Diputaciones provinciales, Ayuntamientos," in Alba, *La constitución en la Nueva España*, I, 148–161, 204–207.

6. Cosme Antonio Urquiola to Francisco Javier Venegas, Presidio del Car-

men, November 30, 1812, in "Instrucción conforme a la cual deberán celebrarse en las provincias de ultramar," vol. 445, leaves 45–46.

7. Manuel A. Lanz, *Compendio de historia de Campeche*, p. 505.

8. "Proclama de la diputación provincial de Yucatán a los habitantes de la provincia," Mérida, April 23, 1813, in Alba, *La constitución en la Nueva España*, I, 209–211.

9. "La diputación provincial de Yucatán avisa al virrey que se installo en 23 de abril de 1813," in ibid., p. 208.

10. It was composed of José de la Cruz, Political Chief of New Galicia, Juan Cruz Ruiz de Cabañas, bishop of Guadalajara; Francisco Antonio de Velasco, intendant; José Crispín Velarde, *alcalde;* Miguel Pacheco, ranking alderman, Pedro Vélez de Zuñiga, attorney general, and Juan José Cambero and Juan Manuel Caballero, the two citizens of good repute.

11. Nueva Galicia, Gefe Político, *Bando de Don José de la Cruz, mariscal de campo de los ejércitos nacionales, comandante general y gefe político del reyno de Nueva Galicia . . .* , Guadalajara, June 21, 1813, a broadside in the Archivo General de la Secretaría del Ayuntamiento de Guadalajara.

12. *Diario de México,* October 23, 1813.

13. "Aviso del resultado de las elecciones de diputados a Cortes y a la diputación provincial en Zacatecas," in Alba, *La constitución en la Nueva España,* p. 180.

14. Libro de actas del ayuntamiento de Guadalajara por el año de 1813, ms., Archivo General de la Secretaría del Ayuntamiento de Guadalajara, legajo 31 (1813), leaf 33; "Aviso de haberse instalado la diputación provincial de Nueva Galicia," in Alba, *La constitución en la Nueva España,* p. 211; Félix María Calleja to the Minister of Overseas Government, México, January 21, 1814, ms., AGNM, Correspondencia Virreyes, Calleja, vol. 6.

15. Junta electoral, Actas de la junta electoral de la provincia de Guadalajara, March 12–14, 1814, ms., AGNM, Ramo de Historia, vol. 445.

16. Actas de la junta electoral de la provincia de Zacatecas, 13 a 15 de marzo de 1814, ms., AGNM, Ramo de Historia, vol. 445.

17. Libro de actas del ayuntamiento de Guadalajara, 1814, ms., Archivo General de la Secretaría del Ayuntamiento de Guadalajara, legajo 32, leaf 172.

18. Ramos Arizpe believed that Saltillo should be the seat of this body. On April 16, 1814, the Cortes approved his bill to locate the Provincial Deputation of the Eastern Interior Provinces at Saltillo (Spain, Cortes, *Actas de las sesiones de la legislatura ordinaria de 1814,* p. 255). But the body continued to hold its sessions at Monterrey.

19. In the latter part of March 1811, when the insurgents were overthrown at Baján, Monterrey, and the state of Nuevo León was without a governor, Francisco Antonio Farías, the acting attorney general, presented to the Municipal Council of Monterrey a plan for a junta to be formed in the capital of the province, in which he proposed that a provincial governing junta composed of six members and a president have authority over all branches of the government in the province ("Expediente formada sobre la instalación de la junta de govierno de esta capital y su provincia por el actual síndico procurador general Don Francisco Antonio Farías ante el Iltre. ayuntamiento de esta ciudad," ms., Archivo General del Estado de Nuevo León). The members of the Municipal Council accepted the plan as wise

and proceeded to elect Blas José Gómez de Castro of Linares as president; Bernardino Ussel y Güimbarda as vice-president; and José León Lobo Guerrero, José Vivero, José Valera, Melchor Núñez de Esquivel, Antonio Silverio de Verridi, and Francisco Bruno Barrera as members. They were put in charge of the political and military government of Nuevo León on April 2, recognized as the governing body by Félix Calleja on April 22 (ibid.), and governed Nuevo León until March 11, 1813, when they turned the government over to the governor appointed by the viceroy (Santiago Roel, *Nuevo León, Apuntes históricos,* I, 101).

20. It was composed of Fernando de Uribe, José León Lobo Guerrero, Juan José de la Garza, Ambrosio María de Aldasoro, José Bernardino Cantú, and Joseph Mier Noriega.

21. La junta preparatoria de Monterrey to the governor of the province of Texas, Monterrey, September 20, 1813, ms., Bexar Archives, University of Texas.

22. Christóbal Domínguez to the Junta of Monterrey, Béxar, October 13, 1813, ms., Bexar Archives, University of Texas; Junta preparatoria de Monterrey to Juan Fermín de Juanicoteña, governor of Nuevo Santander, Monterrey, December 30, 1813, ms., Matamoros Archives (photostats), University of Texas, XVI, 40–41.

23. Governor Christóbal Domínguez estimated in October 1813 that the population of Texas did not exceed five thousand inhabitants (Domínguez to the Junta de Monterrey, Béxar, October 13, 1813, ms., Bexar Archives).

24. That procedure was somewhat irregular: according to the provisions of the Constitution, the district electors of each province were to meet at the capital of the province to elect deputies both to the Cortes and to the Provincial Deputation. In the elections held elsewhere in Mexico during 1813 and 1814, the procedure prescribed by the Constitution was strictly followed.

25. Minutes of the Provincial Deputation of the Eastern Interior Provinces for May 10, 1814, to June 28, 1814, with the title "Oficios y comunicaciones de la Diputación Provincial desde el día 10 de mayo 1814," ms., Archivo General del Estado de Nuevo León. Also found were a number of other documents of this Provincial Deputation, Arredondo's letter to the Provincial Deputation of Monterrey, dated Laredo, June 17, 1814, and Calleja's letter to Arredondo, dated México, August 18, 1814, telling Arredondo to dissolve that body (Libro de actas de las juntas electorales de parroquia, de partido y de provincia, año de 1814, ms., Archivo General del Gobierno del Estado de Nuevo León, legajo 1, no. 2 in 1814; Charles H. Harris, *A Mexican Family Empire: The Latifundio of the Sánchez Navarro Family, 1765–1867* [Austin, 1975], pp. 141–142, 346; Monterrey, September 7, 1814, in Pedro Torres Lanzas, *Independencia de América: Fuentes para su estudio,* IV, 10–11; and Monterrey, August 17, 1814, letter from Diputación Provincial de Monterrey explaining the evils impeding its proper functioning, in Torres Lanzas, *Independencia de América,* III, 515).

26. Durango, April 13, 1814, in Torres Lanzas, *Independencia de América,* III, 478–479; Richard V. Baquera, "Paso del Norte and Chihuahua: Revolution and Constitutionalists," p. 95; Real de Alamos, March 26, 1814, letter of the Junta Electoral de la Provincia de Sinaloa y Sonora with the acts of election of deputies to the Cortes and to the Provincial Deputation of the Western Interior Provinces, in Torres Lanzas, *Independencia de América,* III, 473; Commandant Bernardo Bonavía to the Minister of Overseas Affairs, Durango, March 15 and 16, 1814, in ibid., III,

470–471. Note: Francisco R. Almada (*Resumen de la historia del estado de Chihuahua,* pp. 152–153) says that the Provincial Deputation began to function on January 22, 1814, and that Chihuahua was represented by Francisco Espejo and Juan José Zambrano, but this hardly seems possible since most of the elections for deputies to the Provincial Deputation of the Western Interior Provinces were held in March 1814. He cites no documentation for this.

27. "Instrucción conforme a la cual deberán celebrarse en las provincias de ultramar las elecciones de diputados de Cortes para las ordinarias del año próximo de 1813," ms., AGNM, Ramo de Historia, vol. 445, leaves 10–11; "Elecciones para diputados a las Cortes ordinarias de 1813: Diputaciones Provinciales . . . ," in Alba, *La constitución en la Nueva España,* pp. 154–155.

28. The complete instructions, issued as an official order on November 27, were published in the *Diario de México,* November 30 and December 1–2, 1812.

29. It should be noted that this division was made on the basis of the intendancies of México, Puebla, Valladolid, Guanajuato, Oaxaca, and Veracruz. The same was also true for San Luis Potosí except that the Cortes itself had separated from it the four Eastern Interior Provinces, which had formed a part of that intendancy. Tlaxcala with its district of Huexotzingo was designated a province because of "its peculiar circumstances" and the *corregimiento* of Querétaro with the district of Cadereyta was designated as one, although no reason was given (ibid., December 1, 1812).

30. *Diario de México,* December 2, 1812; Alba, *La constitución en la Nueva España,* p. 162.

31. Alba, *La constitución en la Nueva España,* pp. 159–160; *Diario de México,* December 3, 1812.

32. *Constitución política de la monarquía española* (Cádiz, 1812), Articles 35–103.

33. *Diario de México,* December 3, 1812.

34. Nettie Lee Benson, "The Contested Mexican Election of 1812," *Hispanic American Historical Review* 26 (August 1946): 336–350.

35. Alamán, *Historia de Méjico,* III, 294–297; Niceto de Zamacois, *Historia de Méjico,* VIII, 726–730; Bancroft, *History of Mexico,* IV, 465–466.

36. Bancroft, *History of Mexico,* IV, 502; Alamán, *Historia de Méjico,* III, 409–411.

37. Ramón Gutiérrez del Mazo to Venegas, México, December 27, 1812, and January 3, 1813, in Alba, *La constitución en la Nueva España,* I, 244–246.

38. "Los fiscales to Calleja, México, March 29, 1813," in ibid., pp. 250–255.

39. Minutes of the preliminary electoral council, April 20, 1813, ms., AGNM, Ramo de Historia, vol. 445, leaves 66–67; "México, 30 de Abril," in *Gaceta del gobierno de México,* May 1, 1813.

40. Minutes of the preliminary electoral council, April 23, 1813, ms., AGNM, Ramo de Historia, vol. 445, leaf 68.

41. *Diario de México,* July 7, 1813.

42. Ibid., July 20, 1813.

43. Ciriaco del Llano to Félix María Calleja, Puebla, May 4, 1813, ms., AGNM, Ramo de Historia, vol. 445.

44. José Mariano Marín to Félix Maria Calleja, Puebla, June 24, 1813, ms., AGNM, Ramo de Historia, vol. 447.

45. Ibid., marginal note dated México, July 7, 1813.

46. Junta Electoral de la Provincia de Querétaro to Félix Calleja, Querétaro, June 4, 1813, ms., AGNM, Ramo de Historia, vol. 447, expediente 8.

47. Augustín González del Campillo to Félix María Calleja, Tlaxcala, July 26, 1813, ms., AGNM, Ramo de Historia, vol. 445.

48. Footnote 3 to "Acta de la Junta preparatoria de México de 7 de julio de 1814," in Alba, *La constitución en la Nueva España,* I, 219.

49. "Documentos relativos a las persecuciones de que fué objeto el diputado por la provincia de Tlaxcala: Se declare nula su elección y se decide que se nombre otra persona en su lugar," in Alba, *La constitución en la Nueva España,* I, 213–217.

50. Ramón Gutiérrez del Mazo to Calleja, México, July 23, 1813, ms., AGNM, Ramo de Historia, vol. 445.

51. He was born in Ixtlacuitla, Tlaxcala, on December 26, 1763, and studied at the Seminario Palafoxiano of Puebla, where he later was professor of philosophy and sacred literature. He received the degree of doctor of theology from the University of Mexico, on October 9, 1790. Later he was curate of Tacubaya, where he was at the time of his election to the Cortes in 1810. He set out once for Spain, where he remained until after the signing of the Constitution on March 18, 1812.

52. *Constitución política de la monarquía española,* Article 330.

53. Los Guadalupes to José María Morelos, México, August 5, 1813, ms., AGI, estante 136, cajón 7, legajo 9.

54. Miguel Sandoval to Calleja, May 18, 1814, in Alba, *La constitución en la Nueva España,* I, 48.

55. José de Quevedo, governor of the province of Veracruz to Calleja, Veracruz, March 18, 1814, ms., AGNM, Ramo de Historia, vol. 445.

56. According to Articles 108 and 307 of the Constitution of 1812, deputies to the Cortes and to the Provincial Deputation were to be elected every two years, beginning with 1812.

57. *Diario de México,* March 16, 1814.

58. Calleja to Exmo. Señor Ministro de Ultramar, México, April 30, 1814, ms., AGNM, Correspondencia Virreyes, Calleja, vol. 6, carta no. 178; footnote 3 of "Acta de la junta preparatoria de México de 7 de julio de 1814," in Alba, *La constitución en la Nueva España,* I, 219.

59. "Acta de la junta preparatoria de México de 7 de julio de 1814," in ibid., 218–219.

60. Ibid., p. 220; Calleja to Exmo. Sr. Ministro de la Governación de Ultramar, ms., AGNM, Correspondencia Virreyes, Calleja, vol. 6, carta no. 189.

61. The members were Félix María Calleja, Political Chief; Ramón Gutiérrez del Mazo, intendant; José Angel Gazano, deputy for México; Pedro Acevedo y Calderón, deputy for Querétaro; José Daza y Artazo, deputy for Tlaxcala; Juan Bautista Lobo, elected by the province of México to take the place of the deputy for Oaxaca; and Ignacio García Illueca, alternate for México ("Certificación de haberse instalado la diputación provincial de México," in Alba, *La constitución en la Nueva España,* I, 220–221).

62. Actas capitulares del Exmo. Ayuntamiento constitucional de la ciudad de México, año de 1814, ms., Archivo del Gobierno del Distrito Federal de México, hoja 158.

63. *Diario de México,* August 1, 1814.

64. Ibid., August 11, 1814.

65. Ibid., August 18, 1814.

66. José María de la Canal y Landeta to Fernandó Pérez Marañón, intendant of Guanajuato, Querétaro, October 16, 1813, ms., AGNM, Ramo de Historia, vol. 447, expediente 14.

67. Joseph Ruiz de Aguirre, San Luis Potosí, March 22, 1814, to Félix Calleja, ms., AGNM, Ramo de Historia, vol. 445.

68. Pérez Marañón to Félix María Calleja, San Luis Potosí, March 22, 1814, ms., AGNM, Ramo de Historia, vol. 445; letter of May 7, 1814, San Luis Potosí from Junta Electoral de San Luis Potosí to Spanish Cortes, including act of election of deputies to the Cortes and to the Provincial Deputation for that province on March 14–15, in Torres Lanzas, *Independencia de América*, III, 485.

69. Ruiz de Aguirre to Calleja, San Luis Potosí, March 22, 1814, ms., AGNM, Ramo de Historia, vol. 445.

70. Domingo Juarros, *A Statistical and Commercial History of the Kingdom of Guatemala in Spanish America*, p. 13; Flavio Antonio Pantagua, *Catecismo elemental de historia y estadística de Chiapas*, p. 442.

71. Spain, Cortes, *Actas de las sesiones de la legislatura ordinaria de 1813*, p. 442; Mario Rodríguez, *The Cádiz Experiment in Central America 1808–1826*, p. 117.

72. Spain, Cortes, *Actas de las sesiones de la legislatura ordinaria de 1813*, p. 258; Manuel S. Trens, *Historia de Chiapas desde los tiempos más remotos hasta el govierno del general Carlos A. Vidal*, p. 212.

73. Spain, Cortes, *Actas de las sesiones de la legislatura ordinaria de 1813*, p. 442.

74. Ibid., p. 458.

75. Felipe de la Zúñiga y Ontiveros, *Calendario, guía, manual de los forasteros de México para el año de 1779 al año de 1822*, 1780, 1790–1800, 1811–1813, 1815–1822.

76. Ricardo Rees Jones, *El despotismo ilustrado y los intendentes de la Nueva España*, appendix 1, pp. 211–213 and 313–317.

3. Growth of the Provincial Deputations in Mexico, 1820–1821

1. Decree of March 9, 1820, in Francisco Pi y Margall and Francisco Pi y Arsuaga, *Las grandes conmociones políticas del siglo XIX en España*, I, 126.

2. Ayuntamiento de Campeche to the Conde del Venadito, Campeche, August 7, 1821, in Alba, *La constitución de 1812*, II, 169; Lanz, *Compendio de historia de Campeche*, pp. 166–167, 507–508.

3. Alamán, *Historia de Méjico*, V, 15; Zárate, *La guerra de independencia*, p. 652. Documents of the oath taken at Veracruz are in Alba, *La constitución de 1812*, II, 170–176.

4. *Gaceta del gobierno de México*, June 1, 1820; Alamán, *Historia de Méjico*, V, 16–17; Zárate, *La guerra de independencia*, pp. 652–653.

5. Nueva España (Viceroyalty), Diputación Provincial, *Actas de la diputación provincial de Nueva España 1820–1821*, pp. 27–82; hereafter cited as D. P., *Actas de . . . Nueva España; Gaceta del gobierno de México*, July 20, 1820, and July 25, 1820; *Noticioso general*, January 18, 1821.

6. *Gaceta del gobierno de México*, June 3 and 6, 1820.

7. Ibid., July 13, 1820.

8. Ibid.

9. Guadalajara elected four regular and two alternate deputies (Dr. Toribio González, Juan Manuel Caballero, Dr. José Miguel Gordoa, Matías Vergara and alternates José García and Alfonso Sánchez Leñero); Zacatecas, three regular and one alternate (Lic. Rafael Dionisio Riestro, Lic. José María García Rojas, and Lic. José Crispín Velarde and alternate Agustín de Iriarte) (*Noticioso general* 7, no. 738, September 20, 1820, pp. 1–2). As in 1814, they held separate elections in their respective provinces and not jointly as was done in some places (ibid., September 28, 1820; Diputación Provincial de Nueva Galicia to Diputación Provincial de Monterrey, Guadalajara, September 16, 1820, in Archivo General del Gobierno del Estado de Nuevo León, legajo 1820, carpeta no. 5).

10. In Yucatán the district electors of the three provinces of Yucatán, Campeche, and Tabasco met together in Mérida and elected Pablo Moreno, Pedro Manuel de Regil, José Joaquín Torres, Juan Echánove, Juan Francisco Severo, Sebastián Hernández, and Pablo Lanz deputies and Pedro José Guzmán, Pedro Almeida, and Pedro Cicero alternates (*Semanario político y literario*, September 13, 1820; Juan Francisco Molina Solís, *Historia de Yucatán durante la dominación española*, III, 446; Lanz, *Compendio de historia de Campeche*, p. 171).

11. Veracruz elected Juan Bautista Lobo (*Gaceta del gobierno de México*, September 26, 1820). Michoacán elected Juan José Pastor Morales (ibid., September 28, 1820). México elected José María Fagoaga deputy and José Ignacio García Illueca alternate (ibid., September 19, 1820). Oaxaca elected Lic. Francisco Ignacio Mimiaga as its deputy and Dr. José Mariano Amable as alternate (*Noticioso general* 7, October 4, 1820, p. 2). Puebla elected Patricio Furlong as deputy and José Dionisio Leal as alternate (ibid., no. 739, September 22, 1820, p. 2). Querétaro elected Lic. Juan Nepomuceno Mier Altamirano as deputy and Lic. Juan María Wenceslao Sánchez de Barquera as alternate (ibid., no. 740, September 23, 1820, p. 1). Tlaxcala elected as its deputy Dr. José Miguel Guridi y Alcocer (ibid., p. 1).

12. Guanajuato elected to the Provincial Deputation of San Luis Potosí: the Marqués de San Juan de Rayas, Mariano Marmolejo, Lic. José María Septien and José María Núñez de la Torre and alternates José María Fernández Herrera and Victor Márquez (*Noticioso general* 7, no. 741, September 27, 1820, p. 2). San Luis Potosí elected Juan Vicente Arce, Dr. José María Semper, and Lt. Col. Manuel Ortiz de Zarate and alternate Andrés Pérez Soto (*Noticioso general* 7, no. 744, October 4, 1820, p. 2). See also Manuel Muro, *Historia de San Luis Potosí*, I, 175; Diputación Provincial de San Luis Potosí to the Diputación de las Provincias Internas de Oriente, San Luis Potosí, December 3, 1820, ms., Archivo General del Gobierno del Estado de Nuevo León, legajo año 1820, carpeta no. 5.

13. Aviso de la junta electoral de estas provincias . . . , signed by José Eustaquio Fernández, elector-secretary, Monterrey, October 3, 1820, ms., Archivo General del Gobierno del Estado de Nuevo León, legajo año 1820, carpeta no. 5. As in 1814, they elected two deputies to represent each of the provinces of Coahuila, Nuevo León, and Nuevo Santander and one to represent Texas. They elected Dr. José León Lobo Guerrero and Mauricio Alcocer for Coahuila; Dr. Fermín de Sada and Santos de Uribe for Nuevo León; Dr. Eustaquio Fernández de Lara and Manuel de la Torre for Nuevo Santander, and Ambrosio María de Aldasoro for Texas; and alternates Lt. Col. Juan Fermín de Juanicoteña, José Antonio Rodríguez

Gómez, and José Ignacio de Arizpe (*Noticioso general* 7, no. 754, October 27, 1820, p. 1). The four provinces had their electors meet at Monterrey and elected the deputies as a unit even though they did designate certain deputies to represent certain provinces. The unitary action of these provinces is significant for future developments (Diputación Provincial de San Luis Potosí to the Diputación de las Provincias Internas de Oriente, San Luis Potosí, December 3, 1820, ms., Archivo General del Gobierno del Estado de Nuevo León).

14. New Vizcaya, embracing the provinces of Durango and Chihuahua, also held its election in Durango as a unit. New Vizcaya was allotted three deputies and one alternate. The provinces of Sonora and Sinaloa held their election as a unit and elected two deputies and one alternate. This action of Durango and Chihuahua and Sonora and Sinaloa acting as units and not as four separate provinces at that time had considerable significance for future developments concerning these provinces. New Mexico was allotted two regular deputies and an alternate (*Gaceta del gobierno de México,* November 11 and December 16, 1820; Diputación Provincial de las Provincias Internas de Occidente to Diputación Provincial de las Provincias Internas de Oriente, Durango, December 4, 1820, ms., Archivo General del Gobierno del Estado de Nuevo León, legajo año 1820, carpeta no. 5).

15. José Mariano Michelena was born in Valladolid, Michoacán, in the 1780s. His family was one of the most distinguished of that province. He became a lieutenant in the army and was associated with "Allende and Aldama" and others. Prior to 1808, Michelena spent some time in Mexico City. In that year he was sent to Michoacán to recruit a regiment, but instead became involved in a conspiracy for independence. He was imprisoned for a time, then freed and sent to Jalapa to a division of the army. There he became involved in another conspiracy and was again arrested. He spent the years 1811 and 1813 imprisoned in San Juan de Ulúa, then was sent to Spain, where he joined the Spanish army in the fight against the French. He remained in the Spanish army until 1820, when he was named one of the alternate American deputies to the Cortes.

16. Spain, Cortes, *Diario de las sesiones de Cortes, Legislatura de 1820,* October 4, 1820; hereafter cited as *Diario de las Cortes, 1820.*

17. Ibid., October 13, 1820.

18. Ibid., III, 2037–2038.

19. Ibid., III, 2038.

20. Ibid., III, 2039.

21. Ramos Arizpe was entirely correct in his assertions concerning Arispe. It did have an intendant and governor and met the requirements just as completely as did Valladolid de Michoacán or San Luis Potosí and even more than did the Eastern Interior Provinces. Article 1 of the *Real ordenanzas para el establecimiento e instrucción de intendentes de exército y provincia en el reino de la Nueva España* (p. 3), said, "and the other shall be that one [intendancy] that has already been established in the city of Arispe and which has jurisdiction over the two provinces of Sonora and Sinaloa." The *Calendario, manual y guía de forasteros en México,* which annually listed the intendancies in Mexico, the capitals of each, and the title of the intendant, each year from 1800 to 1821 designated Arispe as the capital of the intendancy embracing the provinces of Sonora and Sinaloa and the title of the intendant, the

same title given to the intendant in Durango, Vallodolid, San Luis Potosí, and so forth. The Eastern Interior Provinces, which had been given a Provincial Deputation in 1812, did not have an intendant. The intendancy of Saltillo, embracing the Eastern Interior Provinces, although created in 1812, was never established.

22. *Diario de las Cortes, 1820,* III, 2040.

23. Spain, Laws, Statutes, etc., *Colección de los decretos y órdenes generales de la primera legislatura de las Cortes ordinarias de 1820 y 1821 (desde 6 de julio hasta 9 de noviembre de 1820),* VI, 295.

24. Miguel Ramos Arizpe to the Ayuntamiento of Puebla de los Angeles, Madrid, July 9, 1821, bound in Libro del cabildo de la muy ilustre ciudad de la Puebla de los Angeles, ms., Archivo General de la Secretaría del Ayuntamiento de Puebla, año 1821, hoja 396.

25. *Representación que hace a S.M. las cortes el ayuntamiento de la Puebla de los Angeles para que en esta ciudad, cabeza de provincia, se establezca diputación provincial, como lo dispone la constitución.* It was signed at Puebla de los Angeles, July 9, 1820, by Ciriaco del Llano, the intendant and governor of the province, Pablo Escandón, José Ignacio Bravo, Joaquín Haro y Portillo, José María de Ovando, Patricio Furlong, José Dionisio Leal, Hilario de Olagüibel, José Domingo Couto, Carlos de Avalos y García, Félix Tequamhuei, Vicente de Ezcurdia, José González, Gregorio Mújica, Manuel Pereza Salazar, Méndez Mont, Rafael Adamo, Antonio Velarde, Matías García de Huesca, Juan Francisco Alduncín, José Marín, Francisco Arregui, and Manuel José Herrera and was printed on the government printing press in Puebla on July 13, 1820.

26. Libro de actas de los cabildos de Valladolid de 1816 a 1821, ms., Archivo del Ayuntamiento de Morelia, Michoacán, no. 5, hoja 32.

27. The attorneys for Mexico City undoubtedly took a more politic view than the Puebla Municipal Council, but they certainly did not offer much of an answer to the Puebla charge of unconstitutionality.

28. Actas ordinarias y extraordinarias del ayuntamiento constitucional de la ciudad de México de 1820, ms., Archives of the Federal District in Mexico City, vol. 140, leaves 127–134.

29. Ibid., leaf 135.

30. Libro de actas de los cabildos de Valladolid de 1816 a 1821, ms., Archivo del Ayuntamiento de Morelia, Michoacán, no. 5, leaf 32.

31. Spain, Cortes, *Diario de las sesiones de Cortes, Legislatura de 1821,* II, 1358; hereafter cited as *Diario de las sesiones de Cortes, 1821;* Spain, Cortes, *Diario de las actas y discusiones de las Cortes, Legislaturas de los años de 1820–1821,* XIII, 7–8.

32. *Representación que hace al soberano congreso de Cortes la junta electoral de la provincia de la Puebla de los Angeles en Nueva España, para que en ella se establezca la diputación provincial conforme al artículo 325 de la constitución,* pp. 1–3.

33. José Nepomuceno Troncoso, *Aviso al público,* Puebla, September 25, 1820.

34. Ignacio de Mora to the Municipal Council of Puebla, Madrid, May 1, 1821, bound in Libro de cabildo del ayuntamiento de Puebla de los Angeles, ms., Archivo General de la Secretaría del Ayuntamiento de Puebla, año 1821, leaf 153.

35. *Diario de las sesiones de Cortes, 1821,* I, 521. The bill was signed by Ramos Arizpe, Michelena, López Constante, Zavala, La Llave, Maniau, Francisco Fagoaga,

Manuel Cortazar, José María Montoya, José María Couto, Nicolás Fernández Pierola, Juan Freyre, José María Arnedo, and Julián Urruela, all American deputies, and read for the first time on March 17, 1821.

36. Ibid., I, 590. Ramos Arizpe was a member of the Committee on Overseas Affairs.

37. Ibid., II, 1131. Patricio López of Oaxaca and José María Puchet of Puebla had entered the Cortes on April 15, 1821.

38. Ibid., II, 1358.

39. Ibid.

40. Spain, Laws, Statutes, etc., *Colección de los decretos y órdenes generales expedidos por las Cortes ordinarias, diputación que comprende desde 25 de febrero hasta 30 de junio del último año,* VII, 72–73.

41. *Diario de las sesiones de Cortes, 1821,* II, 1644.

42. D.P., *Actas de . . . Nueva España,* p. 253. Juan Ruiz de Apodaca, Political Chief of New Spain, published a proclamation calling for the election of deputies to the Cortes for the biennium 1822 and 1823. In New Spain parochial elections were to be held on December 3, 1820, district elections on January 7, 1821, and provincial elections on March 11–13 (*Gaceta del gobierno de México,* November 11, 1820).

43. Libro de actas de los cabildos de Valladolid de 1816 a 1821, ms., Archivo el Ayuntamiento de Morelia, Michoacán, no. 5, leaves 62–65.

44. Ibid., leaves 65–66.

45. The "gacetas and official papers" must have been those published in Spain and probably sent immediately to Valladolid by Michelena. The accounts of the action of the Cortes awarding Valladolid a Provincial Deputation did not appear in print in Mexican papers until late March. The *Semanario político y literario* of Mexico City carried such an account on March 28, 1821, and the decree on November 6, 1820.

46. Libro de actas de los cabildos de Valladolid de 1816 a 1821, no. 5, leaf 66.

47. *Diario de las Cortes, 1820–1821* (June 4, 1821), III, 2046.

48. D.P., *Actas de . . . Nueva España* (April 7, 1821), p. 291; Pedro de Sánchez, "Un precursor ideológico de la independencia mexicana," in *Episodios eclesiásticos de México (Contribución a nuestra historia),* pp. 145–151; *Diccionario Porrúa: Historia, biografía y geografía de México,* II, 1584.

49. Carlos María Bustamante, *Cuadro histórico de México,* 2nd ed., 5 vols. (México, 1846), V, 153–158; William Spence Robertson, *Iturbide of Mexico,* pp. 48–93.

50. Official order signed by Carlos García, Puebla, August 13, 1821; also *Abeja poblana,* supplement to no. 39, August 23, 1821.

51. *Abeja poblana,* no. 41, September 6, 1821.

52. Ibid., nos. 41 and 48 (October 25, 1821).

53. D.P., *Actas de . . . Nueva España,* I–II, 82–246. See also the recent article devoted almost entirely to a listing of the activities of the Provincial Deputation of Nueva España in relation to the Municipal Councils under its jurisdiction by Carlos Herrejón Peredo, "La Diputación Provincial de Nueva España," in *Temas de historia mexiquense,* comp. María Teresa Jarquín Ortega, pp. 195–218.

54. Ibid., pp. 346–348.

55. Ibid., pp. 324–325, 328–333. Note: Timothy E. Anna (*The Fall of the Royal Government in Mexico City,* pp. 214–215) does not mention this act of the Provincial

Deputation of New Spain. He mentions only the later action of the Municipal Council of Mexico City, over which the Provincial Deputation had authority.

56. D.P., *Actas de . . . Nueva España*, pp. 344–345; Anna, *The Fall of the Royal Government in Mexico City*, pp. 211, 217–218.

57. Ibid., p. 219; D.P., *Actas de . . . Nueva España*, pp. 344–345.

58. Ibid., pp. 347–349.

59. Ibid., p. 350.

60. Ibid., pp. 351–352.

61. Jaime Delgado, *España y México en el siglo XIX*, I, 39–55; Pedro Torres Lanzas, *Independencia de América: Fuentes para su estudio*, V, 182, 186, 191–192, 193–196, 201, 233, 237; Zarate, *La guerra de independencia*, III, 735.

62. Delgado, *España y México*, I, 55; José Presas, *Juicio imparcial sobre las principales causas de la revolución de la América española*, pp. 93–95; Robertson, *Iturbide of Mexico*, pp. 102–109; *Idea de la conducta general de don Miguel Ramos Arizpe*, p. 13.

63. Spain, Cortes, *Diario de las cortes* (June 4, 1821), III, 2041–2046.

64. *Diario de las Cortes* (June 25, 1821), III, 2471–2477.

65. *Diario de las Cortes* (June 26, 1821), III, 2496–2497; Delgado, *España y México*, I, 103–108; Carlos A. Villaneuva, *La monarquía en América: Fernando VII y los nuevos estados*, pp. 61–69.

66. Ibid.; Delgado, *España y México*, I, 103.

67. For these plans, see Ramón Esquerra, "La crítica española de la situación de América en el siglo XVIII," *Revista de Indias* 87–88: 159–287; Charles E. Chapman, *A History of Spain;* Manuel de Godoy, *Memorias;* Boleslao Lewis, *Los movimientos de emancipación en hispanoamérica y la independencia de los Estados Unidos;* Elijah Wilson Lyon, *Louisiana in French Diplomacy 1759–1804;* Manuel de Vadillo, *Apuntes sobre las principales sucesos que han influído en el actual estado de la América del Sud;* Demetrio Ramos, "Los proyectos de independencia para América preparados por el Rey Carlos IV," *Revista de Indias* 28, nos. 111–112 (January–June 1968): 85–123; Delgado, *España y Mexico*, I, 103; Villanueva, *La monarquía en América: Bolívar;* William Woodrow Anderson, "Reform as a Means to Quell Revolution," in *Mexico and the Spanish Cortes*, ed. Nettie Lee Benson, pp. 191–207; Timothy E. Anna, *Spain and the Loss of America*, pp. 83–84; Anna, *The Fall of the Royal Government in Mexico City*, pp. 101–102.

68. A manuscript copy signed simply Fernando, without his rubric, to this effect is in the Benson Latin American Collection at the University of Texas. It is written on paper having the same watermark as that of other recognized orders signed by Ferdinand VII. The authenticity of this letter is challenged by some writers, but historians who have reproduced it in full, such as Carlos María Bustamante, *El Nuevo Bernal Díaz del Castillo o sea historia de la invasión de los angloamericanos en México*, I, 135–136, believed it to be authentic. Others who cite or print it in full are Anastasio Zerecero, *Memorias para la historia de las revoluciones en México*, pp. 349–351; Presas, *Juicio imparcial sobre las principales causas de la revolución*, pp. 82–85, who believes it to be authentic; Zamacois, *Historia de Méjico desde sus tiempos más remotos hasta nuestros días*, IX, footnote 1, pp. 565–566, who believes it apocryphal; and Villanueva, who cites it in both *La monarquía en America: Bolívar*, p. 210, and *La monarquía en América: Fernando VII*, pp. 56–57.

69. Delgado, *España y México,* I, 103; Villanueva, *La monarquía en América: Fernando VII,* pp. 66–69.

70. D.P., *Actas de . . . Nueva España,* II, 326.

71. Delgado, *España y México,* I, 54–55; Arrangoiz, *México desde 1808 hasta 1867,* I, 60–61.

72. Ibid., V, 223–226. See also Delgado, *España y México,* I, 55–60.

73. Roberto Olagaray (comp. and ed.), *Colección de documentos históricos mexicanos,* II, 47–58, 73–77.

74. Ibid., II, 52–62; 73–76; Bustamante, *Cuadro histórico,* V, 139–144.

75. Ibid., V, 223–229; Olagaray, *Colección de documentos,* II, 159–161, Delgado, *España y México,* I, 61–65.

76. Bustamante, *Cuadro histórico,* V, 232–234; Olagaray, *Colección de documentos,* II, 165–171; Delgado, *España y México,* I, 67–90; Robertson, *Iturbide of Mexico,* pp. 112–118; *Noticioso general* (Mexico City), supplement to no. 219, October 3, 1821, pp. 3–4.

77. "Junta Guvernativa a que se refiere el Plan de Iguala," in Olagaray, *Colección de dócumentos,* II, 34–35; Bustamante, *Cuadro histórico,* V, 118–119.

78. Bustamante, *Cuadro histórico,* V, 324–325.

79. Ibid., V, 281–282; "De Novella a Iturbide," México, letters fr. Novella to Iturbide August 14 and August 16, 1821, in Olagaray, *Colección de documentos,* II, 239–241.

80. Bustamante, *Cuadro histórico,* V, 281–286.

81. D.P., *Actas de . . . Nueva España,* 361–363; Olagaray, *Colección de documentos,* II, 204–205.

82. "Acta de la Junta de Autoridades de México", México, August 30, 1821, in Olagaray, *Colección de documentos,* II, 221–224.

83. Two communications from "De la Diputación Provincial de Nueva España a O'Donojú," August 31, 1821, in ibid., II, 201–202.

84. "De Novella a O'Donojú," México, August 31, 1821, and "De O'Donojú a Novella," September 4, 1821, in ibid., II, 172–176.

85. "De Novella a O'Donojú," México, September 11, 1821, in ibid., II, 183–184.

86. "Acta de la Junta de Autoridades de México," México, September 9, 1821, in ibid., II, 224–229.

87. "De la Diputación Provincial a O'Donojú," México, September 9, 1821, in ibid., II, 204–205.

88. "De O'Donojú a la Diputación Provincial de Nueva España," Convento de San Joaquín, September 12, 1821, in ibid., II, 205–207.

89. "De O'Donojú a Novella," San Joaquín, Convento de Carmelitas, September 12, 1821, and "De Novella a O'Donojú," México, September 12, 1821, in ibid., II, 189–196. See also "De O'Donojú a los señores Alcocer y Luna Castillo, comisionados de la Junta de autoridades de México," San Joaquín, Convento de Carmelitas, September 11, 1821, in ibid., II, 197–200. It should be noted here that Novella capitulated to O'Donojú in Mexico City on September 12, 1821, and not on September 13 as stated by Anna (*The Fall of the Royal Government in Mexico City,* p. 222), although Novella did not announce his capitulation until two days later in an "Orden al ejército y plaza," signed Novella, México, September 15[?], and

printed in a supplement of the *Noticioso general* (8, no. III), which obviously was printed on the same day.

90. "De la Diputación Provincial a O'Donojú," México, September 14, 1821, in Olagaray, *Colección de documentos,* II, 207–208.

91. These announcements also appeared in the *Gaceta del gobierno de México,* 12, no. 125, September 15, 1821, pp. 976–980.

92. "Habitantes de Nueva España," signed Tacubaya, September 17, 1821, by O'Donojú, in *Noticioso general* 8, no. 114, September 21, 1821, p. 4; and in *Gaceta del gobierno de México* (Mexico City) 15, no. 128, September 22, 1821, pp. 994–995; Robertson, *Iturbide of Mexico,* p. 127.

93. "De O'Donojú a la Diputación Provincial," Tacubaya, September 25, 1821, in Olagaray, *Colección de documentos,* II, 208; Bustamante, *Cuadro histórico,* V, 327; Robertson, *Iturbide of Mexico,* p. 127. Compare Anna (*The Fall of the Royal Government in Mexico City,* pp. 222–223), who states that O'Donojú entered Mexico City on September 24, apparently misreading O'Donojú's statement of September 17, 1821.

94. Bustamante, *Cuadro histórico,* V, 327.

95. Ibid., V, 327–331; Robertson, *Iturbide of Mexico,* pp. 131–132; Anna, *The Fall of the Royal Government in Mexico City,* pp. 223–224.

4. Continued Development of the Provincial Deputations in Mexico, 1821–1823

1. Mexico, Junta Provisional Gubernativa, *Diario de la soberana junta provisional gubernativa del imperio mexicano* (México, 1821), p. 13; hereinafter cited as *Diario de la soberana junta provisional gubernativa.*

2. Ibid., pp. 23–24; Charles W. Macune, Jr., *El estado de México y la federación mexicana, 1823–1835,* p. 193.

3. Matías Romero, *Bosquejo histórico de la agregación a México de Chiapas y Soconusco,* pp. 50–53.

4. *Gaceta imperial de México* I, no. 41, December 20, 1821, pp. 337–339; *Incorporación de Chiapas a México: Discursos leídos en la velada que se verificó en la cámara de diputados en celebración del LXXVIII aniversario de la federación de Chiapas a la república de México,* p. 13; Romero, *Bosquejo histórico,* pp. 56–57; Luis Espinosa, *Independencia de la provincia de las Chiapas y su unión a México,* p. 10.

5. *Gaceta imperial de México,* December 20, 1821.

6. The minutes of the meeting of the Provincial Deputation of October 28, 1821, and the commission given to Solórzano are reproduced in Romero, *Bosquejo histórico,* pp. 56–57.

7. *Noticioso general,* October 1, 1821.

8. Mexico, Junta Provisional Gubernativa, *Diario de las sesiones de la soberana junta provisional gubernativa del imperio mexicano, instalado según provienen el plan de Iguala y tratados de la villa de Córdoba,* p. 4.

9. Ibid., p. 88.

10. Under the provisions of the Spanish Constitution, half of the members of the Provincial Deputation were elected at each election. The other half continued

to serve until the following election, when they were replaced by new members.

As previously mentioned, elections were held on March 11, 12, and 13, 1821, for deputies to the Cortes of 1822 to 1823 and for deputies to the Provincial Deputation for the biennium 1822 to 1823. On March 13, provincial electoral bodies of New Spain elected deputies to replace one-half of the membership of the Provincial Deputation. México elected Manuel de Sotarriba (*Gaceta del gobierno de México*, March 15, 1821); Oaxaca elected José Mariano Fernández Arteaga (ibid., April 3, 1821); Guadalajara named Esteban Huerta, Juan Ceyetano Portugal, and Manuel García Quevedo (ibid., 12, p. 291); Zacatecas, Mariano Iriarte, José Calendonio de Murguía, and Juan María Vélez (ibid., p. 546); San Luis Potosí elected Carlos Flores, José Ildefonso Díaz de León, and Manuel Francisco de Arbide (ibid., pp. 313–314); Sonora and Sinaloa, Juan Gandara and José Subiría (ibid., p. 522); and the Eastern Interior Provinces, Bernardino Cantú, José Melchor Sánchez Navarro, José Antonio Gutiérrez de Lara, and José Vivero, (*Aviso al público*, signed Monterrey, March 13, 1821, Juan Francisco Gutiérrez, elector-secretary, a broadside in the Bexar Archives at the University of Texas at Austin).

11. *Gaceta imperial extraordinaria de México* 1, 228, November 27, 1821.

12. Benson, "The Contested Mexican Election of 1812," p. 337.

13. *Diario de México*, December 1, 1812.

14. *Diario de las Cortes, 1821*, II, 1358.

15. *El sol*, March 2, 1822; *Noticioso general*, March 6, 1822.

16. Mexico, Congreso Constituyente, *Actas del congreso constituyente*, I, 8.

17. The matter was discussed on April 15, April 22, and June 20, 1822 (ibid., I, 37, 77; II, 83, 89; III, 106).

18. *Diario de México*, December 1, 1812.

19. Article 11 of the electoral decree of November 18, 1821, in *Gaceta imperial extraordinaria de México*, November 27, 1821; *Noticioso general*, November 28, 1821.

20. *Diario de las sesiones de la soberana junta provisional gubernativa*, December 20, 1821, p. 168; January 19, 1822, p. 241.

21. Mexico, Laws, Statutes, etc., *Colección de los decretos y órdenes que ha expedido la soberana junta provisional gubernativa del imperio mexicano, desde su instalación el 28 de setiembre de 1821 hasta 24 de febrero de 1822*, p. 183.

22. *Actas del congreso constituyente mexicano*, I, 64.

23. Ibid., II, 69.

24. Ibid., II, 357.

25. Ibid., III, 69.

26. Benjamin Maurice Read, *Illustrated History of New Mexico*, p. 366; Ralph Emerson Twitchell, *The Leading Facts of New Mexican History*, I, 10.

27. *Actas del congreso constituyente*, I, 94.

28. Cf. the records of the deputation in the Surveyor General's Office in Santa Fe, New Mexico.

29. *Actas del congreso constituyente*, I, 94.

30. Ibid., III, 72.

31. Manuel Crescencio Rejón, *Discursos parlamentarios (1822–1847)*, pp. 72–73.

32. *Gaceta del gobierno supremo de México*, June 3, 1823; Manuel Mestre Ghizliazza, *Documentos y datos para la historia de Tabasco*, I, 124, 134–135.

33. Juan Miguel Riesgo et al., *Memoria sobre las proporciones naturales de las*

provincias internas occidentales, causas de que han provenido sus atrasos, providencias tomadas con el fin de lograr su remedio y los que por ahora se consideran oportunos para mejorar su estado, y ir proporcionando su futura felicidad.

34. *Diario de la junta nacional instituyente,* I, 426.

35. Carlos Espinosa de los Monteros, *Esposición que sobre las provincias de Sonora y Sinaloa escribió su diputado* (February 29, 1823), pp. 16–36.

36. *Actas del congreso constituyente mexicano,* IV, 417. This volume of the *Actas* is entitled *Diario de las sesiones del congreso constituyente mexicano.*

37. Manuel Terán de Escalante et al., *Esposición hecha al soberano congreso constituyente mexicano sobre las provincias de Sonora y Sinaloa, por el señor coronel d. Manuel Terán y la mayoría de los representantes de dichas provincias que la subscriben.*

38. *Actas del congreso constituyente,* IV, 417.

39. *Aguila mexicana,* June 2, 1823; *El sol,* June 23, 1823.

40. Nettie Lee Benson, "The Plan of Casa Mata," *Hispanic American Historical Review* 25 (February 1945): 49–50. The Plan and its effects are be dealt with in the following chapters.

41. Ibid.; *Aguila mexicana,* May 23, 1823; Juan A. Mateos, *Historia parlamentaria de los congresos mexicanos de 1821 a 1857,* II, 374.

42. Minutes of the session of Congress of June 12, 1823, in *Aguila mexicana,* June 13, 1823; *El sol,* June 16, 1823.

43. Article 10 listed the Mexican provinces as México, Querétaro, Guadalajara, Puebla, Veracruz, Yucatán, Tabasco, Oaxaca, Guanajuato, Nuevo León, Nuevo Santander, Coahuila, Michoacán, San Luis Potosí, Zacatecas, Texas, Durango, Sonora, Sinaloa, Nuevo México, Antigua California and Nueva California (Mateos, *Historia parlamentaria,* II, 396).

44. *Aguila mexicana,* June 13, 1823; *El sol,* June 16, 1823.

45. Espinosa was referring to those listed as provinces in Article 10 (see note 91, pp. 93–94).

46. *El sol,* June 21, 1823; *Aguila mexicana,* June 18, 1823.

47. *Aguila mexicana,* June 20, 1823; *El sol,* June 23, 1823; Mateos, *Historia parlamentaria,* II, 411.

48. Ibid.; Mexico, Laws, Statutes, etc., *Colección de órdenes y decretos de la soberana junta provisional gubernativa y soberanos congresos generales de la nación mexicana,* II, 184.

49. Mateos, *Historia parlamentaria,* II, 411; *Aguila mexicana,* June 20, 1823; *El sol,* June 23, 1823.

50. "Article 1: The provinces of Sonora and Sinaloa, divided as they have been by right of the former government and the constitutional basis presented to Congress, shall be governed by two Provincial Deputations, each composed of the number of members provided by the Spanish Constitution and elected according to existing laws" (Session of Congress of June 18, 1823, in *El sol,* June 23, 1823; *Aguila mexicana,* June 21, 1823; Mateos, *Historia parlamentaria,* II, 413).

51. Session of July 11, 1823, in *El sol,* July 12, 1823; *Aguila mexicana,* July 13, 1823.

52. *El sol,* July 15, 1823; *Aguila mexicana,* July 15–16, 1823; Mateos, *Historia parlamentaria,* II, 443.

53. *Gaceta del gobierno supremo de México* 2, 213, September 30, 1823; Francisco R. Almada, *Resumen de la historia del estado de Chihuahua,* pp. 172–173; Twitchell,

The Leading Facts, II, 10; Eustaquio Buelna, *Apuntes para la historia de Sinaloa, 1821–1822,* p. 3. The names of the members of the Provincial Deputation of Sonora also have not been located, but they were elected and installed, as witnessed by the Deputation's correspondence with Congress.

54. Ayuntamiento de Monterrey to Servando Teresa de Mier, Monterrey, June 21, 1822, in Mier Papers in the Benson Latin American Collection at the University of Texas at Austin.

55. Gaspar López to Agustín de Iturbide, Monterrey, January 29, 1822; ms. entitled "Minutos de las comunicaciones dirigidas a la diputación de esta ciudad," Archivo General del Estado de Nuevo León, año de 1821, carpeta no. 4.

56. *Diario de las sesiones de la soberana junta provincial gubernativa,* p. 214.

57. Ibid., p. 269.

58. Ibid., pp. 281, 289.

59. *Actas del congreso constituyente,* II, 83; Servando Teresa de Mier (hereafter referred to as Mier) to the Ayuntamiento de Monterrey, México, August 21, 1822, in José Servando Teresa de Mier Noriega y Guerra, *Diez cartas, hasta hoy inéditas de Fray Servando Teresa de Mier,* p. 33.

60. Nuevo Santander elected seven deputies and three alternates to its own Provincial Deputation and reported this action to the central government (*El sol,* March 2, 1822; *Noticioso general,* March 6, 1822). Mier says that the first two deputies elected to the Provincial Deputation of Nuevo Santander were the ones who, according to the committee report, should proceed to take part in the Provincial Deputation of Monterrey (Mier to the Ayuntamiento de Monterrey, México, August 21, 1822, in Mier, *Diez cartas,* p. 33).

61. *Actas del congreso constituyente,* II, 83.

62. Ibid., II, 89–90.

63. Ibid., II, 251.

64. Ibid., III, 73–74, 306.

65. This body had been formally installed long before this, and Gutiérrez de Lara had so informed the Congress on August 26, 1822 (*Actas del congreso constituyente,* III, 89).

66. Mateos, *Historia parlamentaria,* I, 1005.

67. Ibid., I, 1011; *Colección de órdenes y decretos de la soberana junta provisional gubernativa y soberanos congresos generales de la nación mexicana,* II, 85–86.

68. A copy of the complete proceedings of the action of March 6, 1823, is in the Archivo General del Estado de Coahuila, Saltillo, Coahuila.

69. Libro de actas del cabildo que comenzó el día 17 de octubre del año de 1822, ms., Archivo del Ayuntamiento de Monterrey, Nuevo León, leaves 24–25.

70. Mier, *Diez cartas,* pp. 5–6.

71. *Actas del congreso constituyente mexicano,* IV, 133.

72. Official documents of the Provisional Governing Junta of Monterrey, dated Monterrey, March 26, 1823, signed by Miguel Ramos Arizpe, and March 29, 1823, signed José León Lobo and José Antonio Rodríguez, and minutes of the proceedings of April 1, 1823, all with marginal notes in the hand of Ramos Arizpe. These documents are in the Archivo General del Estado de Nuevo León, Monterrey.

73. Mier to the Ayuntamiento de Monterrey, México, August 21, 1822, in Mier, *Diez cartas,* p. 33.

74. Session of July 5, 1823, in *El sol,* July 7, 1823, and *Aguila mexicana,* July 8, 1823.

75. Mier to Bernardino Cantú, México, July 5, 1823, in David Alberto Cossío, *Historia de Nuevo León,* V, 43–44.

76. Session of July 14, 1823, in *Aguila mexicana,* July 16, 1823; Mateos, *Historia parlamentaria,* II, 444.

77. Session of August 18, 1823, in *El sol,* August 20, 1823, and *Aguila mexicana,* August 20, 1823; Mateos, *Historia parlamentaria,* II, 478; *Colección de órdenes y decretos de la soberana junta provisional gubernativa y soberanos congresos generales de la nación mexicana,* I, 159.

78. *El sol,* September 28, 1823.

79. *El sol,* September 28, 1823; *Aguila mexicana,* October 5, 1823; official election report dated September 8, 1823, in Archivo del Municipio de la Ciudad de Saltillo, Coahuila.

80. *Aguila mexicana,* November 13, 1823.

81. Carlos Eduardo Castañeda, *A Report on the Spanish Archives in San Antonio, Texas,* p. 129.

82. Libro de actas de la exma. diputación provincial de Coahuila, año de 1823, photostat of original in University of Texas Archives, pp. 122–123.

83. Cossío, *Historia de Nuevo León,* V, 22, 97.

5. Assumption of Power by the Provincial Deputations

1. J. Lloyd Mecham, "The Origins of Federalism in Mexico," *Hispanic American Historical Review* 18 (May 1938): 165.

2. Nettie Lee Benson, "Washington: Symbol of the United States in Mexico, 1800 to 1823," *Library Chronicle of the University of Texas* 2 (Spring 1947): 175–179.

3. *Semanario político y literario,* December 12 and 19, 1821.

4. José Servando Teresa de Mier Noriega y Guerra, *Memoria instructiva enviada desde Filadelfia en agosto de 1821, a los gefes independientes del Anahuac, llamado por los españoles Nueva España.*

5. *Noticioso general,* June 5, 1822.

6. *Sabatina universal,* June 15, 1822, pp. 8–14.

7. *Noticioso general,* June 17, 1822.

8. Vicente Rocafuerte, *Bosquejo ligerísimo de la revolución de México, desde el grito de Iguala hasta la proclamación imperial de Iturbide por un verdadero americano.*

9. Bancroft, *History of Mexico,* IV, 78.

10. Ibid., IV, 781–782.

11. As will be seen, this was the pattern followed in the capital of almost every province that adopted the Plan of Casa Mata in the early months of 1823.

12. Agustín de Iturbide, *Manifiesto del general d. Agustín de Iturbide, libertador de México,* p. 109.

13. *Gaceta del gobierno imperial de méxico* 2, October 1822, pp. 671–672.

14. The ministry at that time was composed of José Manuel Herrera, José Domínguez Manso, Manuel de la Sota Riva, and Antonio Medina.

15. Iturbide, *Manifiesto,* pp. 104–105; José María Bocanegra, *Memorias para la historia de México independiente 1822–1846,* I, 151–155; Enrique Olavarría y Ferrari,

México independiente, 1821–1855, in *México a través de los siglos,* ed. Vicente Riva Palacio, IV, 83–84.

16. "Proclama de Santa Anna, Veracruz, December 2, 1822," in Bustamante, *Diario histórico de México,* I, 17–18.

17. Antonio López de Santa Anna, *Manifiesto de Antonio López de Santanna a sus conciudadanos,* p. 89.

18. For the confusion of this Plan of Veracruz with the later Plan of Casa Mata, see Benson, "The Plan of Casa Mata," pp. 45–46.

19. Ibid., pp. 45–48; Olavarría y Ferrari, *México independiente,* p. 86; Emilio del Castillo Negrete, *México en el siglo XIX,* XV, 334–343; Carlos María Bustamante, *Continuación del cuadro histórico: Historia del emperador d. Agustín de Iturbide,* pp. 64–71. This last work by Bustamante is sometimes called volume VI of his *Cuadro histórico de la revolución de la América mexicana.*

20. Bustamante, *Diario histórico de México,* p. 102.

21. Alamán, *Historia de Méjico,* V, 695–700.

22. For a detailed study of this error, see Benson, "The Plan of Casa Mata," pp. 45–50.

23. Alamán, *Historia de Méjico,* V, 833; Francisco Banegas Galván, *Historia de México,* II, 271.

24. Alamán, *Historia de Méjico,* V, 711; Lorenzo de Zavala, *Ensayo histórico de las revoluciones de México,* I, 139, 215; Bustamante, *Historia del emperador d. Agustín de Iturbide,* p. 89; Banegas Galván, *Historia de México,* II, 270; William Forest Sprague, *Vicente Guerrero, Mexican Liberator,* p. 54.

25. Benson, "The Plan of Casa Mata," p. 50.

26. José Antonio de Echávarri to Antonio López de Santa Anna, Cuartel de Casa Mata, February 1, 1823, in *Ejército de operaciones,* a circular printed by Priani y Socio.

27. Echávarri to Exmo. Ayuntamiento de la ciudad de Veracruz, Cuartel de Casa Mata, February 1, 1823, in Bustamante, *Diario histórico de México,* I, 170. The Plan as printed in the *Diario de Veracruz* omitted Article 7 of the original Plan and divided Article 11 into two articles.

28. Santa Anna et al. to Echávarri, Veracruz, February 2, 1823, in *Ejército de operaciones.*

29. Bustamante, *Diario histórico de México,* p. 172.

30. This addition was made to Article 5 of the original Plan of Casa Mata, "Libertad de Yucatán," in *Gaceta del gobierno supremo de México* 1, April 12, 1823, pp. 184–186. A copy of the complete Plan adopted by the Municipal Council of Veracruz has not been located.

31. Echávarri to José María Lobato, Cuartel de Casa Mata, February 3, 1823, in Bustamante, *Diario histórico de México,* p. 206.

32. El Puente was a strategic bridge below Jalapa on the highway between Mexico City and Veracruz. It was here that Guadalupe Victoria had made a fortified stand against the armies sent out by Iturbide to subdue Victoria and Santa Anna.

33. Convenio que en lo reservado y con previo conocimiento del gral. Sta. Ana hicieron en el Puente los generales d. José Antonio Echávarri y d. Guadalupe Victoria, ms. N-1-1-9 in Sub-Dirección of the Biblioteca Nacional, Mexico City. The manuscript carries Guadalupe Victoria's signature and is dated February 6, 1823.

34. Echávarri to Lobato, Casa Mata, February 8, 1823, in Bustamante, *Diario histórico de México*, p. 206.

35. Alamán, *Historia de Méjico*, V, 711; Zavala, *Ensayo histórico*, I, 139, 215; Bustamante, *Historia del emperador d. Agustín de Iturbide*, p. 89; Banegas Galván, *Historia de México*, II, 270.

36. *Aviso al público, Oaxaca liberal*, a broadside signed in Puebla, February 15, 1823, by the Marqués de Vivanco, published in Puebla by Pedro de la Rosa; reprinted in Bustamante, *Diario histórico de México*, pp. 204–205. Castillo Negrete, *México en el siglo XIX*, XV, 348, says Bravo entered Oaxaca on February 9.

37. Proclama del Marqués de Vivanco, dando vista que las fuerzas del gral. Echávarri han proclamado el Plan de Casa Mata: Puebla, 8 de febrero de 1823, ms., Hernández y Dávalos Collection in the Benson Latin American Collection at the University of Texas at Austin.

38. This broadside, published in Puebla by Pedro de la Rosa, was reprinted in Bustamante, *Diario histórico de México*, pp. 214–215.

39. Broadsides issued by Don José Morán, Puebla, February 11, 15, and 18 and March 14, 1823.

40. *Bando*, signed Guadalajara, February 27, 1823, Luis Quintanar; *Manifiesto de los gefes que dieron el fausto grito de libertad en Guadalajara*, pp. 2–6; Bustamante, *Diario histórico de México*, pp. 293–294; Luis Pérez Verdía, *Historia particular del estado de Jalisco*, II, 203.

41. Lucio Marmolejo (*Efemérides guanajuatenses, o datos para formar la historia de la ciudad de Guanajuato*, III, 1777) gives February 23 as the date but does not give any particulars concerning the event.

42. *Manifiesto de los gefes que dieron el fausto grito de libertad en Guadalajara*, pp. 2–6.

43. *Querétaro libre*, a printed folder in the Hernández y Dávalos Collection in the Benson Latin American Collection at the University of Texas at Austin; *Manifiesto que al supremo poder ejecutivo, hace de sus operaciones la diputación provincial de Querétaro por el tiempo que tuvo el gobierno administrativo de su provincia*, p. 1.

44. *Acta general de la comisión militar, nombrada por la guarnición de esta plaza, para los usos que adentro se expresan, Zacatecas, 3 marzo de 1823* (this contains a complete documentary account of all action taken by various official bodies of Zacatecas on March 1–2, 1823); Elías Amador, *Bosquejo histórico de Zacatecas*, II, 277; Banegas Galván, *Historia de México*, II, 302.

45. "Acta de San Luis Potosí," March 2, 1823, in Muro, *Historia de San Luis Potosí*, I, 340–343; Bustamante, *Diario histórico de México*, pp. 294–295.

46. Provincial Deputation to the president and chapter of the cathedral, Valladolid, March 3, 1823, in Banegas Galván, *Historia de México*, II, 539 (footnote).

47. Bustamante, *Diario histórico de México*, p. 280.

48. Mexico (Empire, 1822–1823), Junta Nacional Instituyente, *Diario de la junta nacional instituyente del imperio mexicano*, I, 440; hereafter cited as *Diario de la junta nacional instituyente*.

49. "Libertad de Yucatán," in *Gaceta del gobierno de México*, April 12, 1823. The act was signed by Melchor Alvarez (Political Chief), Pedro Bolio (intendant), Pedro Almeida, José Joaquín Torres, Pedro José Guzmán, Basilio María Argaiz, Juan José Espeso, Pablo Moreno, Pedro Pablo de Paz, and others.

50. *Gaceta del gobierno supremo de México,* April 15, 1823.

51. Provincial Deputation of Durango to José Antonio de Echávarri, Durango, March 10, 1823, in *Noticioso general,* April 7, 1823. This communication was signed by Juan Navarro (Political Chief and intendant), Felipe Ramos, Simón de Ochoa, José Francisco del Fierro, José Agustín Gamia, José Miguel de Escontría, Miguel Pérez Gavilán, and Miguel de Zubiría (secretary). Bustamante reported on March 19 that news of the adherence of Durango had reached Mexico City on the preceding day (*Diario histórico de México,* March 19, 1823, p. 319).

52. Ramos Arizpe held the position of precentor of the cathedral of Puebla. He had been greatly disturbed by Iturbide's elevation to emperor. About that time he and Joaquín Leño of Jalapa began to confer about which provinces would be best in which to light the fires of liberty. Ramos Arizpe refused the Cross of Honor of Guadalupe offered him by Iturbide. In August, he left Puebla for Saltillo, where he worked toward the restoration to the nation of the rights usurped by Iturbide. He is said to have been the mind behind the de la Garza revolt (*La verdad destruye a la calumnia,* pp. 1–5). In spite of the failure of the de la Garza revolt, Ramos Arizpe continued to scout for an opportunity to overthrow the Iturbide regime. On November 16, 1822, he wrote from his birthplace (San Nicolás de la Capellanía), in Coahuila, to the ecclesiastical chapter of the cathedral of Puebla asking to be granted a four-month leave of absence, because of ill health (Libro de actas del cabildo eclesiástico de Puebla, años 1821–1824, in the Archives of the cathedral of Puebla). In the same month, according to José Antonio Mejía, a cavalry captain and aide-de-camp of Gen. Nicolás Bravo, Ramos Arizpe had arranged with a Lt. Castillón to keep him informed of conditions in Mexico City and the surrounding provinces with the object of reestablishing liberty in the country and doing away with the despot. Mejía became another of Ramos Arizpe's informants and sent to him through Castillón the Plan of Veracruz, as proclaimed by generals Guadalupe Victoria and Santa Anna and at Chilapa by generals Bravo and Guerrero and an infinite number of other papers and proclamations (Mejía to Manuel Rosales, Tulancingo, April 16, 1823). A manuscript copy of this letter made by Manuel Rosales at Monterrey, May 12, 1824, is in the Bexar Archives at the University of Texas at Austin.

53. *La verdad destruye a la calumnia,* p. 3; Alamán, *Historia de Méjico,* V, 462, pictures Ramos Arizpe, mounted on a mule with a blunderbuss in his saddlebag, going about exciting the people with the most violent language and gestures.

54. (1) Regardless of the bases on which the Congress might be convoked, all electoral councils should be free to instruct their electors and deputies as they saw fit without limitations other than those of sustaining and defending the absolute independence of the country, the Apostolic Roman Catholic religion to the exclusion of all others, the union of the country, and the freedom of the national representation.

(2) Congress within eight days after its installation should review in its entirety the plan of convocation under which it was called and reorganize the national representation along the incontestable principles of natural and public right (*Acta del juramento solemne de adhesión al Plan de Casa Mata, bajo la fórmula que en ella se contiene con las modificaciones que van a su fin por la villa del Saltillo,* 1823, leaf 3).

55. Ramos Arizpe (president), José León Lobo Guerrero (vice-president), José

Vivero, Rafael González, Julián de Arrete, José Antonio Rodríguez, Francisco Eusebio de Arizpe, and José Rafael de Llano (secretary) composed the junta. The original copy of the act is in the Archivo General del Estado de Coahuila, Saltillo, Coahuila. Another copy, Junta Gubernativa de Provincia to Ayuntamiento de Saltillo, Monterrey, March 7, 1823, is in the Archivo General del Estado de Nuevo León, Monterrey.

56. In the Archivo del Estado de Nuevo León, Monterrey, Nuevo León, are the original replies of the various towns to the junta. The dates are from March 7 to March 16, with those of March 7, 8, 9, and 10 predominating.

57. A certified copy made on March 10, 1823, by Joaquín Palou (secretary in charge of the office of the Commandant-General) containing the complete proceedings of the Saltillo junta with the signatures of its members is in the Benson Latin American Collection at the University of Texas at Austin.

58. Ramos Arizpe and Llano to the Junta Gubernativa de la Provincia de Nuevo León, Rinconada, March 10, 1823, ms., Archivo General del Gobierno del Estado de Nuevo León, año 1823, legajo 2, carpeta 2.

59. Lemus to the president and members of the Nuevo León Junta, Hacienda de Santa María, March 11, 1823, and Valle de la Capellanía, March 11, 1823, mss., Archivo General del Gobierno del Estado de Nuevo León, año 1823, legajo 7, carpeta 2, documents 17 and 21.

60. Lemus to the president and members of the Nuevo León Junta, Hacienda de Santa María, March 11, 1823, and Valle de la Capellanía, March 11, 1823, mss., Archivo General del Gobierno del Estado de Nuevo León, año 1823, legajo 7, carpeta 2, documents 17 and 21.

61. Ramos Arizpe and Llano to the vice-president of the Nuevo León junta, Saltillo, March 11, 1823, ms., Archivo General del Gobierno del Estado de Nuevo León, año 1823, legajo 7, carpeta 2, document 12.

62. Ramos Arizpe to Lemus, Saltillo, March 13, 1823, ms., Archivo General del Gobierno del Estado de Nuevo León, año 1823, legajo 7, carpeta 2, document 20.

63. Ramos Arizpe and Llano to López, Saltillo, March 13, 1823, ms., Archivo General del Gobierno del Estado de Nuevo León, año 1823, legajo 7, carpeta 2, document 20.

64. Ramos Arizpe to López, Campo de los Molinos de Arizpe sobre Saltillo, March 13, 1823, ms., Archivo General del Gobierno del Estado de Nuevo León, año 1823, legajo 7, carpeta 2, document 20.

65. Ayuntamiento de Saltillo to Sres. Comisionados por la Junta Gubernativa del N.R. de L., Saltillo, March 13, 1823, ms., Archivo General del Gobierno del Estado de Nuevo León, año 1823, legajo 7, carpeta 2, document 20.

66. Ayuntamiento de Saltillo to Señores Comisionados por la Junta Gubernativa del N.R. de L., Saltillo, March 12, 1823; Pedro Lemus to the president and members of the Governing Junta of Nuevo León, Saltillo, March 15, 1823, ms., Archivo General del Gobierno del Estado de Nuevo León, año 1823, legajo 7, carpeta 2, document 24.

67. Acta del juramento solemne de adhesión al Plan de Casa Mata, bajo la fórmula que en ella se contiene con las modificaciones que van a su fin por la villa del Saltillo, leaf 3.

68. The proceedings of the meetings of the Provincial Deputations are to be

found in *Libro de asientos de órdenes y decretos circulados por el gobierno en este año de 1823 en esta congregación del Refugio*, ms., Alejandro Prieto Papers at the University of Texas at Austin, leaves 82–83. Members of the Provincial Deputation of Nuevo Santander at this time were José María Gutiérrez de Lara, Pedro Paredes y Serna, José Manuel de Zozaya, Juan Francisco Gutiérrez, Ignacio Peña, Juan Bautista de la Garza, and Lucas de la Garza, with José Antonio Guzmán and Joaquín Benítez as alternates. Juan de Echandía was Political Chief of the province.

69. Manuel Gil y Sáenz, *Compendio histórico, geográfico y estadístico del estado de Tabasco*, p. 167.

70. Manuscript circular, signed Gaspar López, Saltillo, March 10, 1823, in Bexar Archives at the University of Texas at Austin.

71. Governing Council of Texas to the Supreme Executive Power, San Fernando de Béjar, June 11, 1823. This document signed by Baron de Bastrop (vice-president), Erasmo Seguín, Juan de Castañeda, José Antonio Navarro, and José Antonio Saucedo (secretary) was published in *Aguila mexicana*, July 18 and 19, 1823, under the title "Oficio dirigido al Supremo Poder Ejecutivo a consecuencias del que con fecha 28 de abril remitió el Exmo. Sr. secretario de estado Don José Ignacio García Illueca a la Exma. Diputación Provincial del Nuevo Reyno de León."

72. Governing Council of Texas to the Supreme Executive Power, San Fernando de Béjar, June 11, 1823, in *Aguila mexicana*, July 19, 1823.

73. José Antonio de Echávarri to Provincial Deputation of México, Casa Mata, February 1, 1823, in [*Official Report of the Provincial Deputation of México of March 6, 1823*], p. 5. This 6-page official report was printed untitled in Mexico by Alejandro Valdés in 1823. It is also to be found under the title "Manifiesto de la Diputación Provincial de México sobre la conducto que observa para lograr el restablecimiento del Congreso constituyente," in José María Luis Mora, *Obra política*, II, 19–29, in *Obras completas*.

74. Bustamante, *Diario histórico de México*, p. 165. Iturbide condemned Echávarri and his supporters for having sent only an officer with the Plan. Iturbide said that by so doing Echávarri did not carry out Article 7, which provided that a *comisión* would be provided to carry the act to Iturbide. He interpreted this to mean that more than one person would be sent with the message. He said also that, by the time the commissioner reached him, Echávarri and his forces had taken over all strategic locations instead of waiting to hear what Iturbide thought of the Plan (Iturbide, *Manifiesto del general d. Agustín de Iturbide*, p. 54). It might be pointed out here that Echávarri and his men sent only one commissioner to Santa Anna and only one to each individual or body to whom they sent the Plan.

75. Provincial Deputation of México to Minister of Domestic and Foreign Affairs, February 26, 1823, in [*Official Report of the Provincial Deputation of México*], p. 6; and Mora, *Obra política*, II, 26.

76. Bustamante, *Diario histórico de México*, p. 138.

77. Ibid., pp. 164–165; Banegas Galván, *Historia de México*, II, 278. The modified version of the Plan of Casa Mata is to be found in Bustamante, *Diario histórico de México*, pp. 170–172 and Olavarría y Ferrari, *México independiente*, p. 88. The complete Plan is given in Miguel M. Lerdo de Tejada, *Apuntes de la heróica ciudad de Veracruz*, II, 262–263; Zavala, *Ensayo histórico*, I, 164–165; Zamacois, *Historia de Méjico*, XI, 449–450; *Diario de la junta nacional instituyente del imperio mexicano*, I,

377–379; Iturbide, *Manifiesto*, pp. 113–116, and *Breve diseño crítico de la emancipación y libertad de la nación mexicana*, pp. 118–121; and an English translation in Benson, "The Plan of Casa Mata," pp. 49–50. Veracruz had adopted the Plan of Veracruz, which had strongly denounced Iturbide. It is not surprising, therefore, that the article stating that a committee should take copies of the Plan of the Casa Mata to Mexico City to be placed in the hands of the emperor was omitted from the printed version issued by the Municipal Council of Veracruz.

78. Alamán, *Historia de Méjico*, V, 715.

79. The Junta Nacional Instituyente came into existence in November 1822. On October 31, 1822, Iturbide declared the first Constituent Congress dissolved and said that until a new Congress could be called the national representation would be invested in a junta composed of two deputies from each province with a large representation in the dissolved body and of one deputy for each province with a small representation. These deputies were to be designated by him (*Gaceta del gobierno imperial de México*, November 5, 1822). Iturbide appointed the forty-five deputies and eight alternates and the junta began its session on November 2 (ibid., November 7, 1822).

80. *Diario de la junta nacional instituyente*, I, 377, 380.

81. Iturbide, from his statement, seems to have expected Echávarri and his army to have sat calmly awaiting a reply while their commissioners negotiated with him.

82. *Gaceta del gobierno imperial de México*, February 11, 1823; Bustamante, *Diario histórico de México*, p. 175.

83. Banegas Galván, *Historia de México*, II, 281; Bustamante, *Diario histórico de México*, pp. 170, 178. Bustamante says that, before the departure of this group on February 11, however, José Demetrio Moreno was named to replace Robles; nonetheless, available documents issued by the commissioners each time list Robles as one of the signers.

84. Manuel Rivera Cambas, *Historia antigua y moderna de la Jalapa y de las revoluciones del estado de Veracruz*, II, 289.

85. *Diario de la junta nacional instituyente*, I, 381–391; *Gaceta del gobierno imperial de México*, February 20 and 22.

86. [*Official Report of the Provincial Deputation of México*], March 6, 1823, p. 5; Mora, *Obra política*, II, 24–25.

87. Ibid., pp. 5–6.

88. Bustamante, *Diario histórico de México*, p. 275.

89. Chiapas never did adopt the Plan. When first presented to that province, it was rejected. Later, when Vicente Filisola proposed that Chiapas join Guatemala, Chiapas also rejected that proposal and began setting up a government independent of both Mexico and Guatemala (Trens, *Historia de Chiapas*, pp. 229–231). Nothing has been found in regard to the acts of the Provincial Deputations of the provinces of Sonora and Sinaloa, New Mexico, and Tlaxcala.

90. *Sin leyes no hay libertad ni hay leyes si no se observen o sea manifiesto que hace la diputación provincial gubernativa de Michoacán a sus habitantes sobre los acontecimientos de estos últimos días*, pp. 6–7. This manifesto was signed by the members of the Provincial Deputation of Michoacán, March 8, 1823.

91. Acta de Toluca sobre la remisión de un diputado a Puebla, leaf 3; Provincial Deputation of Guanajuato to the Provincial Deputation of Querétaro, Guana-

juato, March 10, 1823, mss., Hernández y Dávalos Collection at the University of Texas at Austin.

92. Ibid.

93. Provincial Deputation of Querétaro to Mariano Michelena, Querétaro, March 13, 1823; Provincial Deputation of Querétaro to Provincial Deputation of Michoacán, Querétaro, March 13, 1823; Provincial Deputation of Querétaro to Mariano Michelena, Querétaro, March 12, 1823, mss., Hernández y Dávalos Collection at the University of Texas at Austin.

94. Provincial Deputation of Guanajuato to the Political Chief of the province of Querétaro, Guanajuato, March 14, 1823, ms., Hernández y Dávalos Collection at the University of Texas at Austin.

95. Ibid.

96. Michelena to the Political Chief of the province of Querétaro, San Juan del Río, March 12, 1823. A copy of this letter forwarded from the Provincial Deputation of Querétaro to the Provincial Deputation of the Eastern Interior Provinces is in the Bexar Archives at the University of Texas at Austin.

97. Juan José García to Michelena, Querétaro, March 22, 1823, ms., Hernández y Dávalos Collection at the University of Texas at Austin.

98. José María Ortiz, secretary of the Provincial Deputation of Michoacán, to Michelena, Valladolid, March 28, 1823, ms., Hernández y Dávalos Collection at the University of Texas at Austin.

99. "Comunicación de los comisionados a Echávarri, Puebla, February 13, 1823," in Banegas Galván, *Historia de México,* II, 288–290.

100. Ibid., II, 289–290. Banegas Galván quotes from the minutes of the meeting of February 17 at Jalapa, which he found in the Archivo General de la Nación.

101. Quoted in full in ibid., II, 293.

102. "Convenio," in *Gaceta del gobierno imperial de México,* March 6, 1823.

103. Bustamante, *Diario histórico de México,* pp. 251–252.

104. Session of February 26, 1823, in *Diario de la junta nacional instituyente,* I, 433, 435–436.

105. No account of Iturbide's instructions to his commissioners has been found, but the report of his commissioners published in *Gaceta del gobierno imperial de México,* March 15, 1823, and the account of the conferences in Banegas Galván, *Historia de México,* II, 288–294, make it clear that a change of Article 2, which stated that the convocation of the Congress should be made on the basis prescribed for the first one, was Iturbide's first concern.

106. *Gaceta del gobierno imperial de México,* February 25, 1823.

107. Banegas Galván, *Historia de México,* II, 292.

108. *Gaceta del gobierno imperial de México,* March 15, 1823.

109. Ibid.; Mora, *Obra política,* II, 26–28.

110. *Gaceta extraordinaria del gobierno imperial de México,* March 5, 1823.

111. Bustamante, *Diario histórico de México,* p. 290.

112. Tomás Alamán was the uncle of Lucas Alamán

113. *Actas del congreso constituyente,* IV, 5. Alamán's argument here is most surprising in the light of what Lucas Alamán wrote in his *Historia de Méjico,* V, 739, where he accused Michelena of having initiated federalism in Mexico at the meeting held in Puebla on March 15, 1823, eight days after Tomás Alamán had argued in

Congress that nothing could be done until the provinces had been heard from. Lucas Alamán condemned Michelena for also purportedly having spoken in favor of hearing the provinces before proceeding to recognize Congress (for further details on this matter, see note 118 below).

114. *Actas del congreso constituyente,* IV, 15, 20.

115. Ibid., pp. 44–45.

116. *Acta de la junta de Puebla, sobre la reinstalación del congreso mexicano,* p. 4. Those proceedings were printed in a 2-page folder in Puebla without title or place of imprint and reprinted in Mexico with the above-cited title. Copies of both are in the Bexar Archives at the University of Texas.

117. *Actas del congreso constituyente,* IV, 45–52.

118. Alamán, Bustamante, and Banegas Galván all date the beginning of federalism from this meeting. All say that representatives from other Provincial Deputations took part in it and that Michelena, as a representative of the Provincial Deputation of Michoacán, at that time proposed the federalism of the provinces (Alamán, *Historia de Méjico,* V, 739; Bustamante, *Historia del emperador d. Augustín de Iturbide,* p. 111; Carlos María Bustamante, *El honor y patriotismo del general d. Nicolás Bravo,* p. 35; Banegas Galván, *Historia de México,* II, 323). It appears that Alamán got his authority from Bustamante. He stated that Michelena and the representatives of the Provincial Deputations took part and that "it was said" that Michelena proposed the federation of the provinces at the meeting. But the proceedings of this meeting were printed. They specifically record the names of those who attended and what was said. Bustamante himself preserved for us in his manuscript volume of his "Diario histórico de México, 1822–1823" the printed proceedings of the event, entitled *Firmeza de los poblanos con la comisión de México.* The name of Michelena does not appear, nor do those of representatives of other Provincial Deputations. The entire discussion revolved around whether the recalled Congress should be recognized. Several speakers harshly condemned Iturbide, but no mention was made of federation or of the Provincial Deputations.

It is very doubtful that Michelena had reached Puebla at that time. At nine-thirty on the night of March 12, he was writing a letter from San Juan del Río in the province of Querétaro. To go from there to Puebla entailed a long, circuitous mountain journey, especially considering the fact that Iturbide had issued an order for Michelena's arrest and Iturbide's forces still held Mexico City. To have been in Puebla at the hour of the meeting, Michelena would have to have made the journey either by horseback or by coach in less than forty-six hours.

119. *Firmeza de los poblanos con la comisión de México.* Bustamanate, commenting on the meeting in his diary on March 22, 1823, says: "The act of Puebla of the fifteenth of this month has been republished in Mexico City under the title *Firmeza de los poblanos, con la comisión de México.* That document is worthy of being transcribed in our annals, and therefore we add the imprint to these historical notes" (*Diario histórico de México,* pp. 326–327).

120. *Actas del congreso constituyente,* IV, 55.

121. Ibid., IV, 66–68.

122. Ibid., IV, 68.

123. Ibid., IV, 96–97.

6. Attitude of the Provincial Deputations toward a New Congress

1. Mateos, *Historia parlamentaria*, II, 188.

2. According to the report of these commissioners, they were asked to attend the meeting ("Representación de los comisionados de las provincias, al soberano congreso," in *Aguila mexicana*, May 5, 1823). Bustamante says that they presented themselves asking for a new Congress. Then he continues: "This is a faction of demagogues who are trying to place a large portion of clergymen and monarchists [*serviles*] in the Legislature that they are proposing to form, because they know that their foolish pretension will get nowhere in the present Congress. They speak their mind as if they were possessed by the devil and refuse to listen to reason. We have in these men alone the germ of a frightful revolution, which the Congress will be able to avert by setting the misled provinces right with good writings and by opening a literary fight in which reason will triumph. This America is going to be a theater of discord, stirred up by the clergy and bodies of aristocrats" (Bustamante, *Diario histórico de México*, p. 367).

3. *Aguila mexicana*, May 5, 1823.

4. Valentín Gómez Farías, *Voto particular del sr. Gómez Farías como individuo de la comisión especial nombrada por su soberano congreso, para examinar la cuestión, de si debe o no convocar un nuevo congreso*, p. 1.

5. This report, signed April 12, 1823, and presented to Congress two days later, was printed in full in *Aguila mexicana*, May 11–20, 1823.

6. *Dictamen de la comisión especial de convocatoria para un nuevo congreso*, p. 22.

7. "Voto particular del Lic. D. Carlos María de Bustamante, sobre la ninguna necesidad que hay de formar una nueva convocatoria de congreso," in *Abispa de Chilpancingo, suplemento del 19 de Abril de 1823*, pp. 2–16. This document was written on or before April 4, the date it bears. When Congress failed to order it published and circulated but did order the *Voto particular* of Gómez Farías published, Bustamante himself had his published.

8. *Aguila mexicana*, April 15, 1823; *Actas del congreso constituyente mexicano*, IV, 277.

9. Bustamante, *Diario histórico de México*, p. 367.

10. Mier to the Ayuntamiento of Monterrey, April 23, 1823, in Mier, *Diez cartas*, p. 12.

11. Mier to Cantú, México, June 2, 1823, in Cossío, *Historia de Nuevo León*, V, 36. Cantú was a member of the Municipal Council of Monterrey.

12. Mateos, *Historia parlamentaria*, II, 369.

13. Ibid., II, 369. Godoy made these statements in the session of May 14. On that date José María Bustamante, one of the deputies from the province of Guanajuato, said that he wanted to assure Congress that he had not been responsible for the meeting held by the Provincial Deputation of Guanajuato on April 30 to decide whether the existing Congress should constitute the nation or should call another. He said that, according to the account in *El anunciador mexicano* (no. 11), the meeting was held at the request of the Guanajuato deputies. Godoy immediately arose to say that he was the one who had written to the Deputation for its opinion on the matter.

14. Unsigned manuscript, dated April 1, 1823, giving an account of the installation on that date of the Provincial Deputation of Nuevo León, Coahuila, and Texas. The interlinear notes are in the hand of Ramos Arizpe. The manuscript is in the Archivo General del Estado de Nuevo León, legajo 7, carpeta 2. Another manuscript dated April 4, 1823, signed by Juan Nepomuceno de la Peña and José María Parras y Ballesteros, that contains the instructions of its deputies is in the Bexar Archives at the University of Texas at Austin.

15. A manuscript copy of the minutes of this meeting is in the Bexar Archives at the University of Texas at Austin. The document carries the signatures of José Bernardino Cantú, José Antonio Rodríguez, Juan Nepomuceno de la Peña, Julián de Arrete, José María Parras, and José Rafael de Llano (secretary). It is dated Saltillo, April 23, 1823, apparently the date the document was received in Saltillo. It had been voted at the Monterrey meeting that copies of the minutes should be circulated throughout the provinces.

16. "Representación de los comisionados de las provincias al soberano congreso," signed April 18, 1823, by Martín García for Michoacán, Tomás Vargas and Victor Rafael Márquez for San Luis Potosí, Anastacio Ochoa for Querétaro, Prisciliano Sánchez and Juan Cayetano Portugal for Guadalajara, Francisco de Arrieta and Santos Vélez for Zacatecas, Juan Ignacio Godoy for Guanajuato, and Vicente Manero Enbides for Oaxaca, in *Aguila mexicana*, May 5–6, 1823.

17. *Representación que la diputación provincial de Puebla dirige al soberano congreso pidiéndole se sirva a expedir nueva convocatoria*, pp. 7–11. On November 16, 1821, the Provincial Deputation of Puebla had informed the Sovereign Provisional Governing Junta that it favored the election of deputies to the Congress in conformity with the electoral law set forth in the Spanish Constitution of 1812. It expressed strong disapproval of the election of deputies based on classes, as was being considered.

18. Gómez Farías, *Voto particular*.

19. Mateos, *Historia parlamentaria*, II, 317, 327, 334; *Aguila mexicana*, May 6 and 20, 1823. Bustamante (*Diario histórico de México*, p. 389) says that a committee appointed on May 2 was named to draft a Constitution. He was obviously wrong because Mateos and the *Aguila mexicana* in reporting the minutes of the meeting agreed that the committee was instructed only to study the proposal that a draft be made.

20. Mateos (*Historia parlamentaria*, II, 369) omits the names of Bocanegra and Gómez Farías, but the *Aguila mexicana* (May 16, 1823) included them in its account of that session of Congress, and Mier in his "Voto particular del Doctor Mier" (in *Plan de constitución política de la nación mexicana*, p. 66) said that they were members of the committee.

21. Nettie Lee Benson, "Servando Teresa de Mier, Federalist," *Hispanic American Historical Review* 28 (November 1948): 515–516; José Eleuterio González, *Biografía del benemérito mexicano de Servando Teresa de Mier Noriega y Guerra*, p. 351; *Fray Servando Teresa de Mier*, ed. Edmundo O'Gorman, p. 126; Bustamante, *Historia del emperador d. Agustín de Iturbide*, p. 201.

22. Mateos, *Historia parlamentaria*, II, 372; *Aguila mexicana*, May 23, 1823; *Gaceta del gobierno supremo de México*, May 24, 1823. The "Bases de república federa-

tiva" was completed and signed by Mier's handpicked committee on May 16, 1823. Gómez Farías and Javier Bustamante did not sign the draft (*Plan de constitución política de la nación mexicana*, pp. 64, 65).

23. Mier to Cantú, México, June 25, 1823, in Cossío, *Historia de Nuevo León*, V, 41.

24. It was composed of Luis Quintanar (Political Chief), Antonio Basilio Gutiérrez y Ulloa (intendant), Juan Cayetano Portugal, José Casal y Blanco, José de Jesús Huerta, Urbano Sanromán, Domingo González Maxemin, and Pedro Vélez (secretary).

25. That decree instructed all governmental bodies on the manner in which they were to take the oath of allegiance to the government.

26. "Resoluciones de la provincia de Guadalajara, y sucesos ocurridos en la misma," in *Aguila mexicana*, May 22, 1823.

27. Minutes of the special session of May 12, 1823, of the Provincial Deputation of Guadalajara, in "Resoluciones de la provincia de Guadalajara, y sucesos ocurridos en la misma."

28. *Disolución del congreso mexicano, por los pueblos y manifiesto de la junta provincial de Nueva Galicia*, pp. 1–8.

29. Session of Congress of May 28, 1823, in *Aguila mexicana*, June 1, 1823; Mateos, *Historia parlamentaria*, II, 382.

30. "Acta de Zacatecas," in *Aguila mexicana*, July 3–4, 1823.

31. Eligio Ancona, *Historia de Yucatán*, III, 269; Albino Acereto, "Historia política desde el descubrimiento Europeo hasta 1920," in *Enciclopedia yucatanense*, III, 177.

32. Michoacán's deputies were Francisco Argandar, Juan Nepomuceno Foncerrado y Soravilla, Antonio Castro, Agustín Tapia, Francisco Manuel Sánchez de Tagle, José María Cabrera, Camilo Camacho, José María Abarca, Mariano Anzoreña, Antonio Cumplido, Rudecindo Villanueva, Antonio Aguila, Ignacio Izazaga, and Mariano Tercero; alternates were José Ignacio del Río and José Manuel Galván (*El sol*, February 2, 1822). The Provincial Deputation of Michoacán, like some of the others, felt that such a large number of deputies placed an unnecessary burden on the province.

33. It is not known whether this letter reached the deputies in Mexico City, but it was sent to the editors of the *Aguila mexicana* for publication and appeared May 20, 1823.

34. José María Bustamante told Congress on May 14 that a detailed account of the meeting had been printed in no. 11 of *El anunciador mexicano* (Mateos, *Historia parlamentaria*, II, 369). It has not been located.

35. Chico to Alamán, Guanajuato, May 26, 1823, in *Gaceta del gobierno supremo de México*, June 3, 1823.

36. José Miguel Llorente to editors of *Aguila mexicana*, Guanajuato, May 26, 1823, in *Aguila mexicana*, June 1, 1823.

37. Otero to the Marqués de Vivanco, Guanajuato, May 23, 1823. The original letter is in the Hernández y Dávalos Collection in the Benson Latin American Collection at the University of Texas at Austin.

38. Four Guanajuato deputies (Francisco Uraga, Juan Ignacio Godoy, Miguel Septién, and José Ignacio Espinosa) voted on May 21 in favor of the immediate

issuing of the convocation for a new Congress. Only José María Bustamante voted in the negative (Mateos, *Historia parlamentaria*, II, 374).

39. Chico to Alamán, Guanajuato, May 26, 1823, in *Gaceta del gobierno supremo de México*, June 3, 1823; Llorente to editors of *Aguila mexicana*, Guanajuato, May 26, 1823.

40. Mateos, *Historia parlamentaria*, II, 384; *Aguila mexicana*, June 3, 1823.

41. Municipal Council of Querétaro to the Provincial Deputation of Querétaro, May 17, 1823, in *Contestación que dió el ayuntamiento constitucional de Querétaro a la excma. diputación provincial, manifestando su opinión sobre nueva convocatoria.*

42. Provincial Deputation of Querétaro to Osores, Querétaro, May 20, 1823, in *Gaceta extraordinaria de gobierno supremo de México,* May 28, 1823. A copy of this letter was sent on May 24 by Juan José García, Political Chief of Querétaro, to Alamán, Minister of Domestic Affairs, in reply to his letter of May 21 regarding events occurring in Guadalajara.

43. Minutes of the meeting of the Provincial Deputation of Querétaro, the Municipal Council of Querétaro, and Luis Cortazar, the Commandant-General of the province, Querétaro, June 12, 1823, in *Aguila mexicana,* June 28, 1823.

44. (1) Congress should be made to understand that the sole cause of the evils enveloping the country was its delay in calling a new Congress. (2) Those evils had obliged the Provincial Deputation to adopt measures in order to guard against any aggression and at the same time to prevent anarchy. (3) Congress would not be recognized except as a body to convoke the new Congress; however, orders issued by the restored power and the Supreme Executive Power would be obeyed if approved by the Deputation. (4) The Provincial Deputations of Guanajuato and Michoacán should be invited to join Querétaro in this action.

45. "Triunfo de la razón en la junta promovida por el general Santana en S. Luis Potosí," in *Aguila mexicana,* June 8, 1823.

46. *Aguila mexicana,* June 15, 1823. The above-cited *Voto* was not printed in the *Aguila mexicana,* and no copy of it has yet been located.

47. Santa Anna on orders from Guadalupe Victoria had set sail on March 19, 1823, from Veracruz via Tampico for the Eastern Interior Provinces with the purpose of consolidating opinion there in favor of the revolt against Iturbide (Santa Anna, *Manifiesto,* p. 11; Muro, *Historia de San Luis Potosí,* I, 348; Lerdo de Tejada, *Apuntes de la heróica ciudad,* II, 263; Wilfrid Hardy Callcott, *Santa Anna,* p. 48). In March 1823, from Altamira, above Tampico, he issued a proclamation to the inhabitants of the Eastern and Western Interior Provinces urging them to adhere to the Plan of Casa Mata (Santa Anna, *Manifiesto,* pp. 21–22; cf. Callcot, *Santa Anna,* p. 49, who says he arrived in Tampico on April 1). From Altamira Santa Anna marched to Tula, where he received word of the restoration of the dissolved Congress and of the establishment of the Supreme Executive Power. From there, on April 23, he offered his felicitations to that body and informed it that he had learned that all the Interior Provinces were in complete sympathy with the revolution. He said he was returning to Mexico City by way of San Luis Potosí unless he received orders to the contrary from the national government (Santa Anna to the Executive Power, Tula, April 23, 1823, in his *Manifiesto,* pp. 24–28). The national government replied on May 7, 1823, granting Santa Anna permission to return to Mexico City provided his presence was not needed in Texas, where there had been opposition

to the overthrow of Iturbide (García Illueca to Santa Anna, México, May 7, 1823, in ibid., pp. 23–24). Santa Anna by that date had reached San Luis Potosí. When he received the reply from the government, he set May 30 as the date for his departure for Mexico City with his troops. Events occurred prior to that date, however, that caused him to change his plan. In the first place, he had reached San Luis Potosí with his supplies depleted and many of his men ill. Furthermore, he had difficulty in obtaining supplies for the march across the country. The Provincial Deputation of San Luis Potosí expressed a willingness to cooperate in obtaining supplies, but stated that it could not possibly provide him with the equipment that he requested. Added to the problem of lack of supplies was insubordination of his troops and a fatal clash between the infantry and the cavalry. The bad conduct of the troops greatly displeased the people of San Luis Potosí. It was at that stage that news arrived of events taking place in Guadalajara, and a meeting was called at Santa Anna's request to consider the news.

48. The act was then signed by members of the Provincial Deputation of San Luis Potosí and its Municipal Council and by Santa Anna and the two commissioners, Vargas and Márquez ("Triunfo de la razón," in *Aguila mexicana*, June 8, 1823).

49. Mateos, *Historia parlamentaria*, II, 374. Bustamante in his *Diario histórico de México* (p. 402) says that a group of deputies from the province of México became so angry over the matter that they proposed to withdraw from Congress.

50. Bustamante, *Diario histórico de México*, p. 407.

51. Benson, "Servando Teresa de Mier, Federalist," p. 516.

52. The fact that the *Aguila mexicana* in its report of the May 21 session omitted the word "immediately" from the article in regard to the convocation of the new Congress and stated that it had resolved that "the existing body should form the basis of the future constitution of the nation and have it printed and circulated" no doubt served to confirm that lack of confidence (*Aguila mexicana*, May 23, 1823). The actual wording of the article read: "The project of the 'Bases of a Federal Republic' which has been drawn up by a congressional committee shall be published and circulated immediately" (Mateos, *Historia parlamentaria*, II, 374; *Gaceta del gobierno supremo de México*, May 24, 1823).

The article as a matter of fact did not state that this project should form the basis of the future Constitution. That some members meant and hoped that it would is evidenced by Bustamante, Mier, and Bocanegra, all of whom were members of the committee that had composed it. Bustamante wrote in his *Diario histórico de México* (p. 412) on May 28: "The bases for the future constitution for a federal republic has been read today in Congress. . . ." Mier, on May 14, 1823, wrote to Ramos Arizpe, "Next week the liberal bases for a representative federal republic with its senate and its Congress in each province and everything else that you can crave, all discussed at my home, will appear. Afterward the convocation of your long-desired new Congress will follow" (Cossío, *Historia de Nuevo León*, V, 85). Bocanegra, who had opposed the plan of convoking a new Congress, in explaining why he had done so, said, "by May 16, the basis the congressional committee named to draw up the constitutional bases had already presented its plan of a political constitution for the Mexican nation under the title 'Bases for a Federal Republic'!" (Bocanegra, *Memorias*, I, 219). As Bocanegra himself stated, Congress at the same time that it voted to issue the convocation also voted immediately that, until the new Congress met, the old one should devote its energy to organizing the treasury, the army, and the administration of justice, all of which work was the natural prerogative of a constituent body.

7. Evolution of the Pioneer State Legislatures

1. *Manifiesto de los liberales de Guadalajara, a sus conciudadanos,* pp. 1–2.
2. "Resoluciones de la provincia de Guadalajara, y sucesos ocurridos en la misma," in *Aguila mexicana,* May 22, 1823.
3. Minutes of the special session of May 12 of the Provincial Deputation of Guadalajara, in ibid.
4. *Disolución del congreso mexicano por el voto de los pueblos y manifiesto de la junta provincial de Nueva Galicia,* pp. 1–8.
5. Quintanar to the Governor of Texas, Guadalajara, May 12, 1823. A printed circular in the Bexar Archives, University of Texas at Austin.
6. "Proclama del Sr. Quintanar a los habitantes de Nueva Galicia sobre la separación del Congreso mexicano," in *Aguila mexicana,* May 23, 1823.
7. "Gobierno político superior de Nueva Galicia: Circular," signed Luis Quintanar, May 13, 1823, in *Aguila mexicana,* May 23, 1823.
8. Luis Quintanar to the Municipal Council of Béxar, June 23, 1823, a broadside in the Bexar Archives at the University of Texas at Austin. All the Provincial Deputations in Mexico had adopted a similar practice from the time of their adherence to the Plan of Casa Mata. This correspondence and communication between the Provincial Deputations of the country is reminiscent of the circular letters of the governors of an earlier period in the history of the United States. In the Bexar Archives can be found communications for the period from the Provincial Deputations throughout Mexico. Whenever an important event occurred or a step was taken by one of those bodies, a full account of it was published and copies were sent to all parts of the country.
9. Minutes of the meeting of the Provincial Deputation of Guadalajara of June 5, 1823, in *Gaceta del gobierno supremo de México,* June 5, 1823; *El sol,* June 15, 1823; and Pérez Verdía, *Historia particular,* II, 206–207. A printed folder containing the minutes and issued at Guadalajara is also in the Bexar Archives, University of Texas at Austin.
10. Quintanar to the Minister of Domestic and Foreign Affairs, Guadalajara, June 6, 1823, in *Gaceta del gobierno supremo de México,* June 14, 1823.
11. Minutes of the special session of the Provincial Deputation of Guadalajara of June 16, 1823, pp. 7–9. These minutes were printed in Guadalajara by Urbano Sanromán. The 11-page document has no title.
12. *Manifiesto del capitán-general a los habitantes del estado libre de Xalisco,* signed Luis Quintanar, Guadalajara, June 21, 1823.
13. Quintanar to the Municipal Council of San Fernando de Béjar, Texas, signed Luis Quintanar, Guadalajara, June 23, 1823, a printed circular headed *Gobernación del Estado Libre de Xalisco* in the Bexar Archives, University of Texas at Austin.
14. The printed 12-page official order (*bando*) signed by Quintanar, Guadalajara, July 1, 1823, and headed *El ciudadano Luis Quintanar, Gobernador del Estado Libre de Xalisco* is in the Bexar Archives, University of Texas at Austin. The minutes

of the meeting of June 27 are in the *Aguila mexicana,* July 14–15, 1823; and Bocanegra (*Memorias,* I, 266–267) gives the resolutions adopted at the meeting.

15. Luis Quintanar to the Municipal Council of San Fernando de Béjar, Texas,
signed, Guadalajara, July 1, 1823, an untitled printed circular in the Bexar Archives,
University of Texas at Austin.

16. "Bando publicado el 11 del corriente en la ciudad de Guadalajara," in *Aguila
mexicana,* September 21, 1823.

17. Elected were Prisciliano Sánchez, Pedro Vélez, Dr. José María Gil, Antonio
Méndez, Anastacio Bustamante, José Miguel Gordoa, Esteban Huerta, José María
Castillo Portugal, Juan Nepomuceno Cumplido, Urbano Sanromán, Vicente Ríos,
Manuel Cervantes, Santiago Guzmán, and Ignacio Navarrete; alternates were
Dr. Diego Aranda, José Ignacio Cañedo, Justo Corro, Esteban Arechiga, and
Rafael Mendoza (*Aguila mexicana,* September 19, 1823). It is interesting to note
here that seven of the deputies elected to the first Constituent Congress of Jalisco
had seen prior service in legislative bodies: Gordoa in the Spanish Cortes; Sánchez,
Cañedo, and Castillo Portugal in the national Congress; and Vélez, Gil, and Sanromán in the Provincial Deputation. Two members of the Provincial Deputation—
Jesús Huerta and Juan Cayetano Portugal—won places in the national Congress in
the same election. Gómez Farías and Covarrubias were both reelected to the national Congress; and Juan de Díos Cañedo, José María Castro, Rafael Alderete,
Juan José Romero, José Miguel Ramírez, and Dr. Antonio Montenegro were also
named to the national body.

18. "Manifestación del gobernador del estado al congreso provincial en su in-
stalación," in *Aguila mexicana,* October 4, 1823; "Proclama del ciudadano Luis
Quintanar a los habitantes de Jalisco," in *Aguila mexicana,* September 25, 1823;
"Noticias nacionales," in *Aguila mexicana,* September 21, 1823.

19. "Congreso constituyente del estado de Jalisco," in *Aguila mexicana,* October 15, 1823.

20. Bustamante, *El honor y patriotismo del general d. Nicolás Bravo,* p. 31; Castillo
Negrete, *México,* XV, 348–349.

21. Bustamante, *Diario histórico de México,* p. 303.

22. Banegas Galván (*Historia de México,* II, 404) says the junta was dissolved
early in April. Bustamante (*Diario histórico de México,* p. 381) says it had been dissolved before April 24 and that the Provincial Deputation reassumed its duties.

23. Banegas Galván, *Historia de México,* II, 404.

24. Bustamante, *Diario histórico de México,* p. 388.

25. Bustamante (ibid., p. 425) says that the meeting was called immediately
after the arrival in Oaxaca of the mail carrying the decree of May 21.

26. "Acta de la ciudad de Oaxaca," in *Aguila mexicana,* June 22, 23, and 24, 1823.
The clergy was invited to join in the meeting, but it deferred action until later and
then sent a protest to the national government ("Oaxaca," in *Gaceta del gobierno
supremo de México,* July 3, 1823).

27. The plan did not state how this superior governing junta was to be formed.
The one established by Bravo was composed of members chosen by the Provincial
Deputation of Oaxaca, the Municipal Council of Oaxaca, and the military and ec-
clesiastical officials. Presumably the junta referred to here was similarly constituted.

28. "Bases provisionales con que se emancipó la provincia de Oaxaca," in

Aguila mexicana, June 11, 1823; also issued as a broadside in Oaxaca and republished in Puebla under the title *La provincia de Oaxaca independiente de México.* Lucas Alamán, Minister of Domestic Affairs, reported Oaxaca's action to Congress at a secret session on June 10. On the same day Bustamante told it that Oaxaca had lost its senses and would have to be treated like a crazy person or a child. He asked that no strong measures be adopted against Oaxaca but that the province be tolerated until its federal fever had spent itself; its vertigo had passed; and its reason had returned (Bustamante, *Diario histórico de México,* p. 426). On the same day, however, he wrote a strong reply to Oaxaca's proclamation of independence published under the title *Examen crítico sobre la federación de las provincias* and sent copies to Oaxaca (ibid., p. 427).

29. No account of the call for elections or of their date has been found. Bustamante, on June 18, wrote in his *Diario histórico de México* (p. 440) that Oaxaca had already issued the call for the election of members to its provincial Congress to be installed on July 1. As a rule, at that time it took about ten days for news of events occurring in Oaxaca to reach Mexico City. Hence, it is probable that the call was issued about June 8. Since the Congress was installed on July 6, the elections probably took place during the last two weeks of June. Banegas Galván (*Historia de México,* II, 419) says the final step in the election occurred on July 1. He cites no authority for his assertion.

30. "Bando publicado in Oaxaca," in *Aguila mexicana,* July 15 and 19, 1823; Bustamante, *Diario histórico de México,* pp. 481–482; Victoriano Báez, *Compendio de historia de Oaxaca,* p. 114; Francisco Belmar, *Breve reseña histórica y geográfica del estado de Oaxaca,* p. 26.

31. The third decree issued by the Oaxacan Congress on July 28 set forth the plan of government for the province pending the "proclamation of the general Constitution of the nation and that of the province itself." Article 2 said that the territory previously known as Oaxaca would be called henceforth the "free state of Oaxaca," and Article 3 said that the state of Oaxaca would be composed of twenty districts making up the former intendancy of Oaxaca and listed these districts. Articles 4, 5, 6, 7, and 10 all manifested Oaxaca's intention of remaining a part of the Mexican nation. Oaxaca recognized the existing national government as the center of union of the Mexican federal states until the new Congress had assembled; it recognized the existing body only in the role of convoking a new one and reserved the right to accept or reject all laws issued that might concern the province of Oaxaca. This restriction was applicable only until the new Congress had been installed. All existing laws and orders not contrary to the federal system were recognized as valid, and Oaxaca was not to proclaim its Constitution prior to the adoption of the Constitution of the national government. "Noticias nacionales" (in *Aguila mexicana,* August 13, 1823), "Oficio con que el congreso provincial de Oaxaca da parte de su instalación al Supremo Poder Ejecutivo de la Nación" (in ibid., July 19, 1823), and Bustamante (*Diario histórico de México,* pp. 481–482) all explain Oaxaca's attitude toward the national government.

32. Ancona, *Historia de Yucatán,* III, 265.

33. A manifesto drawn up by the committee, the committee's recommendations, and the acts of the Provincial Deputation were printed in *Aguila mexicana,* May 13, 14, and 15, 1823.

34. Ibid.; Ancona, *Historia de Yucatán,* III, 272–273.

35. Ibid., III, 274–275; "Viva la república federada de Yucatán," in *Aguila mexicana,* June 20, 1823.

36. Manuel León, Pablo Moreno, Perfecto Barranda, José María Meneses, and Benito Aznar were named alternates (ibid.; Ancona, *Historia de Yucatán,* III, 275–276).

37. "Viva la república federada de Yucatán." The acts of the meetings of May 29–30 are given in full. Also see Ancona, *Historia de Yucatán,* III, 277–278; Acereto, "Historia política desde el descubrimiento Europeo hasta 1920," III, 179–180.

38. Ibid.; Ancona, *Historia de Yucatán,* III, 278–279; "Viva la unión del estado yucateco," signed Campeche, May 31, 1823, in *Aguila mexicana,* July 15, 1823.

39. "La junta provisional de la republica de Yucatán a sus habitantes," in *Aguila mexicana,* July 16, 1823.

40. "La honorable junta provisional gubernativa de la república," in *El sol,* July 14, 1823.

41. The deputies were Francisco Genaro Cicero, Eusebio Villamil, Pedro José Guzmán, José Ignacio Cervera, Perfecto Barranda, Manuel Milanes, Juan de Dios Cosgaya, Pedro Manuel Regil, Agustín López de Llergo, Pedro Almeida, Miguel Errasquín, Manuel Jiménez, Pedro Sousa, Juan Nepomuceno Rivas, Juan Evangelista Echanove, José Antonio García, José María Quiñones, Joaquín García Rejón, Manuel León, Pablo Moreno, and Tiburcio López Constante ("Instalación y apertura del congreso constituyente del estado yucateco, verificada el día 20 de agosto de 1823," in *El sol,* September 24, 1823; Ancona, *Historia de Yucatán,* III, 279).

42. Alamán, Minister of Domestic Affairs, reprimanded Yucatán for having proclaimed a federal republic on May 29. He called the action premature and anarchical (Acereto, "Historia política desde el descubrimiento Europeo hasta 1920," III, 180; "Oficio dirigido al diputado d. Manuel Crescencio Rejón por el secretario del H.P.A. de Yucatán," in *Aguila mexicana,* October 25, 1823). The Constituent Congress of Yucatán replied on September 27, denying that Yucatán had any intention of withdrawing from the Mexican nation but maintaining the right to create its own state Constitution and the right of each province or state in Mexico to do the same. To further explain its attitude toward the national government, the Yucatecan Congress included its decree of August 27, which set forth the principles of the state of Yucatán. It declared (1) that the state of Yucatán was sovereign and independent of the domination of any other state, (2) that sovereignty resided in the people of the state, who alone had the exclusive right of directing the provincial government and forming the Constitution and laws of the province, (3) that it was the desire of the state to join in an equitable and just pact with all other independent states of the Mexican nation to form a federal republic, (4) that the legislative, executive, and judicial functions of the state should always remain separate, (5) that the government of the state should be a popular, representative, federal one, (6) that all state employees were agents of the state and responsible to it, and (7) that the state was a refuge for all foreigners, and their person and property were inviolable (ibid.; Ancona, *Historia de Yucatán,* III, 280–283; Acereto, "Historia política desde el descubrimiento Europeo hasta 1920," III, 180–181, 440–441).

43. Gómez Farías, *Voto particular,* pp. 3–4.

44. Session of Congress of May 28, in *Aguila mexicana,* June 1, 1823; Mateos, *Historia parlamentaria,* II, 382.

45. "Acta de Zacatecas," in *Aguila mexicana,* July 3–4, 1823. This document was signed Provincia Libre de Zacatecas, June 18, 1823, by Domingo Velázquez, Manuel de Orive y Novales, Mariano de Iriarte, Juan José Román, José Francisco Arrieta, and Santos Vélez. It was issued as an official order to the province of Zacatecas on June 22. Two days earlier, copies of it with an explanatory note had been sent to the Provincial Deputations throughout Mexico ("Oficio de la Excma. Diputación Provincial de Zacatecas a la de Durango," in *Aguila mexicana,* August 2, 1823).

46. A manuscript copy of the plans, signed Zacatecas, July 12, 1823, by Domingo Velázquez (Political Chief) and Marcos de Esparza (acting secretary) is to be found in the Hernández y Dávalos Collection, in the Benson Latin American Collection, the University of Texas at Austin.

47. Banegas Galván, *Historia de México,* II, 430; Bustamante, *Diario histórico de México,* p. 402.

48. Banegas Galván, *Historia de México,* II, 430; Bocanegra, *Memorias,* I, 225, said that it was reported that Negrete and Bravo were going to San Luis Potosí but their real purpose was to go against Guadalajara and that later events confirmed that fact.

49. Banegas Galván, *Historia de México,* II, 431.

50. The Provincial Deputation of Zacatecas to generals Pedro Celestino Negrete and Nicolás Bravo, Zactecas, July 15, 1823, in "Oficio dirigido a la Excma. Diputación Provincial del Estado de Jalisco por la de Zacatecas," in *Aguila mexicana,* July 31, 1823, and *Gaceta del gobierno de Guadalajara,* July 22, 1823; Banegas Galván, *Historia de México,* II, 431–432.

51. The Provincial Deputation of Zacatecas to the Provincial Deputation of Guadalajara, Zacatecas, July 15, 1823, in "Oficio dirigido"; and *Gaceta del gobierno de Guadalajara,* July 22, 1823.

52. "Manifiesto de governador del estado libre de Jalisco a los habitantes del mismo," in *Gaceta del gobierno de Guadalajara,* July 22, 1823.

53. Bravo to Quintanar, Irapuato, August 7, 1823, in *Sesiones celebradas en la villa de Lagos,* pp. 1–2.

54. *Sesiones celebradas en la villa de Lagos,* pp. 1–15; *El sol,* September 1, 1823.

55. *Proposición hecha al soberano congreso por los diputados que subscriben,* a printed broadside signed August 1, 1823, by Sánchez, Gómez Farías, and García (Bustamante, *Diario histórico de México,* pp. 502–503).

56. José María Covarrubias, *Esposición hecho a soberano congreso por el sr. diputado,* signed August 2, 1823; Mateos, *Historia parlamentaria,* II, 460; Bustamante, *Diario histórico de México,* pp. 504–505.

57. Bustamante, *Diario histórico de México,* pp. 504–505.

58. Mateos, *Historia parlamentaria,* II, 475–476; *Aguila mexicana,* August 17, 1823; Bustamante, *Diario histórico de México,* pp. 517–518. Bustamante asked at this time that amnesty also be extended to Oaxaca.

59. The Zacatecas deputies were Domingo Velázquez, Dr. Juan José Román, Lic. Ignacio Gutiérrez de Velasco, José Miguel Díaz de León, Juan Bautista de la

Torre, Juan Bautista Martínez, María Herrera, and Lic. Miguel Laureano Tobar, with Domingo del Castillo, Eusebio Gutiérrez, José María García Rojas, and Antonio Eugenio Gordoa as alternates (*Aguila mexicana*, September 17 and November 8, 1823).

8. Establishment of Other State Legislatures

1. Pedro Otero to Marqués de Vivanco, Guanajuato, May 23, 1823, ms., Hernández y Dávalos Collection in the Benson Latin American Collection, University of Texas at Austin.

2. Bustamante, *Diario histórico de México*, pp. 376–379.

3. Mier to the Municipal Council of Monterrey, Nuevo León, April 23, 1823, in his *Diez cartas*, p. 9.

4. Stephen F. Austin to J. E. B. Austin, Saltillo, Coahuila, May 10, 1823, in Eugene C. Barker (ed.), *The Austin Papers*, I, 639. It is worthwhile to note that Austin drew up a plan for a central republic for Mexico on March 28, 1823 (ibid., pp. 601–627), and that, before talking to Ramos Arizpe on May 8 to May 10, Austin had not mentioned a federal or federated republic for Mexico. Only after having talked with Ramos Arizpe did Austin speak of a federal republic, whereas Mier's correspondence and that of the Provincial Deputation, of the Municipal Council of Monterrey, and of Saltillo all testify that Ramos Arizpe had been working for the realization of the principles of a federal republic—the division of powers between the central and provincial government—long before March 1823.

5. Bustamante, *Diario histórico de México*, p. 399.

6. Ibid., p. 402. Such a plan first published in Guadalajara was republished in Mexico under the title of *Separación de la Nueva Galicia de todas las provincias de América*.

7. Benson, "Servando Teresa de Mier, Federalist," p. 518; Mateos, *Historia parlamentaria*, II, 382; *Aguila mexicana*, June 1, 1823.

8. Session of Congress of April 18, 1823, in *Aguila mexicana*, April 22, 1823; Mateos, *Historia parlamentaria*, II, 285–286. Mier and Múzquiz, it should be remembered, were the two commissioners appointed by the Eastern Interior Provinces; therefore, it is to be assumed that their information came directly from those provinces. It is known, furthermore, that Mier was kept constantly informed of events occurring in the Eastern Interior Provinces by the Provincial Deputation, the Municipal Council of Monterrey, and Ramos Arizpe, who was directing events taking place in those provinces.

9. Report of the Municipal Council of Monterrey to Servando Mier y Noriega, Monterrey, May 8, 1823, in Actas del cabildo de Monterrey, Libro de 1823, ms., Archivo of the Ayuntamiento de Monterrey, Nuevo León, leaf 39.

10. Municipal Council of San Nicolás de la Capellanía to the Municipal Council of Saltillo, San Nicolás de la Capellanía, April 30, 1823, ms., Archivo of the Ayuntamiento de Saltillo, Coahuila.

11. Quaderno de actas de la junta de este partido del Saltillo, formado para consolidar la opinión de la provincia, ms., Archivo of the Ayuntamiento de Saltillo.

12. Stephen F. Austin to General James Wilkinson, Saltillo, May 11, 1823, pho-

tostat in the Barker History Center of the University of Texas of original letter in the Durrett Collection at Chicago University. Austin arrived in Saltillo on May 8, 1823, where he first met Ramos Arizpe.

13. Minutes of the meetings, Saltillo, May 25–27, 1823, signed by the members of the Municipal Council, Ramos Arizpe, etc., in the Bexar Archives at the University of Texas at Austin.

14. "Acta de la Villa de Saltillo," in *Aguila mexicana,* July 1–2, 1823.

15. Mier to the Provincial Deputation of Monterrey, México, July 5, 1823, in Cossío, *Historia de Nuevo León,* V, 89–90.

16. De la Garza had just arrived in Monterrey from Mexico City, on May 22, 1823. He was named Political Chief at Mier's request. Mier expected de la Garza to counterbalance Ramos Arizpe's influence in the region, but instead he joined with Ramos Arizpe to help him put his ideas into effect.

17. "Acta de Monterrey," Monterrey, June 5, 1823, in *El sol,* July 3, 1823, and in *Gaceta del gobierno supremo de México,* July 3, 1823.

18. De la Garza to the Municipal Council of Saltillo, Monterrey, June 8, 1823, in *Aguila mexicana,* July 4, 1823.

19. Mier to the Municipal Council of Monterrey, México, July 19, 1823, in Mier, *Diez cartas,* p. 14, said that on July 18 the Minister of Domestic Affairs reported that the four Eastern Interior Provinces were establishing a supreme general governing junta. See also Mier to the Provincial Deputation of the Eastern Interior Provinces, México, July 5, 1823, in Cossío, *Historia de Nuevo León,* V, 89–90.

20. Mier to the Provincial Deputation of the Eastern Interior Provinces, México, July 3, 1823, in ibid.; Mier to Cantú, México, July 5, 1823, in ibid., V, 43–45. The project of a Constitution here referred to has not been identified. Mier said that he had received a copy and had notified Congress of it. Stephen F. Austin, who was in Monterrey when de la Garza arrived there, on May 22, hastily drew up a "Plan of Federal Government" between June 5 and June 12. (Note: the date that has been assigned to it, May 1823, cannot be correct, for in it Austin refers to a decree of the national Congress of May 21, 1823, which did not reach Monterrey prior to June 4, 1823.) Austin's plan was drawn as a Constitution not for the Eastern Interior Provinces, but for the Mexican nation as a whole. It is possible, nonetheless, that Mier was referring to this plan by Austin, for during that chaotic period inaccurate references and misinterpretations occurred frequently.

21. Minutes of the Provincial Deputation of Nuevo Santander, San Carlos, June 9, 1823, in the Archivo del Estado de Coahuila, Saltillo, Coahuila.

22. Mier to the Municipal Council of Monterrey, México, July 19, 1823, in his *Diez cartas,* p. 14.

23. Mier to Cantú, México, June 25 and July 5, 1823, in Cossío, *Historia de Nuevo León,* V, 38–39, 43–45; Mier to the Municipal Council of Monterrey, México, July 19, 1823, in his *Diez cartas,* p. 14; Bustamante, *Diario histórico de México,* p. 449.

24. Mier to Cantú, México, June 25, July 13, and July 30, 1823, in Cossío, *Historia de Nuevo León,* V, 41, 50–53; Bustamante, *Diario histórico de México,* p. 450; Mateos, *Historia parlamentaria,* II, 419–420.

25. "Oficios dirigidos por los sres. don Ramón de la Garza and José Antonio

Rodríguez al sr. ministro de relaciones," in *El sol*, September 5, 1823; Felipe de la Garza to Alamán, San Carlos, August 16, 1823, in *Gaceta del gobierno supremo de México*, September 6, 1823.

26. Provincial Deputation of Querétaro to Félix de Osores, Querétaro, May 20, 1823, in *Gaceta extraordinaria del gobierno supremo de México*, May 28, 1823.

27. Minutes of the meeting of the Provincial Deputation of Querétaro of June 11–12, in *Aguila mexicana*, June 28, 1823; Castillo Negrete, *México*, IV, 462.

28. Juan José García to the Minister of Domestic Affairs, Querétaro, June 28, 1823, in *El sol*, July 9, 1823, and in *Gaceta extraordinaria del gobierno supremo de México*, July 2, 1823.

29. "Manifiesto de la Diputación Provincial de Querétaro," Querétaro, July 15, 1823, in *Aguila mexicana*, August 10 and 15, 1823.

30. "Exposición que al supremo executivo hizo la diputación provincial de Querétaro," Querétaro, July 15, 1823, in *Aguila mexicana*, August 14, 1823.

31. Otero to Morán, Guanajuato, May 23, 1823, ms., Hernández y Dávalos Collection in the Benson Latin American Collection, University of Texas at Austin.

32. Llorente to editors of the *Aguila mexicana*, Guanajuato, May 26, 1823, in *Aguila mexicana*, June 1, 1823.

33. Manuel Cortazar to the citizens of Guanajuato, Guanajuato, June 22, 1823, in *Aguila mexicana*, June 29, 1823, and in *El sol*, June 30, 1823.

34. Santa Anna, *Manifiesto*, pp. 28–29.

35. The plan stated that Santa Anna had resolved (1) to form at once an army called "Protector of Mexican Liberty." (2) Its purpose would be to sustain the Roman Catholic religion, to protect its ministers, and to observe strictly the other two guarantees of the Plan of Iguala. (3) The army would request the prompt calling of Congress. (4) The army would preserve and guarantee the right of the provinces to pronounce themselves in favor of a federal republic. (5) Until the new Congress had assembled, the provinces that wished to be independent were to be governed by their Provincial Deputations. (6) The army would take up whatever position it saw fit but would not enter into hostilities except to repel force with force in case of attack or of an attempt against the sacred liberty of the people. (7) A copy of the plan would be sent at once to the acting central government and at the same time it would be asked not to issue any orders against that army or any orders tending to suppress the right of the provinces to act for their own good. (8) Any time an armed force moved against Guadalajara or any other place that desired to be free, the commanding officer of said armed force would be sent a copy of this plan and warned that, if he persisted in his design, he would be responsible before God and the world for the evils that might result. (9) A copy of the plan would also be sent to all of the provinces in the country. (10) Anyone attempting hostilities against the free people would be considered enemies and would be brought to trial before the proper authorities. (11) The army took pleasure in testifying anew to its liberal ideas and would sustain these articles at all costs. (12) The groups composing the army would proceed to their own provinces as soon as the nation was constituted according to the will of the people. (13) Any individuals who, forgetting their duty to their country, worked against the ideas of this plan, either with arms or with the power of sedition, would be tried and judged traitors to their country. (14) If such individuals were employees of the province, they would be removed from office by

the respective Provincial Deputations (Santa Anna, *Manifiesto*, pp. 39–44). Bus-
mante, in his *Diario histórico de México* (p. 499), wrote that Santa Anna was follo
ing in Iturbide's footsteps, but since he did not want to take the title of monar
he had imitated Cromwell and chosen the title of "Protector," a word that ha
much broader meaning.

36. "Noticias nacionales," in *Aguila mexicana*, June 18, 1823. According to B
tamante in his *Historia del emperador d. Agustín de Iturbide* (pp. 154–157), many
the army officers refused to join Santa Anna in his plan; one of them, Lt. Ton
Requeña, stated frankly that the federation did not need Santa Anna's protecti

37. "Noticias nacionales," in *Aguila mexicana*, June 15, 1823.

38. "San Luis Potosí," in *Gaceta del gobierno supremo de México*, July 1, 1823, a
El sol, July 1, 1823.

39. Bustamante in his *Diario histórico de México* (p. 416) wrote that Armijo l
been sent to the interior with the double purpose of being near Nueva Galici;
order to check the aggression of Guadalajara and of curbing the turmoil created
Santa Anna, a man of an antagonistic disposition.

40. Santa Anna to Armijo, San Luis Potosí, June 6, 1823, in *El sol*, June 15, 1;

41. Armijo to Santa Anna, Valle de San Francisco, June 8, 1823, in *El*
June 15, 1823.

42. "San Luis Potosí," in *Gaceta del gobierno supremo de México*, July 1, 1823;
mijo to the Minister of Domestic Affairs, Gogorrón, June 22, 1823, in ibid., an
El sol, July 2, 1823.

43. At least this was Santa Anna's report to the Provincial Deputation of
Luis Potosí, in *Gaceta del gobierno supremo de México*, July 1, 1823. Armijo ga
different interpretation of Santa Anna's actions, however. He said that Santa A
left San Luis Potosí with 400 infantrymen, two cannons, and other arms, wl
caused Armijo to withdraw two leagues into the province of Guanajuato in o
to avoid an outbreak of hostilities (Armijo to Alamán, Gogorrón, June 29, 182
ibid., and in *El sol*, July 2, 1823).

44. *Gaceta del gobierno supremo de México*, July 1, 1823; *El sol*, July 1, 1823.

45. Minutes of the meeting at which this action was taken are to be foun
Gaceta del gobierno supremo de México, July 1, 1823.

46. Santa Anna to the Provincial Deputation of San Luis Potosí, San
Potosí, June 25, 1823, in *Gaceta del gobierno supremo de México*, July 9, 1823.

47. The Provincial Deputation of San Luis Potosí to Santa Anna, San
Potosí, June 24, 1823, in *Gaceta del gobierno supremo de México*, July 9, 1823.

48. Bustamante wrote in his *Diario histórico de México* (p. 470) that the Pro
cial Deputation fled in fear after two of the city's councilmen had been kille
Santa Anna's troops.

49. Muro, *Historia de San Luis Potosí*, I, 362–365; Santa Anna, *Manif
pp. 16–17; "San Luis Potosí," June 28, 1823, in *Aguila mexicana*, July 5, 1823; "S
taría de la diputación provincial de S. Luis Potosí, S. Miguel Misquitic, Jun
1823," in *Aguila mexicana*, July 10, 1823; "Comunicación, San Luis Potosí, Ju
1823," in ibid., July 11, 1823.

50. "Acta de la villa de Celaya," in *Aguila mexicana*, July 12, 1823.

51. García, Gómez Farías, Antonio J. Valdés, Covarrubias, Rejón, and Sár
proposed to Congress (1) that provincial Congresses or Legislatures be establ

at once in the provinces in a manner to be proposed and approved by Congress and (2) that the deficit in funds for the general expenses of the nation be obtained by a proportional levy on the provinces (Mateos, *Historia parlamentaria*, pp. 397–398; *Aguila mexicana*, June 13, 1823).

52. Santa Anna to Congress, San Luis Potosí, July 2, 1823, in Santa Anna, *Manifiesto*, pp. 68–69, and in *El sol*, July 13, 1823.

53. Santa Anna to the Supreme Executive Power, San Luis Potosí, July 3, 1823, in Santa Anna, *Manifiesto*, pp. 68–73, and in *Gaceta extraordinaria del gobierno supremo de México*, July 10, 1823.

54. According to Bustamante (*Historia del emperador d. Agustín de Iturbide*, p. 157), Santa Anna tried in vain to justify his actions by entering the province of Guanajuato, but the Political Chief of that province refused to let him do so. Santa Anna, with an escort of dragoons, arrived in Mexico City on July 27, 1823. According to Callcott (*Santa Anna*, p. 51), Santa Anna had left his command at Querétaro while he went to Mexico City to answer the charges against him. On August 10, he issued his *Manifiesto*. In light of the foregoing facts, it is difficult indeed to see how "the action of Santa Anna crystallized sentiment on all sides," as stated by Callcott (ibid., p. 51). The inference is that Santa Anna's actions crystallized sentiment in favor of a federal republic. Actually, the provinces almost unanimously rejected Santa Anna's overtures as "protector of a federal republic." Sentiment in favor of federalism had already been crystallized to such a degree that as early as May 21 Congress had voted to print and circulate immediately the Mier "Plan for a Federal Republic."

55. Minutes of the meetings of July 10, 1823, in Celaya, are printed in *El sol*, July 24, 1823, and in *Aguila mexicana*, July 23, 1823.

56. The exact date of the first steps taken by Michoacán is not presently known. Since the meeting was the result of the congressional delay in convoking the new Congress, Michoacán probably began working toward the meeting during the close of the month of April when the congressional committee report of April 12 was made known.

57. "Sesiones celebradas en la ciudad de Celaya por los comisionados provinciales de Valladolid, San Luis Potosí, Guanajuato, and Querétaro," in *El sol*, July 24, 1823; "Acta de la junta celebrada al día 8 de julio en la ciudad de Guanajuato," in *El sol*, July 18, 1823.

58. *Manifiesto de la diputación provincial de Veracruz a los pueblos de su distrito*, a broadside, dated April 13, 1823. It was also published in *Aguila mexicana*, May 10, 1823.

59. Eulogio de Villarrutia to Alamán, Veracruz, June 21, 1823, in *Aguila mexicana*, June 30, 1823, and *El sol*, June 28, 1823; "Circular de la diputación provincial de Veracruz," Veracruz, June 30, 1823, in *Aguila mexicana*, July 4–5, 1823.

60. "Circular de la diputación provincial de Veracruz."

61. "Contestación de la diputación provincial de Veracruz a la Excma. de Guadalajara, Veracruz, August 16, 1823," in *Gaceta del gobierno supremo de México*, August 28, 1823, and in *El sol*, August 27, 1823.

62. "Contestación que ha dado la diputación provincial de México a la de Guadalajara," México, July 18, 1823, in *Aguila mexicana*, August 6–7, 1823.

63. "Apéndice a la sesión pública [del congreso nacional] de junio 23, 1823," in *El sol,* June 27, 1823, and in Mateos, *Historia parlamentaria,* II, 490.

64. Mier to Cantú, México June 25, 1823, in Cossío, *Historia de Nuevo Léon,* V, 41; Bustamante, *Diario histórico de México,* p. 450.

65. Mateos, *Historia parlamentaria,* II, 433; *Colección de órdenes y decretos de la soberana junta provisional gubernativa y soberanos congresos generales de la nación mexicana,* II, 146.

66. Bustamante, *Diario histórico de México,* p. 470.

67. *Colección de órdenes y decretos de la soberana junta provisional gubernativa y soberanos congresos generales de la nación mexicana,* II, 126.

68. Mateos, *Historia parlamentaria,* II, 428, Article 1: "The Mexican Congress approves the measure convoking a Congress of Guatemala." Alamán proposed that Congress should consider that, since the people of Guatemala were free to constitute their country as they saw fit, the Mexican troops should be withdrawn from that country.

69. Mier to the editors of *El sol,* July 4, 1823, in *El sol,* July 14, 1823.

70. Trens, *Historia de Chiapas,* pp. 229–231; "La junta suprema provisional de Chiapas a los habitantes de su distrito," in *Aguila mexicana,* September 5, 1823.

71. "La junta suprema provisional de Chiapas a los habitantes de su distrito"; Romero, *Bosquejo histórico,* I, 265–268.

72. Romero, *Bosquejo histórico,* pp. 270–271.

73. Alamán to the provisional governing junta of Chiapas, México, July 9, 1823, in ibid., pp. 271–272.

74. Ibid., pp. 445–446.

75. Ibid., p. 446. A complete documentary account of the period 1823 is to be found on pp. 289–446.

76. Ibid., pp. 460–461.

77. Trens, *Historia de Chiapas,* p. 225.

78. Bustamante, *Diario histórico de México,* pp. 605, 615.

79. Mateos, *Historia parlamentaria,* II, 578; *Aguila mexicana,* November 12, 1823.

80. Eugene C. Barker, *The Life of Stephen F. Austin* (pp. 84–85 in 1st ed. and 75–76 in 2nd ed.), says, "But Austin's connection with the *Acta Constitutiva,* the first form of the federal republican constitution, is very close. . . . Austin at the end of May submitted to Ramos Arizpe, an outline of a federal government. . . . Arizpe was much impressed, made changes and corrections in the copy preserved in the Austin Papers, recommended that it be printed, and said that he would send it to his friends. . . . Arizpe was elected to the new Congress in September and on November 14, and a few days after its organization, offered with the assistance of a competent committee, to prepare within three days a provisional constitution. He was taken at his word and appointed chairman of the Committee on the Constitution, which reported the *Acta Constitutiva* on November 20. . . . Its verbal similarity to Austin's plan is not likely to be the same with two documents drawn independently from a common source, but in substance it is very nearly parallel. Arizpe was much too positive a character to accept any plan without subjecting it to his own analysis, and it is evident that Austin's draft was thoroughly assimilated and coordinated with his own study of the Constitution of the United States, the Span-

ish Constitution and the political history of Mexico, but that the plan should influence him is inevitable."

William Archibald Whatley wrote a master's thesis entitled "The Formation of the Mexican Constitution of 1824" under Barker's direction and also served at that time as Barker's research assistant. Barker cites this thesis as one of his sources for the comments above. Whatley states (pp. 70–72) that Ramos Arizpe's use of "this [Austin's] plan in drawing up the draft of the *Acta Constitutiva* seems likely from the similarity in language which can occasionally be detected. . . . Arizpe's promise to complete a first draft of the *Acta Constitutiva* within three days might be held to argue that he already had a plan in readiness, which might in all probability have been Austin's. . . . Austin himself declares, in a note appended to the copy of the document which he preserved, that Ramos Arizpe had used it as the source of the *Acta Constitutiva*. That Ramos Arizpe and his Committee on the Constitution were influenced in a general way, even if they did not adopt it entire, is betrayed by analogies like that noted above." (The analogy referred to here is cited in note 85 below.)

81. Ramos Arizpe participated in events taking place in Saltillo during all the month of May and through June 5, 1823, for his signature is on the documents recounting the series of events that occurred there during that period.

82. There is no positive evidence that Ramos Arizpe even kept a copy of Austin's plan. Austin states that he gave the plan to Ramos Arizpe, but the plan that he corrected and that he commented on remained in Austin's possession. Furthermore, Ramos Arizpe's name does not appear among the names that Austin mentioned as those to whom he later gave copies (see Barker, 2nd ed., footnote 81, p. 75).

83. James Q. Dealey, "The Spanish Sources of the Mexican Constitution of 1824," *Texas State Historical Association Quarterly* 3 (January 1900): 162.

84. Ibid., pp. 163–164. What Dealey said in regard to the Mexican Constitution of 1824 applies equally to Ramos Arizpe's plan.

85. Since Whatley cited no other article, he apparently concluded this article to be the most perfect example of parallelism. That the article was taken bodily from the Spanish Constitution can be seen at a glance. Besides, it was to be expected that Ramos Arizpe would make use of articles from a Constitution that he himself had helped actively to produce.

Austin's draft	*Ramos Arizpe's draft*	*1812 Constitution*
Para proveer con más seguridad a la defensa, prosperidad y bien común las provincias se unen mútuamente por el más estrecho vínculo de unión y fraternidad bajo el sistema Republicana federada, para formar una grande nación, cuya religión dominante es y será precisamente la Católyca, Apostólyca Romana sin que Estado	La religión de nación mexicana es y será perpetuamente la Católica, Apostólica, Romana, única verdadera. La Nación la protege por leyes sabias y justas y prohibe el ejercicio de cualquiera otra.	La religión de la Nación Española es y será perpetuamente la Católica, Apostólica, Romana, única verdadera. La Nación la protege por leyes sabias y justas y prohibe el ejercicio de cualquiera otra.

alguno pueda proclamar
otra, y todos y cada uno
de por si obligan a pro-
tegerla por medio de
leyes sabias y justas.

86. That fact is revealed both in the Cortes and in *Carta escrita a un americano sobre la forma de gobierno que para hacer practicable la constitución y las leyes, conviene establecer en Nueva España atendida su actual situación,* a printed letter written by Ramos Arizpe to his brother in 1821. Furthermore, there is actually no reason to assume that Ramos Arizpe needed to look to Austin for information in regard to the United States Constitution. Since 1812, it had been printed in Spanish several times and was readily available. See Benson, "Washington: Symbol of the United States in Mexico, 1800–1823," pp. 175–179.

87. More has been made of the brevity of the period in which the *Acta* was drawn up than the facts warrant. It has been implied that Ramos Arizpe and the men on his committee had not even begun to work on a Constitution prior to November 14, but there is no documentation to show that such was the case. The constitutional committee was named on November 10, 1823, according to Mateos (*Historia parlamentaria,* II, 578; *Aguila mexicana* no. 212, November 12, 1823, p. 4). Furthermore, even if it had been named on November 14 (the erroneous date indicated by various authors, including Whatley), that would not preclude the possibility that Ramos Arizpe and others had been working on a constitutional plan from the day they had been elected deputies or even earlier.

For others who assert that the Mexican Constitution of 1824 was patterned largely after the United States Constitution, see Charles Curtis Cumberland, *Mexico: Its Struggle for Modernity;* James Aloysius Magner, *Men of Mexico,* p. 284; George E. Nelson and Mary B. Nelson, *Mexico A–Z, An Encyclopedia Dictionary,* under the name Ramos Arizpe, Miguel; Donald C. Briggs and Marvin Alisky, *Historical Dictionary of Mexico,* pp. 186–187; Rodolfo Reyes' prologue to Emilio Rabasa's reproduced *La organización política de México,* in Andrés Serra-Rojas, *Antología de Emilio Rabasa,* I, 271; Herbert Ingram Priestley, *The Mexican Nation,* p. 262; Carlos González-Salas, *Miguel Ramos Arizpe, cumbre y camino,* p. 106; Alamán, *Historia de Méjico,* V, 717–719; and Meyer and Sherman, *The Course of Mexican History,* pp. 313–314.

88. Article 7 of the *Acta constitucional presentada al soberano congreso constituyente por su comisión el día 20 de noviembre de 1823.*

89. For a detailed discussion of the meaning of Article 5 and the vote on it, see Benson, "Servando Teresa de Mier, Federalist," pp. 514–525.

90. Mateos, *Historia parlamentaria,* II, 620.

91. Ibid., pp. 622–623.

92. On December 8, Espinosa de los Monteros, Lombardo y García, and Zavala asked Congress to declare that strength and victory were to be given to the orders that the provincial Congresses had given their deputies (Mateos, *Historia parlamentaria,* II, 610). Both before and after that date numerous matters presented to the national Congress were declared not within its province and ordered referred back to the provincial Congresses for final decision.

93. Ibid., II, 627.

94. Ibid., II, 630.

95. Ibid., II, 636–641; *Colección de órdenes y decretos de la soberana junta provisional gubernativa y soberanos congresos generales de la nación mexicana*, III, 12–14.

96. *Aguila mexicana*, February 27, 1824; Mateos, *Historia parlamentaria*, II, 698.

97. Mateos, *Historia parlamentaria*, II, 703, 731, 744; *Gaceta del gobierno supremo de la federación mexicana*, March 4, 1824, and March 25, 1824.

98. Mateos, *Historia parlamentaria*, pp. 745, 749, 779; *El caduceo de Puebla*, April 1, 1824; *Aguila mexicana*, March 20, 1824; *Recopilación de leyes, decretos, reglamentos y circulares expedidos en el estado de Michoacán*, I, 11–12; *Gaceta del gobierno supremo de la federación mexicana*, May 4 and 22, 1824; Muro, *Historia de San Luis Potosí*, I, 213.

99. Mateos, *Historia parlamentaria*, p. 646.

100. Ibid., p. 656.

101. *Aguila mexicana*, January 30, 1824; Mateos, *Historia parlamentaria*, p. 663. The name of Nuevo Santander was changed to Tamaulipas at the request of the province (*Aguila mexicana*, January 31, 1824).

102. Mateos, *Historia parlamentaria*, pp. 668–669, 672; *Coleción de órdenes y decretos de la soberana junta provisional gubernativa y soberanos congresos generales de la nación mexicana*, III, 25.

103. Mateos, *Historia parlamentaria*, pp. 818, 853.

104. The intendancy of Saltillo that was to have jurisdiction over the Eastern Interior Provinces, although officially created, was never established, in spite of the fact that an intendant was named to that position in 1814. Before he could assume office, Ferdinand VII had revoked all the acts of the Spanish Cortes; after the restoration of these acts of the Cortes in 1820, the independence of Mexico and the ensuing confusion militated against the actual foundation of an intendancy in Saltillo. Ramos Arizpe had long been working to have northern Mexico divided into three large military, political, and financial entities, and his constitutional committee apparently went along with him in this matter.

105. *Aguila mexicana*, January 31, 1824.

106. Mateos, *Historia parlamentaria*, pp. 698, 708, 729, 737; *Aguila mexicana*, February 24, 1824.

107. Mateos, *Historia parlamentaria*, p. 770.

108. *Aguila mexicana*, February 25, 1824; Mateos, *Historia parlamentaria*, II, 710, 751, 760, 761; "Manifiesto de la diputación provincial de Durango a los habitantes de su comprehensión, Durango," February 21, 1824, in *Observaciones que la diputación provincial de Chihuahua hace sobre el manifiesto que en el 21 de febrero del presente año publicó la excma. de Durango*, pp. 3–9.

109. Mateos, *Historia parlamentaria*, p. 786.

110. Ibid., pp. 815, 828–830.

111. Ibid., pp. 649, 659, 678, 700, 708, 713, 723, 733, 748, 750, 755, 764–766, 808, 810, 813, 842, 867, 884, 886, 906, 911, 914, 970, 972, 1024; *Colección de órdenes y decretos de la soberana junta provisional gubernativa y soberanos congresos generales de la nación mexicana*, III, 125.

112. Carlos Hernández, *Durango gráfico*, p. 62.

113. Cossío, *Historia de Nuevo León*, I, 110–115; Roel, *Nuevo León*, 119.

114. Alessio Robles, *Coahuila y Texas*, I, 190–191; Mateos, *Historia parlamentaria*, II, 899.

115. José N. Ponce de León, *Reseñas históricas del estado de Chihuahua*, I, 155–156.

116. Mateos, *Historia parlamentaria*, p. 966.

Bibliography

Primary Sources

I. *Manuscripts*

Austin, Stephen F. Papers. Mss. in Texas History Center. University of Texas Library at Austin, Texas.

Bexar Archives. Mss. in Texas History Center. University of Texas Library at Austin.

Calleja, Félix María. Letter to Minister of Grace and Justice, México, August 18, 1814. Archivo General de Indias, Seville, Spain, estante 90, cajón 1, legajo 19.

Coahuila (Province), Diputación Provincial. Libro de actas de la excma. diputación provincial de Coahuila, año de 1823. Archivo del Ayuntamiento de Saltillo, Coahuila.

Convenio que en lo reservado y con previo conocimiento del gral. Sta. Ana hicieron en el Puente los generales d. José Antonio Echávarri y d. Guadalupe Victoria. Mss. in Sub-dirección de la Biblioteca Nacional, Mexico City.

Correspondencia Virreyes. Calleja, vol. 6. Archivo General de la Nación, Mexico City.

Eastern Interior Provinces, Diputación Provincial. Actas [Minutes] de la instalación de la diputación provincial de Nuevo León, Coahuila y Texas, el 1 de abril de 1823. Archivo General del Estado de Nuevo León, Monterrey, Nuevo León.

Fernando VII. Carta a Juan Ruiz de Apodaca, signed 24 diciembre 1820. Ms. in the Nettie Lee Benson Latin American Collection at the University of Texas Library at Austin.

Guadalajara (City), Ayuntamiento. Libro de actas del Ayuntamiento de Guadalajara, años 1813 y 1814. Archivo General de la Secretaría del Ayuntamiento de Guadalajara, Jalisco.

Hernández y Dávalos, Juan E. Manuscript Collection. In Benson Latin American Collection at the University of Texas Library at Austin.

Matamoros (City), Ayuntamiento. Archives (photostatic copies). University of Texas Library at Austin.

México, Archivo General de la Nación. Ramo de Historia, vols. 417, 418, 440, 443, and 447. Mexico City.

Mexico (City), Ayuntamiento. Actas capitularios del excmo. ayuntamiento constitucional de la ciudad de México, año de 1814. Archivo del Gobierno del Distrito Federal de México, Mexico City.

————. Actas ordinarias y extraordinarias del ayuntamiento constitucional de la ciudad de México de 1820. Archivo del Gobierno del Distrito Federal de México, Mexico City.

Mier, Noriega y Guerra, José Servando Teresa de. Correspondencia y otros papeles. In Benson Latin American Collection at the University of Texas Library at Austin.

Monterrey (City), Ayuntamiento. Libro de actas del cabildo el día 17 de octubre del año de 1822. Archivo del Ayuntamiento de Monterrey, Nuevo León.

————, Diputación Provincial. Comunicaciones dirigidas a la diputación provincial de Monterrey, 1814. Archivo General del Estado de Nuevo León, Monterrey, Nuevo León.

————, Junta. Actas [Minutes] de la junta de Monterrey del 5 de marzo de 1823. Archivo General del Estado de Coahuila, Saltillo, Coahuila.

Morelia (City), Ayuntamiento. Libro de actas de los cabildos de 1816–1821. Archivo del Ayuntamiento de Morelia, Michoacán.

Nuevo León (Province), Junta Provisional Gubernativa. Actas [Minutes] y correspondencia de la junta provisional gubernativa de Nuevo León (1823). Archivo General del Estado de Nuevo León, Monterrey, Nuevo León.

————, Juntas Electorales. Libro de actas de las juntas electorales de parroquia, de partido y de provincia, año de 1814. Archivo General del Gobierno del Estado de Nuevo León, Monterrey, Nuevo León.

Nuevo Santander (Province), Diputación Provincial. Actas [Minutes] de la diputación provincial de Nuevo Santander, San Carlos, el 9 de junio, 1823. Archivo General del Estado de Coahuila, Saltillo, Coahuila.

Puebla (City), Ayuntamiento. Libros del cabildo del ayuntamiento de la muy ilustre ciudad de la Puebla de los Angeles, año 1821. Archivo General de la Secretaría del Ayuntamiento de la Puebla de los Angeles.

Saltillo (City), Ayuntamiento. Informes oficiales de las elecciones del 8 de setiembre de 1823. Archivo del Ayuntamiento de la Ciudad de Saltillo, Coahuila.

————, Junta del Partido. Quaderno de actas de la junta de este partido del Saltillo, formado para consolidar la opinión de la provincia (1823). Archivo del Ayuntamiento de la Ciudad de Saltillo, Coahuila.

Valle de San Nicolás de la Capellanía (City), Ayuntamiento. Letter addressed to the Ayuntamiento of Saltillo, dated April 30, 1823. Archivo del Ayuntamiento de la Ciudad de Saltillo, Coahuila.

II. Newspapers

La abeja poblana. Puebla, 1820–1821.

La abispa de Chilpancingo, suplemento del 10 de abril de 1823. Edited by Carlos María Bustamante. México, 1823.

Aguila mexicana. México, 1822–1828.

El amigo de la patria, Guatemala, 1821.

El caduceo de Puebla. Puebla, 1824.

El conductor elétrico. Edited by José Joaquín Fernández de Lizardi. México, 1821.

El diario de México. México, 1809–1814.

La gaceta del gobierno de Guadalajara. Guadalajara, 1821–1823.

La gaceta del gobierno de México. México, 1809–1821.
La gaceta del gobierno supremo de la federación mexicana. México, 1823–1824.
La gaceta del gobierno supremo de México. México, 1823.
La gaceta imperial de México. México, 1821–1823.
El hombre libre. México, 1822–1823.
Noticioso general. México, 1820–1822.
Sabatina universal. México, 1822.
Semanario político y literario. México, 1820–1821.
El sol. México, 1822–1823.

III. Books, Broadsides, Documents, Pamphlets

Acta de la junta de Puebla, sobre la reinstalación del congreso mexicano. Puebla, 1823.
Acta del juramento solemne de adhesión al Plan de Casa Mata, bajo la fórmula que en ella se contiene con las modificaciones que van a su fin por la villa de Saltillo. Saltillo, 1823.
Acta general de la comisión militar, nombrada por la guarnición de esta plaza, para los usos que adentro expresan, Zacatecas, 3 de marzo de 1823. Guadalajara, 1823.
Actas de la diputación provincial de Michoacán, 1822–1823. Morelia, 1976.
Alamán, Lucas. *Historia de Méjico desde los primeros movimientos que prepararon su independencia en el año 1808 hasta la época presente.* 5 vols. México, 1849–1852.
Alba, Rafael (ed.). *La constitución de 1812 en la Nueva España.* 2 vols. (Publicaciones nacionales del Archivo General de la Nación, vols. IV–V). México, 1912–1913.
Aviso al público: Oaxaca liberal. Puebla, 1823.
El ayuntamiento de Zacatecas acompaña a su oficio de 24 de enero último las listas de los individuales electos diputados a cortes y vocales para la diputación provincial. México, Feb. 15, 1822.
Barker, Eugene C. (ed.). *The Austin Papers.* 3 vols. Washington, D.C., 1924. Vol. I.
Bocanegra, José María. *Memorias para la historia de México independiente 1822–1846.* 2 vols. México, 1892.
Bustamante, Carlos María. *Continuación del cuadro histórico: Historia del emperador d. Agustín de Iturbide hasta su muerte y sus consecuencias; y establecimiento de la república federal.* México, 1846.
———. *Cuadro histórico de la revolución de la América mexicana, comenzada en quince de septiembre de mil ochocientos diez por el ciudadano Miguel Hidalgo y Castilla.* México, 1827. Vol. V.
———. *Diario histórico de México.* Zacatecas, 1896. vol. I.
———. *El honor y patriotismo del general d. Nicolás Bravo, demostrado los últimos días del fugaz imperio de Iturbide.* México, 1828.
———. *Manifiesto histórico a las naciones y pueblos del Anahuac: Leído en la sesión pública del soberano congreso del 15 de abril de 1823.* México, 1823.
———. *El nuevo Bernal Díaz del Castillo o sea la historia de la invasión de los anglo-americanos en México.* México, 1849.
Calendario, manual y guía de forasteros de México. México, 1800–1823.
Chihuahua (Province), Diputación Provincial. *Observaciones que la diputación provincial de Chihuahua hace sobre el manifiesto que en el 21 de febrero del presente año publicó la excma. de Durango.* México, 1824.

Colección de constituciones de los estados unidos mexicanos. 3 vols. México, 1828.

Constitución política de la monarquía española promulgada en Cádiz al 19 de marzo de 1812. Cádiz, 1812.

Covarrubias, José María. *Esposición hecha al soberano congreso por el sr. diputado José María Covarrubias, 2 de agosto de 1823.* Guadalajara, 1823.

Espinosa de los Monteros, Carlos. *Esposición que sobre las provincias de Sonora y Sinaloa escribió su diputado Carlos Espinosa de los Monteros.* México, 1823.

Firmeza de los poblanos con la comisión de México. México, 1823.

Godoy, Manuel de. *Memorias.* 2 vols. Madrid, 1959.

Gómez Farías, Valentín. *Voto particular del sr. Gómez Farías como individuo de la comisión superior nombrado por su soberano congreso, para examinar la cuestión, de si debe o no convocar un nuevo congreso.* México, 1823.

Guadalajara, Diputación Provincial. *Discusión del congreso mexicano por el voto de los pueblos y manifiesto de la provincia de Nueva Galicia.* México, 1823.

——. [*Actas (Minutes) de la sesión especial de la diputación provincial de Guadalajara del 16 de junio, 1823*]. Guadalajara, 1823 (published without title).

——, Jefe Político. *Bando,* signed Luis Quintanar, Guadalajara, July 1, 1823.

——. *Circular,* signed Luis Quintanar, to the governor of Texas, Guadalajara, May 12, 1823. Guadalajara, 1823.

——. *Circular,* signed Luis Quintanar, to the Ayuntamiento de Béjar, Texas, Guadalajara, July 1, 1823. Guadalajara, 1823.

Heredia, José María. *Himno patriótico que se cantó en el teatro de México la noche del 21 del corriente en celebridad de la instalación de la excma. diputación provincial.* México, 1820.

Hernández y Dávalos, Juan E. *Colección de documentos para la historia de la guerra de independencia de México de 1808 a 1821.* 6 vols. México, 1877–1882.

Idea de la conducta general de don Miguel Ramos Arizpe. México, 1822.

Iturbide, Agustín de. *Breve diseño crítico de la emancipación y libertad de la nación mexicana, y de las causas que influyeron en sus más ruidosos sucesos, acaecidos desde el grito de Iguala hasta la espantosa muerte del libertador en la villa de Padilla.* México, 1827.

——. *Manifiesto del general d. Agustín de Iturbide, libertador de México.* México, 1871.

Jalisco, Captain-General. *Manifiesto del capitán general a los habitantes del estado libre de Xalisco.* June 21, 1823. Guadalajara, 1823.

Jalisco, Gobernador. *Gobernación del estado libre de Xalisco, 23 de junio, 1823.* Guadalajara, 1823.

——. *Manifiesto de los gefes que dieron el fausto grito de libertad en Guadalajara.* Guadalajara, 1823.

——. *Manifiesto de los liberales de Guadalajara, a sus conciudadanos.* Guadalajara, 1823.

Jiménez, Manuel María. *Himno patriótico compuesto por don Manuel Maria Jiménez para que se cantase en este coliseo en la función de la excma. junta provincial, lo que no se verificó por no haberlo permitido el censor.* México, 1820.

Juarros, Domingo. *A Statistical and Commercial History of the Kingdom of Guatemala in Spanish America.* London, 1823.

Lista de los señores diputados de Antequera en el valle de Oaxaca para México. México, 1822.

Lista de los señores diputados para las cortes constituyentes de este imperio mexicano que se han nombrado en las provincias de Veracruz, Querétaro, y Tlaxcala. México, 1822.

Lista de los señores diputados por Puebla. México, 1822.

M., L. *ODA en la instalación de la diputación provincial de México*. México, 1820.

Mateos, Juan A. *Historia parlamentaria de los congresos mexicanos de 1821 a 1857*. 25 vols. México, 1879–1912.

Mestre Ghizliazza, Manuel. *Documentos y datos para la historia de Tabasco*. México, 1916.

Mexico, Congreso Constituyente, 1823, Comisión para Formar un Proyecto de Constitución. *Acta constitucional presentada al soberano congreso constituyente por su comisión el día 20 de noviembre de 1823*. México, 1823.

Mexico (Empire, 1822–1823), Congreso Constituyente. *Actas del congreso constituyente*. 4 vols. México, 1822–1823.

———. *Diario de las sesiones del congreso constituyente de México*. México, 1823. This is actually volume 4 of the above-cited *Actas del congreso constituyente*.

Mexico. *Plan de constitución político de la nación mexicana*. México, 1823.

———, Comisión Especial sobre Convocatoria para un Nuevo Congreso. *Díctamen de la comisión especial de convocatoria para un nuevo congreso*. México, 1823.

———, Junta Nacional Instituyente. *Diario de la junta nacional instituyente del imperio mexicano*. México, 1823.

———, Junta Provisional Gubernativa, 1821–1822. *Diario de las sesiones de la soberana junta provisional gubernativa del imperio mexicano, instalado según provienen el plan de Iguala y tratados de la villa de Córdoba*. México, 1822.

———, Laws, Statutes, etc. *Colección de los decretos y órdenes que ha expedido la soberana junta provisional gubernativa del imperio mexicano, desde su instalación el 28 de setiembre hasta 24 de febrero de 1822*. México, 1822.

———. *Colección de órdenes y decretos de la soberana junta provisional gubernativa y soberanos congresos generales de la nación mexicana*. 8 vols. México, 1829–1840.

———. *Informe oficial [Official Report] de la diputación provincial de México, 6 marzo 1823*. Untitled (it begins "Mexicanos teneis derecho . . ."). México, 1823.

——— (Viceroyalty), Laws, Statutes, etc. *Real ordenanzas para el establecimiento e instrucción de intendentes de exército y provincia en el reino de la Nueva España*. Madrid, 1786.

Michoacán (Province), Diputación Provincial. *Sin leyes no hay libertad ni hay leyes sino se observen o sea manifiesto que hace la diputación provincial gubernativa de Michoacán a sus habitantes sobre los acontecimientos de estos últimos días*. México, 1823.

Mier, Noriega y Guerra, José Servando Teresa de. *Diez cartas, hasta hoy inéditas de Fray Servando Teresa de Mier*. Monterrey, 1940.

———. *Fray Servando Teresa de Mier: Selección, notas y prólogo de Edmundo O'Gorman*. México, 1946.

———. *Memoria instructiva enviada desde Filadelphia en agosto de 1821, a los gefes independientes del Anahuac, llamado por los españoles Nueva España*. Philadelphia, 1821.

Mora, José María Luis. *México y sus revoluciones*. 2 vols. Paris, 1838.

———. *Obras completas*. 6 vols. México, 1986–1988. Compiled, with notes by Lillian

Briseño Senosiain, Laura Solares Robles, and Laura Suárez de la Torre.
———. *Obras selectas*. Paris, 1837.
Nueva España (Viceroyalty), Diputación Provincial. *Actas de la diputación provincial de Nueva España, 1820–1821*. México, 1985.
Nueva Galicia (Guadalajara). *Disolución del congreso mexicano, por los pueblos y manifiesto de la junta provincial de Nueva Galicia*. Guadalajara, 1823.
———, Gefe Político. *Bando de don José de la Cruz, mariscal de campo de los ejércitos nacionales, comandante y gefe político del reyno de Nueva Galicia, gobernador intendente de la provincia de Guadalajara, 21 de junio, 1813*. Guadalajara, 1813.
Olagary, Roberto (comp. and ed.). *Colección de documentos históricos mexicanos*. 4 vols. México, 1925.
La provincia de Oaxaca: Independiente de México. Puebla, 1823.
Puebla, Ayuntamiento. *Representación que hace a S. M. las cortes el ayuntamiento de la Puebla de los Angeles para que en esta ciudad, cabeza de provincia, se establezca diputación provincial, como lo dispone la constitución*. Puebla, 1821.
———, Diputación Provincial. *Representación que la diputación provincial de Puebla dirige el soberano congreso pidiéndole se sirva a expedir nueva convocatoria*. Puebla, 1823.
———, Jefe Político. *Bando* de Carlos García, August 23, 1821. Puebla, 1821.
———, Jefe Político Interino. *Bandos,* de José Morán, February 11, 15, 18 and March 14, 1823.
———, Junta Electoral. *Representación que hace al soberano congreso de Cortes la junta electoral de la provincia de la Puebla de los Angeles en Nueva España, para que en ella se establezca la diputación provincial conforme al artículo 325 de la constitución*. Puebla, 1820.
Querétaro, Ayuntamiento. *Contestación que dió el ayuntamiento constitucional de Querétaro a la excma. diputación provincial, manifestando su opinión sobre nueva convocatoria*. Querétaro, 1823.
———, Diputación Provincial. *Manifiesto que al supremo poder ejecutivo, hace de sus operaciones la diputación provincial de Querétaro por el tiempo que tuvo el gobierno administrativo de su provincia*. México, 1823.
Querétaro libre. Puebla, 1823.
Ramos Arizpe, José Miguel Nepomuceno. *Carta escrita a un americano sobre la forma de gobierno que para hacer practicable la constitución y las leyes, conviene establecer en Nueva España atendida su actual situación*. México, 1821.
———. *Memoria que . . . presenta al augusto congreso, sobre el estado natural, político, y civil de su dicha provincia, y las del Nuevo Reyno de León, Nuevo Santander, y los Texas, con esposición de los defectos del sistema general, y particular de sus gobiernos, y de las reformas, y nuevos establecimientos que necesitan para su prosperidad*. Cádiz, 1812.
———. *Report That Dr. Miguel Ramos de Arizpe . . . Presents to the August Congress on the Natural, Political, and Civil Conditions of the Provinces of Coahuila, Nuevo León, Nuevo Santander, and Texas*. Translation, annotations, and introduction by Nettie Lee Benson. Austin, 1950.
Rejón, Manuel Crescencio. *Discursos parlamentarios (1822–1847), compilación, notas y reseña biográfica por Carlos A. Echanove Trujillo*. México, 1943.
Riesgo, Juan Miguel, et al. *Memoria sobre las proporciones naturales de las provincias internas occidentales, causas de que han provenido sus atrasos, providencias tomadas*

con el fin de lograr su remedio y los que por ahora se consideran oportunos para mejorar su estado, e ir proporcionando su futura felicidad: Formada por los diputados de dichas provincias que la suscriben. México, 1822.

Rocafuerte, Vicente. *Bosquejo ligerísimo de la revolución de México, desde el grito de Iguala hasta la proclamación imperial de Iturbide por un verdadero americano.* Philadelphia, 1822.

————. *Ideas necesarias a todo pueblo americano independiente, que quiere ser libre.* Puebla, 1823.

Romero, Matías. *Bosquejo histórico de la agregación a México de Chiapas y Soconuso y de las negociaciones sobre límites entabladas con Centro América y Guatemala.* México, 1877.

Sánchez, Prisciliano, et al. *Proposición hecha al soberano congreso por los diputados que suscriben.* Guadalajara, 1823.

Santa Anna, Antonio López de. *Ejército de operaciones.* Veracruz, 1823.

————. *Manifiesto de Antonio López de Santanna a sus conciudadanos.* México, 1823.

Separación de la Nueva Galicia de todas las provincias de México. México, 1823.

Sesiones celebradas en la villa de Lagos. Lagos, 1823.

Spain, Constitution. *Constitución política de la monarquía española, promulgada en Cádiz el 19 de marzo de 1812.* Cádiz, 1812.

Spain, Cortes, 1810–1813. *Diario de las discusiones y actas de las Cortes.* 18 vols. Cádiz, 1811–1813.

————. 1813. *Actas de las sesiones de la legislatura ordinaria de 1813.* Madrid, 1876.

————. 1814. *Actas de las sesiones de la legislatura ordinaria de 1814.* Madrid, 1876.

————. 1820. *Diario de las sesiones de Cortes, Legislatura de 1820.* 3 vols. Madrid, 1871–1873.

————. 1820–1821. *Diario de las actas y discusiones de las Cortes, Legislatura de los años de 1820–1821.* 23 vols. Madrid, 1820–1821.

————. 1821. *Diario de las sesiones de Cortes, Legislatura de 1821.* 3 vols. Madrid, 1871–1878.

Spain, Laws, Statutes, etc. *Colección de los decretos y órdenes que han expedido las Cortes generales y extraordinarias.* 9 vols. Madrid, 1820–1822.

Terán de Escalante, Manuel, et al. *Esposición hecha al soberano congreso constituyente mexicano sobre las provincias de Sonora y Sinaloa por el señor coronel d. Manuel Terán de Escalante y la mayoría de los representantes de dichas provincias que la suscriben.* México, 1823.

Tornel y Mendivil, José María. *Breve reseña histórica de los acontecimientos más notables de la nación mexicana desde el año de 1821 hasta nuestros días.* México, 1852.

Torres Lanzas, Pedro. *Independencia de América: Fuentes para su estudio, Catálogo de documentos conservados en el Archivo general de las Indias.* 5 vols. Madrid, 1912.

Troncoso, José Nepomuceno. *Aviso al público, Puebla, 25 de setiembre, 1820.* Puebla, 1820.

Veracruz (Province), Diputación Provincial. *Manifiesto de la diputación provincial de Veracruz a los pueblos de su distrito: Veracruz, 13 de abril de 1823.* Veracruz, 1823.

La verdad destruye a la calumnia. Broadside. Mexico, probably 1823.

Victoria, Guadalupe, et al. *Instrucciones o indicaciones que deben tenerse presentes para la mejor inteligencia del opinión de la acta fecha en Casa Mata el 1 de febrero, y conformidad de esta con el plan formado en Veracruz el 6 de diciembre.* Veracruz, 1823.

Zavala, Lorenzo de. *Ensayo histórico de las revoluciones de México, desde 1808 hasta 1830.* 2 vols. Paris, 1831–1832.

Zúniga y Ontiveros, Felipe de la. *Calendario, guía, manual de forasteros de México para el año del señor de 1779 al año de 1822.* México, 1779–1822.

Secondary Sources

Acereto, Albino. "Historia política desde el descubrimiento Europeo hasta 1920." In *Enciclopedia yucatanense,* vol. III. México, 1947.

Alessio Robles, Vito. *Coahuila y Texas desde la consumación de la independencia hasta el tratado de paz de Guadalupe Hidalgo.* 2 vols. México, 1940–1946.

Almada, Francisco R. *Resumen de la historia del estado de Chihuahua.* México, 1955.

Altman, Ida, and Lockhart, James. *Provinces of Early Mexico: Variants of Spanish American Regional Evolution.* Los Angeles, 1976.

Amador, Elías. *Bosquejo histórico de Zacatecas.* 2 vols. Zacatecas, 1943.

Ancona, Eligio. *Historia de Yucatán desde la época más remota hasta nuestros días.* Barcelona, 1889.

Anderson, William Woodrow. "Reform as a Means to Quell Revolution." In *Mexico and the Spanish Cortes,* ed. Nettie Lee Benson. Austin, 1966

Anna, Timothy E. *The Fall of the Royal Government in Mexico City.* Lincoln, Neb., 1957.

———. *Spain and the Loss of America.* Lincoln, Neb., 1963.

Arrangoiz y Berzabal, Francisco de Paula. *México desde 1808 hasta 1867.* 4 vols. México, 1871.

Báez, Victoriano. *Compendio de historia de Oaxaca.* Oaxaca, 1909.

Bancroft, Hubert Howe. *History of Mexico.* 6 vols. San Francisco, 1883–1887.

Banegas Galván, Francisco. *Historia de México.* 3 vols. México, 1923–1940.

Baquera, Richard V. "Paso del Norte and Chihuahua: Revolution and Constitutionalists." M.A. thesis. University of Texas at El Paso, 1977.

Barker, Eugene C. *The Life of Stephen F. Austin.* Nashville, 1925.

Belmar, Francisco. *Breve reseña histórica y geográfica del estado de Oaxaca.* Oaxaca, 1901.

Benson, Nettie Lee. "The Contested Mexican Election of 1812." *Hispanic American Historical Review* 26 (August 1946): 336–350.

———. "La elección de Ramos Arizpe a las Cortes de Cádiz en 1810." *Historia mexicana* 33, no. 4 (April–June 1984): 515–539.

———. "The Plan of Casa Mata." *Hispanic American Historical Review* 25 (February 1945): 44–56.

———. "Servando Teresa de Mier, Federalist." *Hispanic American Historical Review* 28 (November 1948): 514–525.

———. "Texas' Failure to Send a Deputy to the Spanish Cortes." *Southwestern Historical Quarterly* 64, no. 1 (July 1960): 1–12.

———. "Washington: Symbol of the United States in Mexico, 1800–1823." *Library Chronicle of the University of Texas* 2 (Spring 1947): 175–182.

——— (ed.). *México and the Spanish Cortes, 1810–1822: Eight Essays.* Austin, 1966.

Berry, Charles R. "The Election of the Mexican Deputies to the Spanish Cortes, 1810–1822." In *Mexico and the Spanish Cortes,* ed. Nettie Lee Benson. Austin, 1966.

Briggs, Donald C., and Marvin Alisky. *Historical Dictionary of Mexico*. Metuchen, 1981.
Buelna, Eustaquio. *Apuntes para la historia de Sinaloa 1821–1822, con una introducción y notas de Genaro Estrada*. México, 1924.
Callcott, Wilfrid Hardy. *Santa Anna: The Story of an Enigma Who Once Was Mexico*. Norman, Okla., 1936.
Carr, Raymond. *Spain 1808–1939*. Oxford, 1966.
Castañeda, Carlos Eduardo. *A Report on the Spanish Archives in San Antonio, Texas*. San Antonio, 1937.
Castillo Negrete, Emilio de. *México en el siglo XIX*. 26 vols. México, 1875–1892.
Chapman, Charles E. *A History of Spain*. New York, 1938.
Cossío, David Alberto. *Historia de Nuevo León*. 5 vols. Monterrey, 1925.
Cumberland, Charles Curtis. *Mexico: Its Struggle for Modernity*. New York, 1964.
Dealey, James Q. "The Spanish Sources of the Mexican Constitution of 1824." *Texas State Historical Association Quarterly* 3 (January 1900): 161–169.
Delgado, Jaime. *España y México en el siglo XIX*. 3 vols. Madrid, 1950–1954.
Diccionario Porrúa: Historia, biográfia y geografia de México. 3rd ed. 2 vols. México, 1964.
Espinosa, Luis. *Independencia de la provincia de las Chiapas y su unión a México: Síntesis de aquellos dos sucesos memorables extractados de los documentos coleccionados por los excelentes señores Manuel Larrainizar y Matías Romero*. México, 1918.
Esquerra, Ramón. "La crítica española de la situación de América en el siglo XVIII." *Revista de Indias* 87–88 (1962): 159–287.
Fisher, Lillian Estelle. *The Intendant System in Spanish America*. Berkeley, 1929.
———. *Political Administration in the Spanish American Colonies*. Berkeley, 1926.
Gil y Sáenz, Manuel. *Compendio histórico, geográfico y estadístico del estado de Tabasco*. Tabasco, 1872.
González, José Eleuterio. *Biografia del benemérito mexicano de Servando Teresa de Mier Noriega y Guerra*. Monterrey, 1876.
González-Salas, Carlos. *Miguel Ramos Arizpe, cumbre y camino*. México, 1978.
Gortari Rabiela, Hira de. "Julio–Agosto de 1808: La lealtad mexicana." *Historia mexicana* 39, no. 1 (153) (July–August, 1989): 181–203.
Gutiérrez del Arroyo, Isabel. "El Nuevo Régimen institucional bajo la real ordenanza de intendente de la Nueva España (1786)." *Historia mexicana* 39, no. 1 (153) (July–December 1989): 89–122.
Haring, C. H. *The Spanish Empire in America*. New York, 1947.
Hernández, Carlos. *Durango gráfico*. Chihuahua, 1903.
Herrejón Peredo, Carlos. "La diputación provincial de Nueva España." In *Temas de historia mexiquense*, comp. María Teresa Jarquín Ortega. Toluca, 1988.
Incorporación de Chiapas a México: Discursos leídos en la velada que se verificó en la cámara de diputados en celebración del LXXVIII aniversario de la federación de Chiapas a la república de México. México, 1902.
Jarquín Ortega, María Teresa (comp). *Temas de historia mexiquense*. Toluca, 1988.
Lanz, Manuel A. *Compendio de historia de Campeche*. Campeche, 1905.
Lerdo de Tejada, Miguel M. *Apuntes de la heróica ciudad de Veracruz*. México, 1857. Vol. II.

Lewis, Boleslao. *Los movimientos de emancipación en hispanoamérica y la independencia de los Estados Unidos.* Buenos Aires, 1952.

Lovett, Gabriel H. *Napoleon and the Birth of Modern Spain.* 2 vols. New York, 1965.

Lyon, Elijah Wilson. *Louisiana in French Diplomacy 1759–1804.* Norman, Okla., 1954.

Macune, Charles W., Jr. *El estado de México y la federación mexicana, 1823–1835.* México, 1978.

Magner, James Aloysius. *Men of Mexico.* Milwaukee, 1942 and 1964.

Marmolejo, Lucio. *Efemérides guanajuatenses o datos para formar la historia de la ciudad de Guanajuato.* 4 vols. México, 1883–1884. Vol. III.

Mecham, J. Lloyd. "The Origins of Federalism in Mexico." *Hispanic American Historical Review* 18 (May 1938): 164–189.

Meyer, Michael, and William L. Sherman. *The Course of Mexican History.* 3rd ed. New York, 1987.

Molina Solís, Juan Francisco. *Historia de Yucatán durante la dominación española.* 2nd ed. 3 vols. Barcelona, 1889. Vol. III.

Muro, Manuel. *Historia de San Luis Potosí.* 2nd ed. 3 vols. San Luis Potosí, 1910. Vol. I.

Navarro García, Luis. *Intendencias en Indias.* Seville, 1959.

Nelson, George E., and Mary B. Nelson. *Mexico A–Z, An Encyclopedic Dictionary.* Cuernavaca, 1978.

Olavarría y Ferrari, Enrique. *México independiente, 1821–1855.* In *México a través de los siglos,* ed. Vicente Riva Palacio, vol. IV. México, 1889.

Pantagua, Flavio Antonio. *Catecismo elemental de historia y estadística de Chiapas.* San Cristóbal, 1876.

Pérez Verdía, Luis. *Historia particular del estado de Jalisco.* Guadalajara, 1910. Vol. II.

Pi y Margall, Francisco, and Francisco Pi y Arsuaga. *Las grandes conmociones políticas del siglo XIX en España.* 4 vols. Barcelona, n.d. Vol. I.

Ponce de León, José N. *Reseñas históricas del estado de Chihuahua.* 2nd ed. Chihuahua, 1905.

Presas, José. *Juicio imparcial sobre las principales causas de la revolución de la América española.* Burdéos, 1828.

Priestley, Herbert Ingram. *The Mexican Nation.* New York, 1938.

Ramos, Demetrio. "Los proyectos de independencia para América preparados por el rey Carlos IV." *Revista de Indias* 28, nos. 111–112 (January–June 1968): 85–123.

Read, Benjamin Maurice. *Illustrated History of New Mexico.* Santa Fe, 1912.

Rees Jones, Ricardo. *El despotismo ilustrado y los intendentes de la Nueva España.* México, 1979.

Riva Palacio, Vicente (ed.). *México a través de los siglos.* 4 vols. México, 1888–1889. Vols. III–IV.

Rivera Cambas, Manuel. *Historia antigua y moderna de la Jalapa y de las revoluciones del estado de Veracruz.* 3 vols. México, 1869.

Robertson, William Spence. *Iturbide of Mexico.* Durham, N.C., 1952.

Rodríguez, Mario. *The Cádiz Experiment in Central America 1808–1826.* Berkeley, 1978.

Roel, Santiago. *Nuevo León, apuntes históricos.* 2 vols. Monterrey, 1938.

Romero Flores, Romeo. *Historia de la ciudad de Morelia.* Morelia, 1928.

Sánchez, Pedro de. "Un precursor ideológico de la independencia mexicana." In *Episodios eclesiásticos de México (Contribución a nuestra historia)*. México, 1948.

Serra-Rojas, Andrés. *Antología de Emilio Rabasa*. 2 vols. México, 1969.

Sprague, William Forest. *Vicente Guerrero, Mexican Liberator*. Chicago, 1939.

Trens, Manuel B. *Historia de Chiapas desde los tiempos más remotos hasta el govierno del general Carlos A. Vidal*. S. Turanzas del Valle, 1942.

Twitchell, Ralph Emerson. *The Leading Facts of New Mexican History*. Vol. II. Cedar Rapids, Ia., 1911.

Vadillo, Manuel de. *Apuntes sobre los principales sucesos que han influído en el actual estado de la América del Sud*. Cádiz, 1836.

Velázquez, María del Carmen. "La comandancia general de las Provincias Internas." *Historia mexicana* 28, no. 2 (October–December 1977): 160–177.

Villanueva, Carlos A. *La monarquía en América. Bolívar y el general San Martín*. Paris, n.d.

———. *La monarquía en América: Fernando VII y los nuevos estados*. Paris, n.d.

Washburn, Douglas Alan. "Institutional Change and Political Development: The Interior Provinces in Late Colonial New Spain." Master's thesis. University of Texas at Austin, 1977.

Whatley, William Archibald. "The Formation of the Mexican Constitution of 1824." Master's thesis. University of Texas at Austin, 1921.

Zamacois, Niceto de. *Historia de Méjico, desde sus tiempos más remotos hasta nuestros días*. 22 vols. México, 1878–1879. Vols. VII–XI.

Zárate, Julio. *La guerra de independencia*. In *México a través de los siglos*, ed. Vicente Riva Palacio, vol. III. México, 1888.

Zerecero, Anastasio. *Memorias para la historia de las revoluciones en México*. 2 vols. México, 1869.

Index

Lightning Source UK Ltd.
Milton Keynes UK
UKHW010045211221
396012UK00001B/11